SOUTH AFRICA

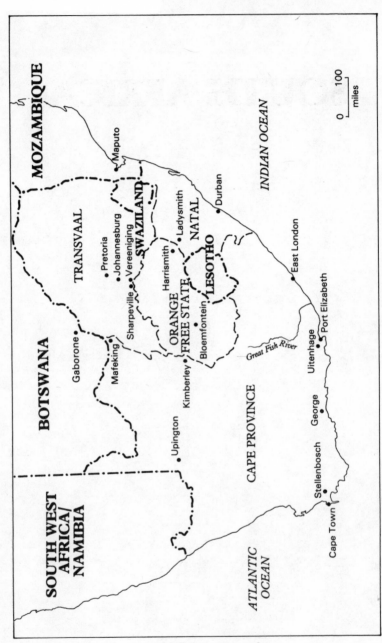

South Africa – general

SOUTH AFRICA
No easy path to peace
Graham Leach

Routledge & Kegan Paul
London, Boston and Henley

First published in 1986
by Routledge & Kegan Paul plc

14 Leicester Square, London WC2H 7PH, England

9 Park Street, Boston, Mass. 02108, USA

Broadway House, Newtown Road,
Henley on Thames, Oxon RG9 1EN, England

Set in Sabon, 10 on 12 pt
by Inforum Ltd, Portsmouth
and printed and bound in Great Britain

Library of Congress Cataloging in Publication Data

Leach, Graham.
   South Africa.
   Bibliography: p.
   Includes index.
   1. South Africa—Politics and government—1978—
   2. South Africa—Economic conditions—1961—
   3. South Africa—Social conditions—1961—
   4. Apartheid. 5. Namibia—Politics and government—
   1946-   . 6. National liberation movements—South
   Africa. I. Title.
   DT779.952.L43   1986   968.06   85–25665

British Library CIP data also available

ISBN 0–7102–0848–0

FOR RUTH, A LOYAL FELLOW-TRAVELLER,
THOMAS, WILLIAM AND OLIVER

Contents

Plates

Maps

Preface

On Saturday 2 June 1984 the South African and British prime ministers stood together on the steps of the British premier's country retreat at Chequers in Buckinghamshire. P.W. Botha and Margaret Thatcher had just completed an historic meeting, part of the first tour to Europe by a South African leader since the early part of the century. Looking at the photographs of the meeting in their next day's newspapers many white South Africans must have wondered whether the country had at last turned the corner and whether the path back to international acceptance for their 'pariah state' now lay open before them.

Botha had embarked upon his European tour with an impressive record of breaking the logjam of South African politics. He had introduced a new constitution for South Africa, under which non-whites were for the first time given a limited share of power. In the foreign field he had signed a peace treaty with President Samora Machel of Mozambique, South Africa's Marxist neighbour. P.W. Botha appeared to be at the pinnacle of his power. He seemed to be steering his country in a new direction, one which was not dreamt of five years previously. Though not satisfied with the pace of change, the Europeans wanted to reward him, to dangle the carrot of international recognition if and when South Africa relinquished its apartheid policy for good.

Within two months of returning, however, it all began to fall apart. The worst violence yet seen in South Africa claiming more than 800 lives between September 1984 and September 1985 was unleashed in some of the country's black townships, while hopes that the Mozambique peace treaty would bring about a new era of peace in southern Africa were soon disappointed.

For the outsider it has been a confusing period. On the one hand, this is the first South African government to initiate significant reform since the National Party came to power in 1948 armed with its apartheid policy. On the other hand it has clamped down on dissent, often using methods which the international community has condemned as the same repressive techniques of previous Pretoria governments. This phenomenon, of reform and repression existing side by side, needs explaining. I hope this book goes some way towards enlightening the general reader who wishes to understand more of the complicated situation which lies behind the daily news headlines about South Africa.

I was first in South Africa in 1976 and 1977, covering the turbulent events which flowed from the uprising in Soweto in 1976. I returned here in mid-1983, since when I have been reporting on the events covered in this book. To be able to interview many of the key figures involved – the Bothas, the Tutus, the Tambos – has been a gripping experience. I hope, too, that I have conveyed some of the excitement of being a first-hand witness to history in the making, whether it has been in Soweto and Sharpeville, or in private conversations with decision-makers and influential figures across the political spectrum.

As a foreign correspondent who earlier spent some considerable time in both Northern Ireland and the Middle East it is my humble conclusion that the world's trouble-spots, where violence is part of everyday life, very often produce the finest and friendliest people it is possible to meet. South Africa is no exception and in reporting from here I have had the pleasure of meeting many such individuals – black and white, rich and poor, famous and not-so-famous. It is in the hope that these people will one day resolve their problems that this book is written.

Graham Leach, Johannesburg
December 1985

Acknowledgments

For his initial encouragement to write the book and for his later thoughtful comments on the script and editorial advice, I should like to thank Thomas Thomson, Chief Correspondent, Reuters News Agency, South Africa. Thanks are due also to the two doyens of the southern Africa foreign correspondents – Christopher Munnion, Southern Africa Correspondent of the London *Daily Telegraph*, and Peter Hawthorne, Correspondent in Johannesburg for *Time* magazine – for their cogent and informed comments on the book and for the benefit of their experience of the region over many years. Similar thanks are owed to François Marais, cameraman for BBC Television News in South Africa, whose breadth of knowledge of the region extends far beyond what he shoots so brilliantly through his camera lens.

Michael Spicer, formerly Deputy Director of the South African Institute of International Affairs, read the book and offered several informed comments based on his wide knowledge of southern African affairs which during his period at the Institute made him one of the foremost commentators in his field.

To the staff of the South African Institute of Race Relations in Johannesburg I should like to express my gratitude for their invaluable assistance on numerous occasions over the past couple of years. A special word of thanks is due to the Librarian, John Morrison, who also read the script, and to Jennifer Shindler who has been particularly helpful providing facts and figures about the background to the unrest in South Africa.

Special thanks are owed to Patricia Thomson for her editorial assistance and for compiling the index.

Despite the opinions offered by other observers, I take full responsibility for the views expressed in this book.

I am indebted to Julian Kerr, Chief Representative, Reuters News Agency, South Africa, for making a Reuters word-processor available. I am grateful to Jacqueline Holmes, Jessie Hawthorne and Ann Roberts for their long labours in typing the script.

I would also like to thank the following picture libraries for permission to reprint the photographs which appear in the plates section: Afrapix, Johannesburg for figs 1, 2a, 3, 4, 5b, 6a and b and 12b; Associated Press for figs 2b and c, 5a, 7a, 8a and b, 9a and b, 10, 11a and b and 12a, and Popperfoto for figs 7b and 12c.

Finally, a word of appreciation to Ray Gowdridge, Foreign Editor of BBC Foreign News (Radio) in London for his support and encouragement while I wrote the book.

Glossary

SOUTH AFRICA

Official figures for the population of South Africa in mid-1984 were:

Race group	Number	Percentage of population
African	24,103,458	73.8
White	4,818,679	14.8
Coloured (mixed race)	2,830,301	8.7
Indian	890,292	2.7

Of the African population, the number living in the 'independent' homelands of Transkei, Bophuthatswana, Ciskei and Venda was 5,865,458.

Those living in the non-independent homelands of Lebowa, Kwa-Ndebele, Gazankulu, KaNgwane, Qwaqwa and KwaZulu were 7,226,453.

> South Africa has three capital cities:
> Pretoria – seat of government
> Cape Town – seat of parliament
> Bloemfontein – seat of justice

The main political parties and groupings in South Africa are:

National Party – the ruling white party which entrenched statutory apartheid.

Progressive Federal Party – the liberal opposition party advocating a qualified franchise within a federal system.

Conservative Party – a right-wing party for whites founded in 1982 following a defection from the National Party by MPs protesting against reforms to apartheid.

Herstigte Nasionale Party – an earlier right-wing breakaway party holding to traditional hard-line apartheid.

New Republic Party – a small Natal-based party fighting to maintain a separate identity from the Nationalists.

Afrikaner Weerstandsbeweging – a group of neo-Nazi style right-wing whites.

Afrikaner Broederbond – a secretive Afrikaner organization which influenced government policy for many years from behind closed doors.

Afrikaner Volkswag – a right-wing breakaway group from the Broederbond.

African National Congress – the outlawed nationalist organization fighting to end apartheid and supported by many blacks inside South Africa.

United Democratic Front – formed 1983, now the largest anti-apartheid organization in South Africa. Multi-racial membership.

Black Consciousness – founded by the late Steve Biko, believed in the black man waging his own struggle against white rule.

Azanian People's Organization – present-day heir to the Black Consciousness tradition.

Inkatha – Zulu-dominated organization prepared to dilute black nationalist demand for one man, one vote.

Labour Party – main party in parliament for the coloured or mixed-race people.

South African Indian Council – government-created representative body for Indians replaced by Indian chamber in parliament.

Natal Indian Congress – anti-apartheid Indian organization, based in Natal, rejecting Indian participation in the new parliament.

Transvaal Indian Congress – same as above, based in Transvaal.

Some of the major political figures in South Africa are:

P.W. Botha – state president, who introduced power-sharing with coloureds and Indians although not blacks.

R.F. 'Pik' Botha – Minister of Foreign Affairs.

Dr Gerrit Viljoen – Minister of Co-operation and Development, in charge of black affairs.

Chris Heunis – Minister of Constitutional Development and Planning, the architect of the new constitution.

F.W. de Klerk – Minister of National Education, leader of the National Party in the Transvaal.

Louis le Grange – Minister of Law and Order.

General Johan Coetzee – Police Commissioner.

General Constand Viljoen – former chief of the Defence Force (now replaced by General Jannie Geldenhuys).

Dr Frederik van Zyl Slabbert – leader of the Progressive Federal Party.

Helen Suzman – PFP member of parliament for the Houghton constituency of Johannesburg.

Dr Andries Treurnicht – leader of the Conservative Party.

Nelson Mandela – black nationalist leader, imprisoned for life in 1964. Opinion polls have shown he commands most support among blacks.

Oliver Tambo – leader of the African National Congress in Zambia.

Steve Biko – Black Consciousness leader who died in police detention in 1977.

Chief Mangosuthu Buthelezi – chief minister of the KwaZulu homeland and head of Inkatha.

Bishop Desmond Tutu – Anglican Bishop of Johannesburg, winner of the Nobel Peace Prize 1984, formerly general secretary of the South African Council of Churches.

Dr Allan Boesak – president of the World Alliance of Reformed Churches and prominent (coloured) anti-apartheid churchman.

Lucas Mangope – president of the 'independent' homeland of Bophuthatswana.

Chief Lennox Sebe – president of the 'independent' black homeland of Ciskei.

Rev. Allan Hendrickse – leader of the Labour Party and first coloured minister in a South African cabinet.

Amichand Rajbansi – first Indian in a South African cabinet.

Mewa Ramgobin – prominent anti-apartheid Indian campaigner, one of the Durban Six who occupied the British consulate in Durban.

MOZAMBIQUE

Capital: Maputo (formerly Lourenço Marques).
President: Samora Machel.
Ruling Party: FRELIMO (Front for the Liberation of Mozambique) – Marxist.
Anti-government rebels: RENAMO (Mozambique National Resistance).

ANGOLA

Capital: Luanda.
President: Eduardo dos Santos.
Ruling Party: MPLA (People's Movement for the Liberation of Angola) – Marxist, backed by estimated 30,000 Cuban troops as well as Soviet and eastern bloc technicians and advisers.
Anti-government forces: UNITA (National Union for the Total Independence of Angola) led by Jonas Savimbi – pro-western, anti-Marxist, supported by South Africa.
FNLA (National Front for the Liberation of Angola) led by Holden Roberto – anti-Marxist, supported by Zaire.

ZIMBABWE

Capital: Harare.
Leader: Robert Mugabe.
Ruling Party: ZANU (Zimbabwean African National Union).
Anti-government party: ZAPU (Zimbabwean African People's Union) led by Joshua Nkomo.

SOUTH WEST AFRICA/NAMIBIA

Capital: Windhoek.
Foreign policy, security, defence and other major policy areas controlled by South Africa.
Local areas of administration controlled by an 'interim government' formed by Namibia's Multi-Party Conference which comprises

internal parties which Pretoria regards as moderate.
Anti-South African guerrillas: SWAPO (South West African People's Organization) led by Sam Nujoma.

Other major leaders of southern Africa:

President Kenneth Kaunda of Zambia.
President Julius Nyerere of Tanzania (retired November 1985).
President Quett Masire of Botswana.
Chief Leabua Jonathan, prime minister of Lesotho.
President Hastings Banda of Malawi.

In July 1985 the South African currency (the rand) was worth £0.34 and $0.50. By September 1985 the rand had fallen to £0.30 and $0.38.

CHAPTER 1

This Land is Whose Land?
South Africa's racial cauldron

Johannesburg. Saturday 12 March 1985. The city has an air of tense expectation this morning. Thousands of blacks are pouring into downtown Johannesburg from the black township of Soweto, scene of the violent rioting in 1976. They march through the streets in gangs, swaggering past anxious-looking whites.

From elsewhere in the racially-segregated city, thousands of whites make their way into town. Roads from coloured and Indian suburbs are jammed. By mid-morning 150,000 people from different races are converging. Police are taking up positions, nervously, expecting trouble. The temperature is rising. Johannesburg is waiting for an explosion . . .

The explosion came at 2.30 in the afternoon when the first of twenty-five local rock bands started pumping out the decibels at the Ellis Park sports stadium. 'The Concert In The Park', the largest-ever rock concert on the African continent, had begun.

For the next ten hours thousands of young people – blacks, whites, mixed-race coloureds and Indians – linked arms and swayed in time to the music. Blacks and whites forgot their differences. There were Boy George look-alikes, breakdancers, all brands of punks. Their line in eccentricity was what differentiated them, not the colour of their skin.

The bands included multi-racial Juluka, South Africa's most successful musical export in recent years, and others with names like Harari, the Working Girls, and Hot Line. The atmosphere became frenzied when a group calling itself Brenda and the Big Dudes took the stage. Each of the twenty-five bands was performing free in the concert to raise funds for 'Operation Hunger', the aid organization which is run from a small Johannesburg office by a dedicated white lady, Ina Perlman. It is trying to alleviate the suffering of the thousands of undernourished and impoverished blacks, especially children, living in South Africa's forgotten tribal homelands where drought and government policies have caused widespread suffering.

Concert-goers paid R5 per head. By the end of the day 'Operation Hunger' had seen its bank account swell by over half a million rand. Food for a few more bellies.

The concert organizers knew they were taking a major risk in arranging a 'South African Woodstock' in the land of apartheid with the ever-attendant likelihood of racial violence. As things turned out, there were no major incidents. Police, who broke up minor trouble, were cheered by the multi-racial audience and encouraged to remove offenders whatever their colour.

How could it happen in a country depicted as wracked by racial division and confrontation, where violence is seen almost nightly on the world's television screens, where the black revolution and a holocaust are predicted for any moment? How could so many people, black and white, come together, and share such an experience? Is this really the South Africa the world knows?

Of course, Johannesburg, with its liberal, English-speaking traditions, is not typical of the rest of South Africa. It was founded less than 100 years ago, a klondike shanty town which just kept growing and growing after the discovery of gold on the Reef, the gold belt running east to west across the city. Man-made mountains of waste rock dominate the city's southern rim, evidence of the unashamed pursuit of wealth which has been the pulse of the city since the first foreign prospectors, the 'uitlanders' as the Afrikaners called them, started arriving with their pans and shovels in the 1880s. These waste dumps are now being recycled to extract gold deposits which were missed the first time round because of inferior equipment. The refining of low-grade ore has now become economic because of the higher gold price.

Johannesburg retains much of the atmosphere of that period. Approaching the city from the south, the headgear of the Village Main Reef gold mine stands out in the foreground; behind it are the modern skyscraper blocks which mark the new American-style

Johannesburg of the 1980s.

There are poor whites, of course, living in white suburbs like Bezuidenhout Valley, whose standard of living may be lower than that of the more prosperous blacks. There is a white middle-class belt running across the southern suburbs of the city, populated to a large extent by mainly Afrikaner civil servants and public service workers, as well as factory workers who are at the sharp end of the economic recession fighting with up-and-coming blacks for semi-skilled jobs. But in the main, Johannesburg is the home of the rich, the very rich, whites of South Africa. In the northern suburbs of the city, with names like Sandringham, Hurlingham, and Hyde Park, is the kind of wealth most people can only dream about: vast, opulent mansions, with swimming pools and beautiful, lavish gardens, bordered by bougainvillæa or jacaranda trees which each October bear their famous purple blossom and in the shade of which families sip their 'sundowner' drinks each evening.

It is here in the northern suburbs that the men nurse their ulcers, worry about the gold price, and complain that the government is failing to introduce reform quickly enough. Many of them are awake at the crack of dawn to go jogging; the whites of Johannesburg are manic about jogging and the agony on their faces suggests they may be convincing themselves it is worthwhile but they know they're not fooling anybody else.

Their wives are obsessed about fitness and about maintaining a general appearance of well-heeled good living. They spend most mornings at the aerobics class perhaps, then a game of tennis at home (many whites have their own tennis courts) followed by a visit to one of the many American-style shopping precincts with their vast hypermarkets. Rule Number One is to shop still wearing the tennis outfit . . . it indicates the family is so well-off the wife does not have to work and provides an opportunity for exhibiting well-tanned legs and arms, not to mention expensive jewellery.

Homes are normally wired up for security like Fort Knox: large brick walls and thick gates; dobermann pinschers patrolling the grounds to tear an unexpected visitor to shreds; and often search-lights. Many whites keep firearms by their beds. For extra security, some white families seal off the bedroom areas with an iron grille gate; intruders can steal the video or the radio but at least the chances of being murdered in bed are reduced.

The whites of the northern suburbs know their liberalism does not protect them from the crime, often violent crime, which is rife among the black population. A better political deal for the blacks they certainly believe in, but they still would not open the door to a black man at night, or even during the day.

And yet most whites in Johannesburg and elsewhere give the run of their homes to the blacks every day of the week in the shape of the domestic servant or servants, something no self-respecting white family can be without. If they did but know it, the black maids of Johannesburg are the blacks' most powerful political weapon in their struggle for freedom. Forget the African National Congress which is fighting to end white minority rule or the anti-apartheid United Democratic Front – a strike by black maids would be the quickest method blacks have of achieving one man, one vote.

The white ladies of Johannesburg entrust their maids with responsibility for running most of the household including laundry, cleaning, cooking and looking after the children. In some cases the good ladies of the northern suburbs even pay for their maids to have driving lessons so as to relieve themselves of some of the more burdensome chores; some go so far as to buy their maid her own car. On Thursdays, 'maids' day off', the take-aways and fast food restaurants of Johannesburg are packed with white families. After all, with no maid on duty, the white housewives cannot possibly be expected to cook a meal and do the washing-up afterwards.

But while domestic servants are part of the family by day, by night they are despatched to the servants' quarters at the back of the house, usually a single room with a bathroom. It is amazing how many people can squeeze into these small rooms. The maids frequently have visits from sisters, cousins, aunts, each of whom can pitch up with a retinue of dependents.

Much of the time the visitors are there illegally under South African laws which racially zone residential areas, and the house might be raided by the police. The white owner can face a substantial fine, even though, as he rarely ventures 'out back', he hasn't the faintest clue how many people might be spending the night there.

The lack of racial friction in these families may surprise many. It could be argued that black domestic servants toe the line because they depend financially on white employers. But the warmth and affection they show towards the white children who spend many hours in their care tends to negate this argument. The close relationship between a white child and its black maid or nanny is established from a very early age when the child is carried around African-style on the maid's back, held by a blanket tied across the nanny's breastbone.

Black servants are permitted to live in designated white areas because they have a bona fide white employer, who requires them to live on the premises. Without this guarantee they would have to return to their tribal homeland located many miles away from the big city, an area where there is unlikely to be much work.

This applies to the remainder of the black workforce who are employed in Johannesburg. In recent years the blacks have made significant strides in improving their job opportunities. Most still work in the service industries at a low grade and with very little responsibility. But some are moving up the ladder. It is not unusual to see a black bank clerk or a black cashier in a supermarket. The whites, at least the more enlightened, are now allowing blacks to fill jobs they would not have dared trust them with ten years ago.

But however trustworthy the black employee may be, however well he or she is doing, however clean and tidily dressed, however prosperous or however cultured, at the end of the day, when the office or the shop closes, the black worker must head off in a separate direction to that of his white colleagues. People who talk and joke with one another throughout the day must, under South Africa's apartheid laws, spend the evening and the night in their separate residential areas. And for most blacks of Johannesburg that means Soweto.

Protea police station, Soweto. 2000 hours. Christmas Eve 1983.
A black policeman checks our credentials and admits us into Soweto's police headquarters through an iron gate. A patrol car carrying one white and three black officers passes us in the opposite direction about to do a tour of the township.

We are shown into the office of Brigadier Johan Viktor, a tall, craggy figure, and a veteran of the Soweto police force. The brigadier has allowed myself and a colleague to spend Christmas Eve on patrol with the Soweto police. 'It's going to be a big night tonight,' he tells us. 'They'll all be drinking and celebrating. There are bound to be a few murders. We're going to try to stop a few of them getting killed.'

Tonight's operation is against the illegal shebeens which provide the blacks of Soweto with the opportunity for after-hours drinking, which in turn leads to many of the murders and robberies, the victims

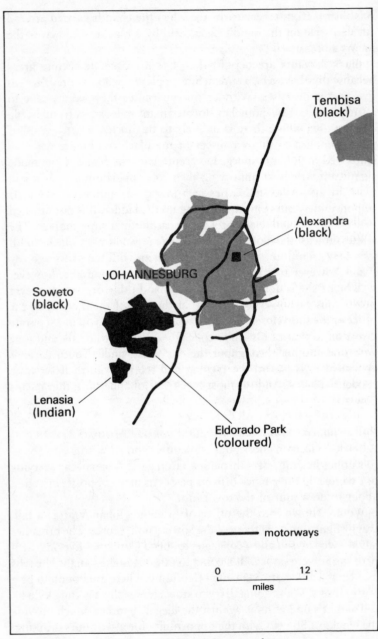

Johannesburg and its townships

often being drunks staggering their way home during the early hours of the morning through dark streets.

We are handed over to Colonel Brown, another white Sowetan police veteran. With him we watch the plain-clothes detectives (many of them black) being given their final instructions and off we go.

Colonel Brown takes us on a 'Soweto by night' tour of the township. Every so often we hear someone whistle by the side of the road as our police car goes by. 'That's the signal,' says the colonel, 'the warning that there's a police car in the neighbourhood.'

We have not been driving for long when a car comes speeding towards us and then suddenly veers off, knocking over a passer-by. The driver does not stop. Colonel Brown slams on the brakes, gets out of the car, checks the pedestrian is not dead or seriously injured, calls for an ambulance on his two-way radio and then gives chase. 'Which way did they go?', he shouts to us, peering into the distance. It's a very dark night; a few street lamps throw an eerie light across the township. Visibility is hazy, anyway, because of the smoke belching out from thousands of coal fires. We lose track, give up the hunt. Another unsolved crime.

Ten minutes later our headlights pick up a middle-aged woman swaying across a lonely side street, obviously drunk. A couple of women come by who say they vaguely know her. The colonel gets an undertaking from them that they will see her home. Back in the car he says: 'In that condition she wouldn't have reached home without being robbed and murdered, or raped.'

It's eleven o'clock. All over Soweto Christmas Eve parties are in full swing. We visit a few. Rooms or garages packed with hundreds of sweating, swaying bodies dancing to the beat of reggae music blasting out over loudspeakers. The cops invite themselves in. The locals know them, offer them a Coke, and we're on our way again.

Come midnight, it's time to bust the shebeens. The clever ones among the shebeen owners expected the call and have shut up shop for the night. A few minor offenders are given a warning. A couple of store-rooms hiding dozens of crates of illegal liquor are broken into by the police who take away the goods and ask after the owner.

Colonel Brown takes us over to the police station in Eldorado Park, the nearby coloured township. It's all quiet there, says the duty officer. Just an average night. In a corner, the victim of a street attack lies slumped on a bench. His teeth have been knocked out and there is blood all over him.

As our night with the Soweto police draws to an end we see a few people still preparing to leave for the Christmas holiday, probably going back to the homeland to spend a few days with their families. But they are not loading just a suitcase or two into their vehicle, but appear to be taking the entire household possessions; chairs, a fridge, a table, etc. 'Every holiday-time they take the house with them,' says the colonel, 'in case they get burgled.'

Soweto stands for South Western Townships. A fairly functional name, one might think, but an improvement on some of the other names which were suggested, like Sawesko and Swestown, when the decision was taken in 1963 to rid the area of what was considered to be the impersonal title South Western Bantu Township. Somebody actually put forward Hendrik Verwoerdville as a possible name (after the prime minister who was the architect of apartheid) but, not surprisingly, it was felt this would not be entirely to the liking of the people who have to live in the place.

Much like Johannesburg itself, the shanty town which was to become Soweto sprang up towards the end of the last century as blacks from all over southern Africa flocked to the City of Gold ('Egoli', as the Africans call it) in search of work.

Its population expanded rapidly during the Second World War when laws controlling the inflow of blacks were suspended as companies manufacturing war materials needed cheap black labour. The official population of Soweto now stands at around 900,000 although most people regard that figure as laughable; the actual population is more like two million, most of these being in the township illegally, according to South Africa's apartheid laws governing how many blacks and which blacks are allowed to reside in the urban areas as opposed to the rural homelands.

The township is a huge area, and is linked to Johannesburg by an extensive road and rail network. The daily transportation of hundreds of thousands of black workers from Soweto into Johannesburg and back out again without any major congestion is a feat of modern urban planning. One factor may be that many of Soweto's blacks start work in the city very early in the morning, cleaning offices or sweeping the streets, for example, so that commuter traffic is staggered. Nevertheless at the height of the rush hour it is by no means unusual to see blacks hanging onto the handrails of already over-crowded buses and trains.

As black townships go in South Africa, Soweto is among the most affluent. There is a prosperous black middle class living there, whose houses are congregated in an area known by the locals as Beverly Hills. The majority of blacks, though, live in rudimentary, but not necessarily squalid, conditions; a two- or three-roomed house, sometimes with a small plot of garden in front. Electrification is gradually being introduced into Soweto, and more and more blacks have telephones. The streets are not particularly tidy, compared to the aesthetically-landscaped white suburbs.

But compared to most shanty towns in Africa (and not a few of the black ghettos in the United States) Soweto could be a lot worse. South African government ministers frequently declare that 'ours are the best-off blacks in Africa'. But then most blacks living in Soweto have not been to Lagos or Cairo. Their point of comparison is the rich white suburbs in which, under apartheid, they are not allowed to live.

Whether, in order to foresake the apartheid burden, the comparatively prosperous blacks of South Africa would prefer to live in one of the black African states, where they would enjoy fuller political rights but might live in relative poverty, is an argument which occupies many of the dinner-table conversations among liberal whites who are concerned about the blacks' future.

Whatever the economic well-being of the blacks, Soweto has experienced several periods of political violence, most notably in 1976 when school pupils clashed with the police on 16 June of that year, setting off a nationwide wave of violence which left 575 people dead.

But it is the non-political crime, the day-to-day violence, which takes up most of the time of police officers like Brigadier Viktor and Colonel Brown. Soweto is possibly the most violent city in the world, worse even than New York.

Every Monday morning the South African Press Association transmits on its news agency teleprinters the weekend crime report compiled by the police chief in Soweto. This, as an example, was his report for the weekend 19–21 April 1984:

> Seven people were murdered and eight women were raped
> including an eight-year-old hostel child and a thirty-four-year-
> old white woman who was picked up by her attackers in a
> city-centre hotel and taken to Soweto where she was raped.

There were twenty street robberies and four armed robberies. There were twelve cases of theft, fifteen thefts from cars and seven cars were stolen. Police arrested two men in a stolen car and recovered twenty-four stolen cars.

Two business premises were burgled and five burglaries of homes were reported. Police also arrested twenty-two shebeen owners, confiscating 129 bottles of beer.

One man was arrested for dealing in dagga [marijuana], five for possessing dagga and two for dealing in mandrax tablets.

All in all, a fairly quiet weekend, nothing exceptional.

The police, almost to a man, attribute the violent crime in Soweto to two factors: faction-fighting between rival gangs or tribal clans, particularly among the Zulu migrant workers living in all-male hostels, and illegal drinking. Colonel Brown said that during the whole of 1983 the police had seized 13,000 bottles of malt liquor.

But black leaders in Soweto dismiss these reasons. Dr Nthato Motlana, a leading activist, believes black deprivation is behind the violence. 'The fact is that thousands of young people are here illegally, desperately searching for work, who resort to robbery with murder to survive.' He also blames the heavy drinking on the lack of recreational facilities.

Cross the motorway from Soweto and you experience the kind of culture shock which so often strikes the foreigner living in South Africa. Suddenly you are in the Orient. For this is the township of Lenasia, where Johannesburg's Asian, mainly Indian, population must live, having been removed over the years from their traditional residential areas of Johannesburg under apartheid.

Some houses in Lenasia, many situated close to Hindu temples or Muslim mosques, are well up to the standard of those in the wealthier white suburbs, better than the homes in which most people in Europe live. This is because many Indians are in the professional class, lawyers or doctors, for example, and are doing as well as their white counterparts.

I once gave a lift to a young man whose job was installing swimming pools. He told me that most of his work these days was in Lenasia and that the Indians wanted only the very best pools.

Like Indian communities all over the world, the Indians of Johannesburg work mainly in the service industries like furniture removals, or as shopkeepers. The city's Oriental Plaza comprises 300 Indian-run shops where many whites go to purchase cloth and pots and pans far more cheaply than at their own overpriced shopping malls.

This, then, is Johannesburg, a place where all the races come together by day and where they all go their separate ways at night. I am often asked why foreign correspondents in South Africa base themselves in Johannesburg and not in Pretoria, the country's administrative capital, or in Cape Town, the legislative capital. The answer is simple. It is in and around Johannesburg that one has the largest concentration of whites and non-whites. This is South Africa's racial front line.

It is when the blacks of Soweto start marching on the white suburbs of Johannesburg that we will know the revolution has really started.

But what of South Africa's other major urban centres?

A two-hour flight from Jan Smuts airport, Johannesburg, is Cape Town. As the South African Airways Airbus makes its final approach the sights which have made Cape Town famous and infamous come into view: Crossroads squatter camp and Robben Island prison camp, vineyards stretching for miles, the docks and of course Table Mountain beneath which the 'Mother City' nestles.

Visible from over 100 miles out to sea, Table Mountain provides one of the most stunning backdrops to any of the world's major cities. From its summit (reached by cable car) the entire Cape peninsula as far as the Cape of Good Hope opens up, as well as the Cape Flats where the non-white housing zones are located, the mountains which lie beyond the wine-producing centre of Stellenbosch, and the north coast as far as South Africa's first nuclear power station at Koeberg which came on stream in 1984.

It was Table Mountain which provided a kind of homing signal for the first Dutch settlers in 1652 as they sailed towards the Cape. It was in Table Bay that they landed and hoisted the Dutch flag and on its shores that they constructed a fort and erected their first humble abodes.

Shortly after landing at the Cape the white settlers were mixing freely with the indigenous Hottentots and nomadic Bushmen, as well as with the imported slaves from Mozambique, Madagascar, India, Ceylon and what is now Malaysia. The result is South Africa's 2.8

million mixed-race or coloured people, 87 per cent of whom live in the Cape Province, half of these in the western Cape where the first white settlements sprang up.

Today most coloureds live in the huge township of Mitchells Plain and, like their black counterparts in Soweto, form a satellite work-force which supports the white city. The coloureds speak Afrikaans (the language spoken by the descendants of the early Dutch, German and French settlers) as their first language and many bear Afrikaner names, taken from the white parent who fathered their ancestors two or three centuries ago. They form a curious halfway-house kind of people, never quite certain, many of them, whether their real interests lie within the white man's system or with the struggle for black rights.

It's a dilemma which faces South Africa's other major population group, the Indians, the majority of whom are located on the country's eastern seaboard around the port city of Durban, probably South Africa's best-known holiday resort, famous for its warm but shark-infested waters, its long beaches and its surfers (the 'waxies', as they are called, after the wax they smear on their surfboards to provide a firmer foot-grip).

Away from the beaches, around the outskirts of the city or tucked into the rolling hills of Natal which stretch back for miles inland, are the Indian residential areas, places like Chatsworth where one Sunday in October 1983 I was invited to the home of Mr P.I. Dervan, an Indian politician who believes the Indians of South Africa should seek to better the lot of non-whites by working within the white man's system instead of trying to overthrow it.

The Indians first arrived in South Africa in 1860 as imported labourers for the Natal sugar farms. Over a curry lunch Mr Dervan recounted the story of his father who at the age of eighteen walked the 300 miles from his home in the Indian village of Arasapatti to the city of Madras on the strength of a vague promise of work. Soon he found himself on a boat crossing the Indian Ocean, arriving five months later in a country he knew nothing about.

Mr Dervan's father spent five years as a sugar-worker and then began a new career with the railways. Like many of the 800,000 Indians in South Africa, his children and grandchildren have now spread their wings, taking up jobs which in many cases place them higher up the economic ladder than many of the local black population who are mostly Zulus, South Africa's largest black tribe.

The Indians and the Zulus live cheek-by-jowl around Durban. After lunch Mr Dervan took me to watch a competition for Indian dance groups. An Indian dance teacher had been flown in from Bombay to do the judging. As we drove around Chatsworth, my host pointed out the proximity of the Zulu areas. It's possible to listen to Tamil, Hindi or Urdu one moment and then a short time later be surrounded by people speaking Zulu.

Relations between Zulu and Indian are generally good on the shop floor; it is in those situations where the Indians are in a supervisory role over the blacks that tensions can arise. Also black domestic servants feel more humiliated working for an Indian family than for whites.

The most serious outbreak of inter-communal violence broke out in 1949 after a black youngster suspected of shoplifting was given a hiding by an Indian shopkeeper. Word quickly spread that an Indian had killed or maimed a young black and within an hour Zulu impis or war parties were on the rampage. At the end of the day the official death count was ninety though many people thought the number killed was considerably higher.

It is an incident which still lives in the collective memory of the Indian community of Natal and one which is perhaps on their minds when they contemplate whether their political interests lie with the whites or with the blacks. During 1983, when Indians were deciding whether or not to join Prime Minister Botha's new power-sharing parliament which admits coloureds and Indians, but excludes the blacks, the Zulu leader, Chief Mangosuthu Buthelezi, issued what was described by some commentators as a 'veiled threat' against the Indians when he warned of the danger of racial violence erupting, saying he was not advocating violence but that 'we live in a violent situation and we cannot carry on blissfully unaware of this fact.' Indeed, in August 1985 another murderous round of intercommunal violence flared between blacks and Indians following the death of a black anti-apartheid campaigner. It left over fifty people dead.

Leaving Mr Dervan I drove north of Durban, past the holiday resort of Umhlanga Rocks, then turned inland to the Indian location of Verulam, to meet another Indian leader, Mr Mewa Ramgobin. He lives in a luxurious house on a hilltop with a magnificent view of the surrounding countryside.

Despite his obviously comfortable existence, Mr Ramgobin is one of the most ardent campaigners against apartheid. He despises those Indians who have agreed to take part in Mr Botha's new parliament, describing them as quislings who are failing to address black rights.

Mr Ramgobin is married to the grand-daughter of Mahatma Gandhi, who spent some of his early years in South Africa as a lawyer and later led the campaign of passive resistance against British rule in India. Ramgobin and his opponents contest bitterly which of them are the true heirs to the Gandhi tradition. Would Gandhi have compromised and joined the white man's system in the hope of winning a better deal for his people? Or would he have hung on to the bitter end until full political rights had been granted to all of South Africa's people?

In the year ahead we were to hear a lot more of Mr Ramgobin.

Between them, Johannesburg, Cape Town, Durban and the major city of the eastern Cape, Port Elizabeth, comprise the main urban centres of South Africa. But given the affinity of many South Africans (black and white) for the land, no picture of the country could be complete without mentioning the vast open spaces which afford South Africa some of its most majestic scenery.

Places like the western Transvaal with its mile upon mile of maize fields and its Magaliesberg mountain range. The Transvaal is where the heart of the Afrikaner lies, reflected in the old Boer War song 'Sarie Marais', which was sung by the commandos when they were many miles from home and thinking about the families and farms they had left behind:

O take me back to the old Transvaal
That's where my Sarie dwells,
Down there in the maize lands by the green thorn tree,
That's where my Sarie dwells.

The Transvaal and the Orange Free State, the former Boer republics, were explored and opened up by the Afrikaner pioneers during the last century and remain the most conservative parts of the country. They are where the 'whites only' signs are still fairly prominent.

The rest of the country consists of vast stretches of wilderness like the Great Karoo, a timeless expanse of desert and rock, and areas of great natural beauty, many of them the home of South Africa's wild life, places like the Kruger National Park bordering Mozambique which is roughly the size of Wales. These wide-open landscapes are enjoyed only infrequently by the country's black population, most of whom are consigned to the tribal homelands dotted around the fringes of South Africa. Under the apartheid system, as originally conceived by the National Party after 1948, these 'bantustans' were eventually to become the home for all of South Africa's blacks. They would be allowed into white areas, including the cities, only when their labour was required.

There are ten of these homelands, representing the various black tribes which live in South Africa. They are:

Homeland	*Tribe*
Transkei	Xhosa
Bophuthatswana	Tswana
Ciskei	Xhosa
Venda	Venda
Lebowa	North Sotho
KwaNdebele	Ndebele
Gazankulu	Shangaan and Tsonga
KaNgwane	Swazi
Qwaqwa	South Sotho
KwaZulu	Zulu

Four homelands (Transkei, Bophuthatswana, Ciskei and Venda) have been made fully independent national states by the Pretoria government, although only South Africa recognizes them as such. But this does not deter their leaders from conducting themselves as if they were the heads of some of the most powerful nations on earth.

Money is no object when it comes to acquiring the trappings of power. The legislative assembly building in KwaZulu, financed by local contributions, would outstrip any parliamentary building in the West for luxury. The carpet pile is so deep one's shoes almost disappear into it. Most of the homeland leaders drive around with fleets of limousines; they have their own security forces, not to mention grandiose plans for international airports and such like. The 'independent national states' also have their embassies in Pretoria, though because they represent what are, as far as the international community is concerned, 'non-countries', their 'ambassadors' do not get invited to many diplomatic cocktail parties.

South Africa maintains that the homeland borders conform to the

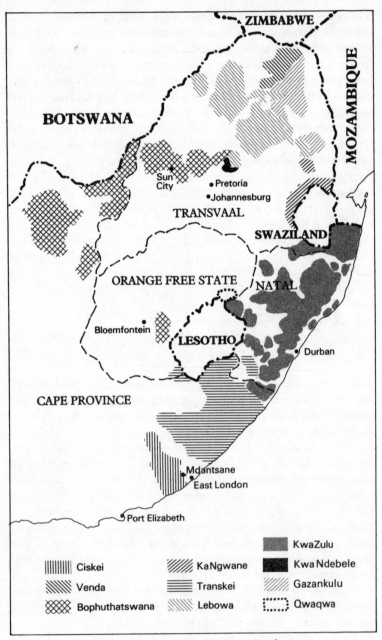

South Africa's black homelands

areas where the various tribes have traditionally lived. The problem is that these areas do not form one solid chunk of territory. One part of Bophuthatswana is hundreds of miles from the other bits and pieces of the same homeland. KwaZulu is divided up into so many little segments that one can drive through much of Natal and not know whether one is in 'white-ruled South Africa' or 'black-ruled KwaZulu'.

The homelands, or some of them, have gradually become the playground of white South Africans, the places they can do things they are not allowed to do in their own country: watch soft-core pornographic films, for example, or gamble. The most famous homelands pleasure palace is Sun City, about two hours drive from Johannesburg in Bophuthatswana. Sun City has two luxury hotels, a casino, and the Superbowl amphitheatre where international stars like Frank Sinatra, Shirley Bassey, Elton John and Rod Stewart have performed in defiance of a United Nations blacklist of sportsmen and entertainers who visit South Africa.

Apartheid has been banned by President Lucas Mangope of Bophuthatswana, and the whites who visit Sun City think nothing of rubbing shoulders with blacks on an equal basis. It is only when they return to their homes in 'white South Africa' that race becomes an issue once more.

Within South Africa – this country of dramatic landscapes, cities old and new, prosperity and poverty, palaces and shanty towns – live people of many different races, a 'mini-United Nations' government ministers often call it.

And yet South Africa is not a country where racial hatred is a dominant aspect of everyday life. Men like P.W. Botha and others who maintain the apartheid state do not hate the blacks. They look northwards to the inter-tribal violence which erupted in many black African states when the whites surrendered power and conclude that the blacks are not fit to govern themselves, at least not yet, and that in South Africa's multi-tribal society one man, one vote would lead to chaos as it would result in one tribe coming to dominate the others. Other systems have to be found, they believe.

Similarly, men like Bishop Desmond Tutu, Oliver Tambo (the ANC leader), Nelson Mandela (despite being incarcerated in prison for over twenty years) and even the young black agitators on the streets do not hate the whites. Their anger is mainly directed at the system and those who enforce it, a system which has in their view brutalized the whites, rendering them oblivious to the demands for justice by their black fellow-countrymen.

It is quite remarkable that the expression of black anger in recent years has rarely been directed at whites as individuals. Black mobs have seldom marched on white areas seeking revenge for their political inferiority. The recent unrest has, however, tested such tolerance to the extreme. A sign that some blacks may be more inclined to turn their anger on individual whites came in May 1985 when, at the height of the disturbances in the townships, a mob of blacks halted a car being driven by a white nurse east of Johannesburg, pulled her out and stoned her. She died shortly afterwards in hospital. But such acts are still infrequent as are personal displays of overt racism by the whites. It varies, of course, from area to area. In the big cities, where blacks and whites rub shoulders every day, there is a high degree of mutual tolerance and respect. But in the more conservative white areas the master-servant ingredient of race relations is more to the forefront, tempered often by the paternalistic affection a white will display towards his 'boys' (as black employees are still called in these areas even if they are sixty years old) as individuals.

A leading black activist once told me that the biggest racists he had ever met in South Africa were the emigrants from Britain who had arrived in the country in recent years. 'They come out here, see the lifestyle, the swimming pools in the gardens, the luxurious homes and the blacks working as servants and assume that the accepted way of treating the blacks is to insult them. They are far worse than most of the Afrikaners!' There are, however, growing signs of increasing friction between the lower middle-class Afrikaners in the urban areas who, in a time of recession, see their economic position threatened by up-and-coming blacks. But here again such friction has not generally expressed itself in violent attacks on the blacks.

There is far more racial tension in the big cities of Britain, where there are large immigrant populations, or in America.

Maybe that is because each race group knows that the other is here to stay. Perhaps, also, over 300 years of living together has established a common African consciousness in the minds of blacks and whites which even the harshest aspects of apartheid have failed to obliterate.

CHAPTER 2

Boers, British and Blacks
The tribes of South Africa

Ringing out from our blue heavens, from our deep seas breaking
    round:
Over everlasting mountains where the echoing crags resound;
From our plains where creaking wagons cut their trails into the
    earth —
Calls the spirit of our Country, of the land that gave us birth.
At thy call we shall not falter, firm and steadfast we shall stand,
At thy will to live or perish, O South Africa, dear land.

These words are from the first verse of the South African national
anthem 'Die Stem van Suid-Afrika' ('The Voice of South Africa'),
declared the official national anthem in 1938 by the then prime
minister J.B.M. Hertzog. He had no right to make such a declaration
as South Africa was still a British dominion, but as the old imperial
relationship began to wither the call among Afrikaners for a truly
South African anthem became ever stronger. In 1938 Hertzog
decreed that 'Die Stem' should be played at the opening of parliament as well as 'God Save The King'. Almost twenty years later, on 2
May 1957, Prime Minister J.G. Strijdom announced in parliament
that the government had accepted 'Die Stem' as the official national
anthem of South Africa. The English translation came later.

Although it is the national anthem for all South Africans it is
essentially the anthem of the Afrikaners: a hymn of thanksgiving to
the land which they pioneered and opened up, suffering deprivation,
hardship, humiliation, misery and death in the process. It evokes
resolution, pride, and nationalism without xenophobia. Because of

South Africa's international isolation, 'Die Stem' is rarely heard outside the country. But it is one of the most stirring anthems in the world.

Equally stirring is 'Nkosi, sikelel' iAfrika' ('God bless Africa') which has become the black nationalist anthem. Its English translation is this:

Lord, our God, bless Africa our home.
May her head be lifted up on high.
Let your ear be open to our cry
That your blessing may come.

Bless the chiefs and leaders of our land;
Since you made them, may they always hear
Your commandments and your name revere,
Bless them, under your hand.

The anthem was first sung as a black nationalist hymn in 1912 at the inaugural meeting in Bloemfontein of the South African Native National Congress, the forerunner of the African National Congress. It has since been sung wherever the call for political justice is made. Part of it is sung in Zulu, part in Sotho, and part in Xhosa.

The excerpt above is followed by a call to God to guide all the people and all the rulers of Africa towards a greater goodness.

Two national anthems, then: one of a people fighting to survive in what it perceives as a hostile environment, the other of a people struggling to achieve political rights for all the people of South Africa, both invoking the spirit of the Lord as their inspiration.

Somewhere along the line God might have ordered things differently so as to have avoided such an explosive confrontation.

Long before the arrival of the white man, the land that is now South Africa was peopled by yellow-skinned Hottentots and Bushmen, whose ancestors had inhabited most of sub-Saharan Africa for thousands of years. Bartholomew Diaz rounded what was to be named the Cape of Good Hope in 1488, followed ten years later by Vasco da Gama who opened up the route to India for the Portuguese. South Africa's strategic importance as the guardian of the Cape sea routes and as the halfway-house to the East was therefore established.

By the 1600s, however, other countries among the imperial powers, notably the English, the Dutch and the French, had set up their own chartered companies to explore the East Indies. The bay beneath Table Mountain became an important stop for vessels en route to the Indies to pick up provisions and for medical facilities. One company which used the station was the Dutch East India Company whose powerful directors, the Council of Seventeen, decided that a more established settlement should be founded to service the company's vessels.

On Christmas Eve 1651, a young Dutch employee of the company, Jan van Riebeeck, and his wife set sail from Holland on board the *Drommedaris*, accompanied by the *Reygar* and the *Goede Hoop*, arriving at Table Bay on 6 April 1652. It was a calm and peaceful evening when they landed, yet the events which followed were to be anything but tranquil. The company had not intended that van Riebeeck and those who followed him should become settlers or colonizers; they were sent to construct a fort, build a hospital, ensure plentiful supplies of fruit and vegetables for ships and barter with the local Hottentot cattle-breeders. But by 1657 soldiers who were released from service were being granted the status of 'free burghers' and allowed to cultivate the land and raise cattle, thereby establishing early on the close affinity between the settlers and the land.

Over the next century they ventured further and further into the interior, establishing their homesteads in the shade of trees or on the lower slopes of mountains. By this time they were proud to call themselves 'Boers' (farmers); having firmly identified themselves with the country that had become their new home, they were pledged to carry with them the traditions they had brought from Europe as they inched deeper into the heart of the country.

As with any pioneers, their life was not easy, driving their wagons and their cattle through mountain passes or across swirling rivers. But it was, nevertheless, an undisturbed life. The colony was expanding; it seemed to be a land of endless horizons and opportunities. Two events were to change this dramatically.

With the outbreak of the Napoleonic wars in Europe, a British expeditionary force seized the Cape of Good Hope in September 1795. Britain held the colony on behalf of the Prince of Orange who became an exile in England when the Netherlands slipped under the tutelage of revolutionary France. Britain handed back the Cape under the terms of the Peace of Amiens (1803).

But three years later the British returned to the Cape, a temporary reoccupation in theory, to secure the sea routes to India during the war. At the European Convention at the end of the war the Cape was ceded formally to Britain. The temporary occupation had become permanent and Britain had acquired a new piece of empire.

For the Afrikaners the arrival of the British meant a dramatic change in their lives. No longer were they the deciders of their own destiny as the British, faced with the problem of coping with a foreign population, enforced a vigorous policy of anglicization. The Dutch language was abolished as a medium in the administrative service and in the judicial system, and its use in schools and in the churches was gradually phased out. Then in 1820, the British government granted funds for large-scale emigration to the Cape. The first arrivals landed in April of that year at Algoa Bay, later renamed Port Elizabeth; 4,000 of them, over half males, had sailed in twenty-one ships from London, Bristol, Liverpool, Portsmouth and Cork.

The arrival of the 1820 settlers marked the true beginnings of the English-speaking population of South Africa. There were now two language groups in the Cape. English settler towns sprang up in Port Elizabeth and Grahamstown. English homesteads appeared, matching the Cape Dutch houses of the Afrikaners. The arrival of the settlers increased the demands for a more democratic form of administration with the result that fully responsible government came to the Cape in 1872. Both communities have grown and prospered in their separate ways. The Afrikaners, who now comprise 56 per cent of the white population, became the backbone of the administrative class, leaving the English, forming 38 per cent of whites, to lead the business community.

But the British had not sent the emigrants to the Cape simply to bestow the traditions of parliamentary democracy upon the colony. Nor was it by accident that the new arrivals were settled in the eastern Cape. For since occupying the Cape the British had been desperately trying to secure the eastern frontier of the colony, close to the Great Fish River, against black raiders belonging to the Xhosa clans.

The first meeting of the white man and the black man in South Africa had already taken place before the British had arrived at the Cape, when the Boers, establishing their farms further eastwards, came across men of negroid extraction who were obviously of a different race to the Hottentots and Bushmen they had encountered previously. The early contacts across the Fish River were cautious and there was considerable conflict as both sides trespassed across the unofficial boundary. These blacks were the vanguard of a great sweep south by the black tribes of Africa which dated back centuries and the Boers correctly guessed that, behind this advance guard, there existed black empires of as yet unknown power.

If the arrival of the British was the first shock to the Boers' way of life, depriving them of their political independence, their coming face-to-face with the 'kaffirs' (non-believers), as the natives were called, brought home to them that the country was no longer open to them alone. The constant raids on their farms in the border areas, coupled with the apparent failure of the British administration to bring the situation under control, led the Boers to think about moving elsewhere to fulfil their aspirations.

But who were these people who had stopped the Boers in their tracks and who for over a century were to provide what was then known as a 'kaffir problem' in the eastern Cape?

The blacks who live in South Africa today belong to a family of over 70 million, the negroid tribes who inhabit the continent south of the Equator. Between them they speak 200 to 300 related languages which are referred to philologically as 'bantu', a derivation of 'abaNtu' which means 'people'. Nobody is absolutely certain where they came from originally although many anthropologists place their ancestors in the area around Lake Chad between present-day Nigeria and Sudan several centuries before the birth of Christ.

Their progress south – no doubt prompted in part by the pasturing requirements of their cattle and the simple human desire to explore – was one of history's monumental human migrations. When exactly they crossed the Limpopo River into what is present-day South Africa is an open question, but by the fifteenth century, if not earlier, they appear to have settled as far south as the area which is now Transkei. What would have happened had they migrated more quickly? What would be the shape of South Africa's politics today had the bantu-speaking tribes peopled the entire sub-continent as far as the Cape before the white man rowed his first boats ashore? Would the sight of a firmly-rooted black civilization have deterred the white man from establishing a foothold in the south of Africa? The historical possibilities are endless, although it does seem unlikely that the age of imperialism would have come and gone without touching the foot of Africa in some shape or form.

The bantu-speakers came south in various migrations and belonged to four main language groups: the Nguni, the Sotho, the Tsonga and the Venda. It is uncertain which group arrived first and which route they took, but by far the most important are the Nguni and the Sotho. Within them are nearly all the major black tribes which live in South Africa today. The Nguni, who account for 66 per cent of the black population, comprise the Zulus, the Xhosas, the Swazi, and the Ndebele. The Sotho, which includes the North and South Sotho and the Tswana, account for most of the rest. The Nguni languages, Xhosa in particular, are punctuated by strange clicking noises produced by placing the tongue at various points inside the wall of the mouth.

Nearly all these languages are related. So a Zulu, for example, can make himself reasonably well understood to members of most of the other tribes. In a place like Soweto where most tribes are represented in the shape of migrant workers from the bantustans, all the tribal languages can be heard and many of the blacks living in the township can speak several of them fluently. One language common to all blacks is Fanakalo, the spoken tongue of South Africa's mines where a uniform language is required for reasons of safety. Even white mine employees learn Fanakalo.

The traditional centre of family life among the blacks is the kraal, an enclosure comprising several huts for the head of the family, his wife or wives and children, as well as several other relatives, the extended family being the custom.

The blacks have traditionally been subsistence farmers. Cattle are the most important animals, reared mainly for their milk, skins and horns. Their dung is also used in building huts. Herding of cattle and hunting other animals is the responsibility of the men, leaving the women to till the fields, the most important crop being sorghum and then maize.

It was these tall, well-built, often handsome African warriors whom the Boers confronted at the historic meeting place along the Great Fish River. The two great tribes of southern Africa – the Boers and the blacks – sized each other up and the Boers took a decision which would change the direction of the country's history.

Threatened by the marauding warriors on the one hand, and

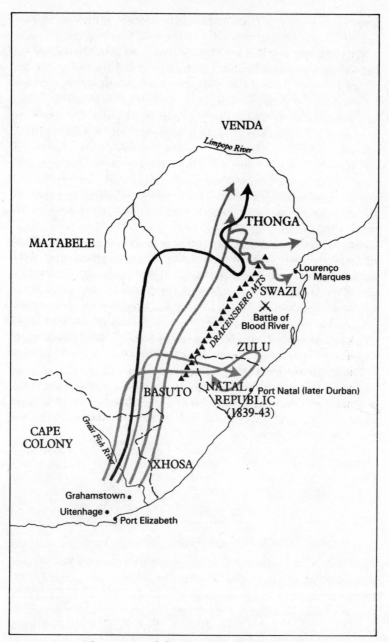

VENDA

Limpopo River

MATABELE

THONGA

Lourenço
Marques

SWAZI

DRAKENSBERG MTS

✕
Battle of
Blood River

ZULU

BASUTO

NATAL
REPUBLIC
(1839-43)

Port Natal (later Durban)

CAPE
COLONY

Great Fish River

XHOSA

Grahamstown •

Uitenhage •

Port Elizabeth

The routes of the Great Trek 1834–54

constrained in their political and social freedom by the British authorities, the Boers looked towards the interior. Scouting parties were
secretly sent out north of the Orange River and into Natal where in
1824 a small group of English traders had settled at what is now the
city of Durban. Soon the decision to move on was taken.

Leaving behind their homes and the fields they had cultivated,
bidding farewell to the land they had believed was theirs, the Boer
families, 6,000 fugitives altogether accompanied by 4,000, mainly
coloured servants, packed their belongings onto their ox wagons and
set off north to begin a new life. They were armed with muskets and
their Bibles and a firm conviction that God had chosen them to
explore new territories and to create a new independent nation in
Africa. What became known as the Great Trek took the Boers on an
often arduous and dangerous journey across the Drakensberg mountains into Natal, north across the Orange River into the Transvaal, as
far north as the Limpopo, and east to Lourenço Marques. They
became known as the 'voortrekkers', 'voor' meaning 'in front' or
'ahead' in Afrikaans. Eventually some of them were to explore as far
afield as present-day Angola, Botswana, Lesotho, Malawi, Zimbabwe, Swaziland and Zaire. The number of Dutch Reformed
Churches in black Africa is evidence of how far they spread their
wings.

The reasons for their going were perhaps most accurately reflected
in a manifesto drawn up by one of the Boer leaders, Piet Retief, and
published in the *Grahamstown Journal* on 2 February 1837. It read:

> We quit this colony, under the full assurance that the English
> government has nothing more to require of us, and will allow us
> to govern ourselves without its interference in future.
>
> We are now quitting the fruitful land of our birth, in which we
> have suffered enormous losses and continual vexation, and are
> entering a wild and dangerous territory; but we go with a firm
> reliance on an all-seeing, just, and merciful Being, Whom it will
> be our endeavour to fear and humbly to obey.

The Great Trek, when the Boers migrated to escape the British, and
the war with the British almost seventy years later, are arguably two
of the three most important events in Afrikaner history, events
whose significance for the emergence of the Afrikaner people is
indelibly printed on the mind of each of them. Piet Retief's manifesto
also stated:

We purpose, in the course of our journey, and on arriving at the country in which we shall permanently reside, to make known to native tribes our intentions, and our desire to live in peace and friendly intercourse with them.

It was a pledge which was soon to be put to the test. Unknown to the Boer voortrekkers, deep within the area settled by the blacks momentous events were taking place in which they too would soon become embroiled and which would add another tragic day of remembrance to Afrikaner history.

A series of inter-tribal wars had brought to the throne of the Zulu people a young warrior named Shaka. Personal humiliations which he and his mother had suffered during his early years (not least the taunting he regularly received over the smallness of his penis) had left Shaka determined to seek revenge. He proved to be one of the greatest of modern generals but at the same time a brutal dictator.

Shaka's mother, to whom he was deeply attached, died in 1827 and her funeral triggered off one of the most remarkable outbreaks of mass hysteria on the African continent. As if bent on convincing their chief of their extreme grief, the multitude commenced a general massacre, which set off a chain reaction of wars making what had gone before seem tame by comparison. The Zulu impis, whom Shaka had built into one of the most formidable of armies, swept aside everything that lay before them. Those clans who feared Shaka's rule fled from the war zone. Huge tides of migration were set in motion. South into the Transkei they moved to escape the dragnet, or else north into present-day Zimbabwe. One of the chiefs, Moshweshwe, established a kingdom in what is now Lesotho, a sea of tranquillity in the midst of madness. Mzilikazi took his dispirited tribe north but was defeated by the voortrekkers; in order to preserve his kingdom he crossed the Limpopo and founded a new royal kraal and named it Kwa-Bulawayo – 'The Place of the Persecuted One' – after Shaka's own palace in Natal. His tribe were called the Ndebele; the site of his kraal is now the provincial capital of Matabeleland.

Shaka was assassinated in 1828, stabbed with two assegais (native spears). The turbulent events of the previous decade had possibly accounted for the lives of two million people; smaller clans had perished or had fled; only a few mighty ones remained of which the mightiest were the Zulus. Shaka had brought the Zulu empire to the height of its power by a combination of brilliant strategy and total ruthlessness. As with many military dictatorships, it was discontent within the army, coupled with murmurings among the ruling élite, which brought about the coup which led to his death. When the Boers trekked north across the central plains they found the area virtually depopulated, but they too were to experience similar horrors at the hands of the Zulu warriors.

On 3 February 1838 a party of sixty-nine Boers and a number of Hottentot servants led by Piet Retief arrived at the Zulu kraal where Dingane (Shaka's successor) received them. Their business was to negotiate a land transfer, which Dingane duly agreed to the next day when he put his mark on a document Retief had drafted. Two days later, amid the festivities arranged by Dingane, Retief became unnerved by the menacing sound of the wardrums, especially as he and his fellow-Boers had deposited their weapons at the entrance to the kraal. Suddenly Dingane leapt to his feet and shouted: 'Kill the wizards!' They were dragged away to a nearby hill and butchered.

A few hours later Dingane sent his men out to massacre the Boer families who were camped a few miles away awaiting the return of their leaders. At the end, 41 men, 56 women, 185 children and 250 servants had been slain. The Boers' revenge came the following December when under Andries Pretorius they camped in one of their 'laagers' (a camp formed by a circle of ox wagons) on the banks of the Ncome River. It was a particularly strong defensive position. They woke on the morning of the 16th to find 'all Zululand out there' – around 12,000 warriors. Despite repeated attacks, the Zulus failed to take the camp. Only four voortrekkers were wounded in the two-hour battle, but the Zulus were annihilated, losing more than 3,000 of their men. The Ncome River has since become known as Blood River, and the Boer victory is recalled every year on 16 December, a national holiday known as the Day of the Vow after the oath sworn by the Boers shortly before the battle, in which they pledged themselves to build a church and to remember the day as one of deliverance if God were to grant them victory.

Despite their defeat the Zulus remained a formidable force in Natal until 1879 when they were finally conquered by the British, but not before the British army had suffered one of its worst defeats at Isandhlwana. They were overrun by Cetshwayo's armies, a humiliation which was redeemed only when a detachment of the 24th Regiment put up a truly heroic resistance at Rorke's Drift. With the subjugation of the Zulus, the field was now clear for the final struggle between the Boers and the British for the ultimate sovereignty of the territory which is now South Africa.

The Boers who had mounted their Great Trek north briefly declared a republic in Natal but this was annexed by Britain after only four years. By the 1850s, however, two independent republics had been established: the South African Republic in the Transvaal and the Orange Free State between the Orange and Vaal rivers. So twenty years after the Great Trek had begun the country was divided into four separate entities: two Boer republics and two British colonies, Natal and the Cape. Tentative steps were undertaken to create a federal relationship between the four but these foundered with the discovery of diamonds between 1857 and 1859 in Griqualand West, an area to the west of Kimberley. Disputes between the Boer republics and the Griqua and Tswana chiefs over the ownership of the diamond fields were ended by Britain through the simple stroke of annexing the territories. Renewed efforts at federation were made but these came to nought, so that in 1877 the Transvaal was annexed as well. The discovery of the diamonds had resulted in a sudden change of policy on the part of the British government; the policy of benign indifference towards the Boer republics suddenly became one of profound concern about their future.

But having trekked north to escape British rule and having lived in their own independent republics, the Boers were not about to surrender to renewed British domination. The cause of regaining independence united the Afrikaner people in the Transvaal even though a few years earlier the Boers had suffered a divisive civil war.

Enter a man who was to dominate the fortunes of the Boers for the next quarter of a century: Paul Kruger, descendant of a Prussian immigrant, whose family had trekked across the Orange Free State in 1835. Despite his limited education, Paul Kruger played a part in many of the political crises during the early years of the Transvaal Republic. He undertook two missions to England where he pleaded with Queen Victoria to revoke the annexation of the Transvaal. Her refusal prompted the outbreak of the first Anglo-Boer War in December 1880. It ended with a resounding defeat for the British at the Battle of Majuba Hill, with the British losing ninety-four soldiers. Within a month a peace treaty had been signed and independence was restored to the fledgling Boer state. Kruger was elected state president in 1883. He presided over the spectacular economic explosion set off by the discovery of gold, while at the same time striving to defend the republic's independence against a British imperial administration which coveted the Transvaal for its wealth and for its strategic position straddling the route leading further north into Africa. He guided his nation through the tumultuous years of the Boer War.

But if the Afrikaners had produced their own titan so had the British. Cecil John Rhodes was the son of an Anglican churchman and had emigrated to South Africa in 1870 in the hope of recovering from tuberculosis. For a time he worked on his brother's farm in Natal, but with the discovery of diamonds the brothers quickly gave up their farming to join the rush of hopeful prospectors. By 1880 Rhodes had founded the De Beers Mining Company, which was eventually to control the world's diamond industry, and in 1887 he expanded his interests to form the giant Gold Fields of South Africa Company. The British South Africa Company which he also formed had by 1893 turned into a vast empire with enormous political, economic and social influence over those areas of southern Africa which were controlled by the British.

These were the two men who held the fortunes of the British and the Boers in their hands and whose determination to protect and further the interests of their countries was certain to lead to a clash. Rhodes, who by 1890 was the prime minister of the Cape Colony, wanted to see an uninterrupted swathe of pink across the map of Africa, while Kruger was determined to resist the Boer republics becoming the sacrificial lambs to British imperial interests.

Developments came to a head in 1896. Rhodes, supported by the mining lords in Johannesburg, saw in the presence in the mining city of thousands of British subjects (the 'uitlanders') a vehicle for drawing the Transvaal into a conflict which he hoped the Boers were bound to lose. In an ill-conceived piece of machiavellianism, Rhodes plotted an uprising among the British in Johannesburg, to be supported by an attack on the city by British soldiers based in Bechuanaland, led by his accomplice Dr Jameson. This attempt to overthrow the Kruger government ended in a fiasco; the uprising never materialized and Jameson was arrested near Johannesburg along with his 'rebels'. Although the Jameson raid had the makings of high comedy, its most serious consequence lay in placing both powers on a path leading irrevocably towards war.

On 9 October 1899 the Boer republics presented the British

government with an ultimatum: that all mutual differences should be made subject to an arbitration committee and that all British troops then posted along the Transvaal borders or on their way to the Transvaal should be withdrawn or turned back; failure to comply with these demands within forty-eight hours would be regarded as a declaration of war. The British were unmoved and on 11 October 1899 the Boer War began.

The Boer leaders saw the British presence in neighbouring Natal as the most serious threat to their vastly outnumbered forces. The Boer commandos were sent across the border to attack British forces at Talana Hill and to sever communications between Ladysmith and Dundee. The British fell back into Ladysmith and relief forces sent up from the south suffered serious reverses at Spion Kop and Vaalkrans. On the western front the British experienced similar setbacks as they moved up from the Cape to relieve the siege of Kimberley. But under a new commander, Field Marshall Lord Roberts, who was sent out from London to bring some order to the chaos, the tide turned. Kimberley was relieved, Bloemfontein fell, and on 31 May 1900 the British entered Johannesburg. A week later they rode into Pretoria. Roberts was soon to return to a hero's welcome in London, leaving Lord Kitchener behind to bring the war to its conclusion. The British clearly felt the war was over, bar the mopping-up.

The fall of Pretoria did not, however, mark the end of the war. The Boers increasingly perfected their techniques of guerrilla warfare, harassing the British forces at every opportunity and withdrawing before a substantial British counter-attack could be mounted. Kitchener's response to this was to launch a 'scorched-earth' policy, destroying farmhouses, food supplies, and indeed everything which could offer support to the commandos. The suffering of the guerrillas was bad but so was that of the civilian population left behind. The policy of denuding the countryside of everything from which the Boers could gain succour included rounding up the womenfolk and children. The problem Kitchener had was where to put them. The idea he came up with created another legacy of bitterness between the Boers and the British, one that still lingers today in the soul of the Afrikaner, and one that bestowed upon Britain a place in history as inventors of the 'concentration camp'.

Twenty-six thousand women and children died in the British concentration camps, most of them the victims of epidemic diseases. But Kitchener's tactics achieved results.

The Peace of Vereeniging, ending the war and imposing colonial status upon the republics for a time at least, was signed on 31 May 1902. Britain had committed half a million troops to the war, against a Boer force of less than 100,000. There were almost 23,000 British dead, while the Boers had lost an estimated 4,000 men. The war, like the Great Trek, like the battle at Blood River, was of crucial importance in the shaping of modern South Africa, not only for the later political developments but also because it brought the Afrikaners closer together than they had ever been. The Boers had been forced through overwhelming odds to become part of the British empire. The emergence of a strong Afrikaner nationalism, already evident before the Boer War, was now a vital element for Boer survival.

Instrumental to that survival was the protection and the promotion of the Afrikaans language, the only Germanic-based tongue to have originated in Africa. Much of the Afrikaner's history, his struggle for survival, his affinity with the land, his yearning for independence and security, is expressed through his language.

When the first Dutch settlers arrived in the Cape in 1652 they spoke High Dutch and were determined to preserve their language in its pure form. The Dutch East India Company was insistent that a localized dilution of High Dutch should not emerge. It was company policy that all non-Dutch immigrants together with the indigenous inhabitants should learn Dutch. It was also stipulated that slaves could only purchase their freedom if they spoke fluent Dutch and were members of the Dutch Reformed Church. Company officials who were responsible for trading with the Hottentots were under strict instructions not to learn the local languages in case they would gradually cease speaking Dutch. But with each new wave of European settlers, the French Huguenots for example, and with each new contact with the locals and with imported slaves the language was refined.

Despite being demoted to second-class status under the British the language did not disappear; rather it continued to evolve, so that by the middle of the nineteenth century what is today recognized as the Afrikaans language, that is to say a European language transposed into an African setting, had become entrenched. In 1876 the first Afrikaans newspaper *Die Afrikaanse Patriot* appeared with the aim of promoting the language; grammar books in Afrikaans followed, as did a history of the Afrikaner volk (people). The Boer War coincided with the rise of the first serious Afrikaans language movement, so that by the mid-1920s the language was fully restored. The Bible was translated into Afrikaans in 1933.

Eight years after the Boer War ended the *South Africa Act*, passed by the British parliament, established a Union embracing the two former Boer republics and the two British colonies. The document had been drawn up at a National Convention at which former enemies from the Boer and British camps shaped a future for the country. Thus South Africa became a self-governing dominion within the British Empire. At a stroke the British government washed its hands of all responsibility for the country's non-white population.

The former Boer leader, General Louis Botha, became the first prime minister. His first cabinet contained two other Boer commanders, Jan Smuts and J.B.M. Hertzog. Botha and Smuts adopted a conciliatory line towards the British, while Hertzog pursued a strong defence of the national aspirations of the Afrikaner people. This division was to surface again and again during the next fifty years, especially in the debate over whether South Africa should support Britain in the two world wars against Germany, and over whether the country should remain within the British Empire and later the Commonwealth.

Then, in 1938, all the passions surrounding the issue of national independence came to a climax when a symbolic ox-wagon trek was mounted from various parts of the country to converge on a hilltop near Pretoria where a site had been reserved for the erection of a monument to commemorate the centenary of the Great Trek. Inside this solid-looking monument, a shrine to the courage of the Afrikaner, is a marble frieze depicting the struggles of the voortrekker families. At noon on 16 December each year, the anniversary of the Battle of Blood River, a shaft of sunlight suddenly beams through a hole in the roof, symbolizing the civilization the Afrikaner believed he was creating in Africa. As 200 Afrikaners 'trekked' towards the proposed site, a wave of patriotism swept the country, a desire for national unity which the ensuing divisions over participation in the Second World War could not destroy. The upsurge of nationalism brought more support for a dissident National Party led by D.F. Malan, who was advocating a policy of separating the races in South Africa to ensure the survival of the Afrikaner. In the first general election following the war, held in 1948, Malan went to the country proposing a policy of 'apartheid' (apartness), a programme of separate racial development. Malan also exploited some of the wartime grievances against the Smuts government. When the votes were counted Smuts was defeated, against all expectations. The Nationalists and a coalition partner squeezed in by the narrow margin of five seats, but in they were.

The most controversial period of South Africa's history, one which was to turn it into the world's outcast state, had begun. During it, the blacks were hived off into tribal homelands and deprived of South African citizenship. Those blacks who were allowed into white areas, under a kind of *gastarbeiter* (foreign worker) status, were condemned to a separate existence at every level of their political and social lives. It was not intended to be a policy of suppression. It was, rather, an honestly-held belief that apartheid was the only way of avoiding friction between those whom God had created differently. The Dutch Reformed Church, with its Calvinist theology and its strong connections with the National Party, saw no reason to doubt that apartheid was in keeping with the scriptures. It was, after all, a nation's Christian duty to defend its identity, to honour its history. Certainly apartheid was aimed at enshrining white supremacy, but not through any Nazi- or fascist-style desire to persecute an entire race of people, rather through a paternalistic self-assurance that the white man had been granted a God-given assignment to civilize southern Africa; it was under his guidance that the black peoples of the sub-continent would attain their political and social fulfilment, albeit on a basis separate to that of the whites.

The attitude of the church towards apartheid was captured in the report of a commission of the Nederduitse Gereformeerde Kerk (the largest Afrikaans church) which met in the 1950s:

Every nation and race will be able to perform the greatest service to God and the world if it keeps its own attributes, received from God's own hand, pure with honour and gratitude. . . . God divided humanity into races, languages and nations. Differences are not only willed by God but are perpetuated by Him. Equality between Natives, Coloureds and Europeans includes a misappreciation of the fact that God, in His providence, made people into different races and nations. . . . Far from the word of God encouraging equality, it is an established scriptural principle that in every community ordination, there is a fixed relationship between authorities. . . . Those who are culturally and spiritually advanced have a mission to leadership and protection of the less advanced. . . . The Natives must be led and formed towards independence so that eventually they will be equal to the Europeans, but each on his own territory and each serving God in his own fatherland.

It was a policy steeped in the Afrikaner's 300 years of history. The Great Trek, Blood River, the Jameson Raid, the Boer War, the commemorative ox-wagon trek had all taught the Afrikaner that nothing was more sacred than ensuring his own survival at the foot of the dark continent where he was surrounded by far larger numbers of Africans. Above all, there was the certain knowledge that the Afrikaners had nowhere else to go. Unlike other Europeans who have settled in Africa they did not have British, French, Belgian or Portuguese passports tucked inside their jacket pockets ready for the day when the blacks took over. They would survive, or be engulfed, on the land where they stood.

The Afrikaners of today are as divided as they have been at several stages throughout their history: there are those who cling to the old values, and those who recognize the dynamics of change which have to be accommodated. The old school are essentially puritan in spirit – a puritanism founded in their religion, in their sense of mission, and in the deep-seated belief that in coming to South Africa to escape persecution in their own countries, as many of their forefathers did, it was entrusted to them to create a more perfect order of society.

In its religious context, this search for a purity of spirit is reflected in some of the most stringent rules governing public morals that exist in any western society. Not for South Africa are the Reeperbahns, the Sohos, the pornographic cinemas, the massage parlours; at least not unless you go looking for them. Photographs of naked ladies in the popular newspapers and in girlie magazines appear daubed with a black stripe across the offending parts of the female anatomy. When the Johannesburg evening newspaper *The Star* published a photograph of the French actress Brigitte Bardot lying in a hammock with her uncovered breasts exposed to the camera, the editor was taken to the Press Council by a private citizen who claimed *The Star* was a family newspaper and that the paper was treating Miss Bardot as a 'sex object' and a 'plaything', thereby seeking to deprave and corrupt. In its defence, the paper said it had published the picture because Miss Bardot had been in the news and because her body was her main claim to fame. In rejecting the complaint, the Press Council ruled that the picture was not suggestive because Miss Bardot's legs and arms were in the normal position of anybody sleeping in a hammock. One cannot imagine the editor of *The Sun* newspaper in Britain having to submit to such scrutiny. Yet in South Africa the Press Council ruling was seen as a milestone, although the Council warned that its decision should not be regarded as a carte blanche signal for newspapers to publish photographs where breasts and nipples were clearly visible.

Standards of theatre and cinema censorship have also reflected the puritan ethic. It was not until December 1983 that Stanley Kubrick's film *A Clockwork Orange* was unbanned by the Publications Appeal Board. Kubrick had refused to allow his film to be cut when it was released in 1972 and so it had never been shown in South Africa. But the official who heads the board is sensitive to changing times and to what can be allowed now which would not have been permitted a decade ago. Indeed in its 1983 decision the board came out in favour of the film saying 'it was of excellent artistic and psychological merit' and that 'the violence was necessary to the film, while the scenes of nudity were portrayed surrealistically and in a caricatural nature'. Other films were unbanned at about the same time; *Easy Rider* was one, so was Bertolucci's *1900* which traces the rise of Italian communism. On the latter decision, the Appeal Board said: 'We cannot ignore a fact [i.e. communism] because it does not fit in with our way of life.'

But the relaxation of film censorship did not extend to *Dear God*, because the Lord was depicted wearing a baseball cap, nor to *The Happy Hooker* which 'contained cheap sex without dramatic merit'.

In its political and social context, the near-absolutist search for a pure society has extended to the belief that a mixing of the races could lead only to a breakdown of established order. The theory of separation, in its ultimate form, decreed that even sex between the races should be prohibited. The idea of the pure Aryan blood of the Afrikaner being diluted by non-white blood was anathema, as this too was seen as another threat to the survival of the race.

One can imagine the outrage, therefore, when one of South Africa's best known Afrikaner actresses, Sandra Prinsloo, appeared on stage with black actor John Kani in a production of Strindberg's *Miss Julie*, the study of a master-servant relationship which was adapted to South Africa's racial situation. Miss Prinsloo, who was seen on stage in a stylized seduction of her black co-star, received several threatening telephone calls, one caller saying: 'How dare you, Afrikaner daughter.'

A similar outcry greeted the publication by Dr Hans Heese of the University of the Western Cape of a book which claimed to prove that at least 1,000 well-known Afrikaner families were the descendants of unions between whites and non-whites. He stated bluntly that there was no such thing as pure, 100 per cent Afrikaner blood. Dr Heese argued that many of the early marriages and relationships at the Cape were between whites and slave women. He argued that the children of these relationships were frequently taken in by the white families and many of today's Afrikaners descended in this way from Asian ancestors. Several Afrikaner families announced that they were taking Dr Heese to court following the publication of his book.

This then is the traditional face of the Afrikaner: doctrinaire, conservative, resolute, uncompromising. It is people of such outlook who run the bureaucracy, who administer the policies of apartheid, whether at senior civil service level or in the local pass office where blacks go to obtain pass books and other documents regulating their lives. But, in recent years, a new breed of Afrikaner has arisen: sophisticated, travelled, enlightened, and increasingly moving into the world of commerce and business, an area which has traditionally been the preserve of the English-speakers. Afrikaner businessmen control some of the country's leading commercial enterprises including Federale Volksbeleggings, one of the top industrial holding companies in the world, Volkskas (the People's Bank), a huge life assurance society (Sanlam), a major building society (Saambou), Trust Bank, the mining company Gencor and several others. Anton Rupert, head of Rembrandt Tobacco, is one of the country's most influential industrialists, and Afrikaners fill senior positions in the parastatal companies, ISCOR and SASOL, which produce iron and steel, and oil, respectively.

Afrikaner businessmen are arguably one of the most important groups in South African society today. Having visited other countries, having addressed meetings in Europe and America, having listened to the arguments abroad about South Africa, they have come to realize that the world does not end if a white man has to stand behind a black in a bus queue. They now constitute one of the greatest forces for change in South Africa at present. When Afrikaner business leaders talk to government, government listens. Increasingly they are moving towards a position of parity with the heads of the giant English-owned companies who have until now been in the vanguard of those calling for reform to the apartheid system.

One thing unites Afrikaners of whatever disposition: a stubborn refusal to be lectured to by the outside world. As one government official explained it to me:

> We don't mind anyone sitting down with us over a glass of beer and giving us his opinion on where we have gone wrong and making suggestions as to what we should do. We're prepared to listen. But we are not impressed by those who get up on their soap boxes and start giving us moral lectures and ordering us to do what they say.

The Nationalist government, which came to power in 1948, was the first in South Africa which did not feel in any way tied by a colonial link with Britain (even though South Africa remained in the Commonwealth until 1961). The policy of apartheid was therefore South Africa's first attempt at solving its racial problem. There is now an increasing recognition that the policy has failed, not because it is seen both abroad and by most South Africans as morally indefensible, but because it did not allow for the pressures which any country will experience during a period of change, growth, industrialization, economic boom, and the attendant movements of population. The policy had no safety valve; it was immutable.

Something else had to be found, a new approach which would recognize the deficiencies of the past while accommodating the demands of the future. After thirty-five years South Africa was about to move into uncharted waters.

CHAPTER 3

The Ballot, not the Bullet
Power-sharing with non-whites

On 13 July 1984 the sole remaining whites-only parliament in Africa dissolved itself for the last time. Established in 1910 after the *South Africa Act*, the House of Assembly had met for seventy-four years in an enlarged section of the building in Adderley Street, Cape Town, first used by the parliament of the Colony of the Cape of Good Hope on 15 May 1885.

The House of Assembly had since 1948 passed the major pieces of legislation under which the whole apartheid policy was enforced: the exclusion of non-whites from parliamentary representation, the laws relegating blacks to second-class citizenship, the maze of security legislation aimed at netting opponents of the government. The House had also seen the rise and fall of some of South Africa's most controversial leaders: Hendrik Verwoerd, who was assassinated on the floor of the House on 6 September 1966 by a temporarily-employed messenger who was later committed to an institution (a replacement piece of green carpet now covers Verwoerd's blood stains); John Vorster, the prime minister who presided over the Soweto riots of 1976, the death in police custody of the Black Consciousness leader Steve Biko in 1977, and South Africa's early overtures towards black Africa, but who was brought down in the infamous 'Muldergate' scandal in which vast amounts of money were laundered from the budget of the Department of Information and other ministries into secret propaganda funds, aimed at improving the country's international image.

The dissolution of the House clearly marked the end of an era. MPs said goodbye to their longest-serving member, Prime Minister

P.W. Botha, who was destined for higher office, although he would retain the right to address parliament. The second-longest-serving member sat on the opposition benches. Since 1961, Helen Suzman of the Progressive Federal Party (PFP) has mounted a valiant campaign against the policies of the Nationalists; for thirteen of those years she was the only liberal opposition voice in the House.

Mrs Suzman and most of her fellow-white MPs would be returning to the House a few weeks later, by which time the South African parliament would have turned into a less exclusive institution.

Two months later, on 18 September, two sergeants-at-arms led a procession of MPs into the House at the beginning of a new session. They passed the pictures on the wall of all the previous parliaments as they walked solemnly into the white chamber. This time, though, there was a difference. The MPs were no longer whites on their own: there were gentlemen of mixed-race origin with tan-coloured skins and others of Asiatic appearance. Upstairs in the gallery the MPs' wives were adorning the occasion with their best twin sets and pearls, but saris and exotic dresses were also in evidence. This was, quite clearly, a new era and the ghost of Verwoerd lurking in the parliamentary corridors must have wondered what on earth was going on. Non-whites in the South African parliament indeed!

Extra chairs had been brought in to seat the new arrivals for the joint opening of the new three-chamber legislature. A liberal opposition MP, commenting on the exclusion of the majority black population from the new legislature, was later to compare these joint sittings with the rearranging of the deck chairs on board the *Titanic*. Nevertheless, the older generation of Nationalists probably had to look twice to believe it was really happening, especially when Mr Botha entered the chamber and had to walk past coloureds and Indians on either side of him to reach his seat.

If South Africa, in the future, does arrive at a system of government which is agreed upon peacefully and which provides for a share in power for all the country's peoples, 18 September 1984 may well be looked back upon as the date when this country turned the corner – away from imposed political discrimination towards a path of negotiated political rights for all.

Alternatively, if the much-predicted black revolution ever consumes South Africa, the same day may come to be seen as the moment when blacks finally realized that they were not to be a part of the white man's club, that they would always be left out in the political wilderness.

Whatever happens in the future, the opening of the new parliament, and the admission of coloured and Indian MPs, marked a distinct shift in government thinking compared to what had gone before.

The 'brown Afrikaners', as South Africa's coloured population are frequently referred to, have always constituted something of a skeleton in the cupboard for many white Afrikaners, given that their ancestors helped create the coloured race in the first place. The belief in a pure white race means the Afrikaners like to maintain a distance between the two races; but there is a feeling, not often acknowledged, that the Afrikaners owe something to the mixed-race people. This dilemma has been reflected over the past decades in the confusion among whites as to what sort of political representation the coloureds should enjoy.

Prior to 1910, coloureds living in the Cape could obtain the franchise and be elected to parliament according to certain property and wage qualifications, although none had stood for election. In Natal a small number of black people had secured voting rights. But no such arrangement existed in the Boer republics in the Transvaal and the Orange Free State. Clearly, when the four states sat down at the National Convention a formula had to be agreed on the sensitive issue of non-white voting rights.

The result was a compromise. The Cape retained its franchise system for non-white voters but had to give up the provision which could allow a coloured person to stand for election to parliament. At the insistence of the Cape, the franchise rights for non-whites were entrenched in the constitution, thereby protecting these rights in the event of the conservative Boer republics ever gaining a position where they could outvote the more liberal former British colonies.

But then in 1931 the British government renounced its legislative authority over the dominions by virtue of the Statute of Westminster. Suddenly there was a very large question mark hanging over the entrenched clauses in the 1909 Act which were aimed at guaranteeing non-whites' voting rights. In 1936 parliament passed the *Representation of Natives Act*, thereby removing black voters from the common roll and placing them on a separate roll which could elect white members to represent them. A black voter who was affected by this took the matter to court but his application was defeated by the Appeal Court, which ruled that the South African parliament was now supreme and could lay down its own procedures.

In 1951 the Nationalist government moved once more against the entrenched clauses, this time passing an act to remove coloured voters from the common roll, placing them on a separate voting list with the right to elect four white MPs. Again the move was challenged in the courts and this time it was the court ruling that the act had not been adopted by the required two-thirds majority. Amid considerable political turmoil, the government resorted to a series of parliamentary manœuvrings including the enlargement of the Senate, in order to achieve its two-thirds majority. The government thereby got its way and the *Separate Representation of Voters Act* took effect in 1956. It was to fight against the passage of this bill that the Black Sash civil rights organization was founded, whose membership at that time consisted of white women. The organization gets its name from the black ribbons the women wore on protest marches and vigils to symbolize what they regarded as the death of the South African constitution. The organization, which now includes non-white women, has provided considerable assistance to those who have suffered under apartheid, without being able to turn back the policy itself. Indeed in 1969 coloured people lost the right even to be represented by white MPs.

But this still left the government with the problem of providing the coloureds with some sort of representative body. Unlike the blacks, who, under the government's apartheid plan, had recognizable tribal areas where they could exercise their political rights, the coloureds had no such territorial heartland. They were spread throughout many parts of the Cape and elsewhere. The answer the government came up with was the creation of a Coloured Representative Council which, they clearly hoped, the coloureds would regard as their equivalent to a fully-fledged legislature. The government was to be disappointed.

The Council was eventually dissolved in 1980 by act of parliament because the Labour Party, the largest coloured party, had rejected the body by refusing to co-operate in efforts to make it workable.

So the question of coloured representation was still unresolved. With the Coloured Representative Council having clearly proved itself inadequate, the government in 1973 appointed a commission of inquiry into 'Matters Relating to the Coloured Population Group' under the chairmanship of a Stellenbosch sociologist, Professor Erika Theron. The committee, which comprised six coloureds and twelve whites, was charged with investigating the development of the coloured people at the political, economic and social level, as well as any other points of contention which might come to the committee's attention. Questioned in the House of Assembly in April 1976 about the commission's brief, the then prime minister, Mr Vorster, said the commission had not been appointed to devise a coloured policy for the government, as the government already had one. He simply wanted the commission to identify points of friction so that they could be dealt with, but within the terms of the government's overall policy.

The commission's report was tabled in the House the following June. It consisted of five parts, analysing those issues it had investigated, and also a sixth part in which the commission's members made a total of 178 recommendations. These included the abolition of the *Prohibition of Mixed Marriages Act* and the clause in the *Immorality Act* prohibiting sexual relations between whites and non-whites, the opening-up of a number of amenities like sporting facilities, beaches, etc. on a selective basis to people of all races and, most importantly, the establishment of satisfactory forms of direct coloured representation and decision-making. The commission said that the Westminster-style type of government might have to be altered to accommodate the demands of South Africa's multi-racial society.

The government's provisional reaction to the report of the Theron Commission was contained in a subsequent White Paper. It did not bode well for a fundamental change of policy which would allow coloureds what they would regard as a meaningful share in government. The White Paper said:

> The government is convinced that . . . recommendations that would amount to the recognition and development of the identity of the various population groups in the republic being broken down are not conducive to the orderly and evolutionary advancement of the various population groups. . . . For this reason the government is not prepared to change its standpoint . . . in regard to the Immorality Act and the Prohibition of Mixed Marriages Act. Any recommendation to the effect that direct

representation be granted to coloureds in the existing
parliamentary, provincial and local institutions is . . . not
acceptable to the government.

However the government did acknowledge that the Westminster
style of government did not have 'to be followed slavishly'. A cabinet
committee under Minister of Defence P.W. Botha had been set up
and its terms of reference were expanded to include the constitutional future of the Indian population. The National Party's policy
towards the Indian community, since it came to power in 1948, had
been to regard them as temporary immigrants, 'a strange and foreign
element which is not assimilable' as the report of a party commission
described them. The commission recommended the repatriation of
Indians to India or elsewhere, with financial assistance from the
state, and a ban on further immigration. They would also be denied
all forms of political representation. Under a law dating back to
1891 Indians (and Chinese) are prohibited from living and working in the Orange Free State (although President Botha has said this
law is to be repealed). Gradually, though, it became evident that
most Indians now regarded South Africa as their own country
despite the continuing links with India. They wished to remain in
South Africa and saw themselves as being as much part of the
country as the whites, the blacks or the coloureds. Clearly, they
could not be swept under the political carpet; some form of representation had to be found for them as well as for the coloureds.

Although between the years 1975 and 1982 many leading experts
were to consider the subject of a constitutional reform, in which the
coloureds and the Indians would be accommodated alongside the
whites, the driving force was without question P.W. Botha both as
chairman of the cabinet committee and, from 1978, as prime minister. So who is this man who was to set South Africa on a new
course?

Pieter Willem Botha was born in 1916 into a solid Afrikaner family.
During the Boer War his mother had hidden in a cave for three
months until she was captured by the British and incarcerated in a
concentration camp where two of her children died. Her husband
was captured by the British and imprisoned in Ceylon. Botha's
family was ardently committed to the Afrikaner cause, so much so
that Botha cut short his university career in 1936 without gaining a

degree when approached by Prime Minister Malan to work for the National Party. He was appointed the party's information officer in 1946 which meant he co-ordinated the nationwide publicity campaign which helped prepare the way for the Nationalist victory in the 1948 election in which he was elected as MP for the Cape constituency of George, a seat he held until 1984 when he became the state president. P.W. Botha is very much in the 'strong man' mould of most of South Africa's previous seven prime ministers. He earned this reputation largely during his twelve years as Minister of Defence during which he had the image of being a 'hawk', especially when he sent South African forces deep into Angola in 1976 during the civil war in that country, a mission which ended in a humiliating withdrawal by South African troops under pressure from the Americans. When he was elected prime minister on 28 September 1978 there were many who feared that, under his leadership, South Africa would be placed on a path of further confrontation, both externally and internally.

But, installed in his new office, the hawk appeared to some as though he were becoming a 'dove'. Mr Botha became the first Nationalist prime minister to visit Soweto; he presided over the extension of black trade union rights; and he visited Taiwan, reacting a little stiffly at first, but by the end of the visit he was dancing to Chinese music with young ladies who, in his own country, would be categorized as mixed-race and therefore out of bounds as far as any significant socializing was concerned. The most important clue to Botha's outlook is that he is a man of the Cape, the first Cape Nationalist to become prime minister since D.F. Malan. During the early years of his political career he was regarded with suspicion by many of the hard-liners among the Transvaal Nationalists who thought of him as a 'Cape liberalist'. Representing a Cape constituency, P.W. Botha came into contact with coloured people more than most Nationalist politicians and, at several private functions during the late 1970s, he clearly revealed something of a soft spot for the coloureds whenever the conversation came round to discussing their political future in South Africa.

Attacks from the right-wingers because of his attitude towards the coloureds had left him unmoved. He had been instrumental in having the Nico Malan Theatre in Cape Town opened to people of all races. In 1977, amid a nationwide blaze of publicity, he effectively ordered the agricultural society in his constituency of George to open its annual show to coloured people. There might also have been a degree of guilt over his instrumental role as a member of the Nationalist government which had deprived the coloureds of the vote. So the signs were there early on that Mr Botha wanted to do something for the Afrikaners' skeleton in the cupboard.

Of course, a role for the coloureds and by extension for the Indians in the politics of the country conformed to the government's wider plans for the constitutional shape of a future South Africa. The country's black population was gradually being deprived of its South African citizenship; their political representation was destined to lie in the tribal bantustans, not in 'white South Africa'. While that took care of the problem of the blacks, the coloureds and the Indians could not then remain in the white heartland but be left voteless. Consequently, following his election as prime minister, Botha pushed hard for a new constitutional deal involving both minority communities. There were several rounds of discussions at government and party level, culminating in June 1980 with the passing by parliament of the *Republic of South Africa Constitution Fifth Amendment Bill*. This paved the way for the abolition of the upper house (the Senate) and its replacement with a multi-racial President's Council consisting of sixty white, coloured, Indian, and Chinese representatives appointed by the state president. They were charged with the task of drawing up a new constitution for the country, one which would take account of the requirements for coloured and Indian representation.

The President's Council reported in May 1982. In summary, its proposals were for an electoral college to be established comprising white, coloured and Indian members who would elect an executive president for a period of seven years, the executive presidency to be created from the existing offices of prime minister and state president (the non-political head of state). The council made no specific proposals on the composition of the new legislative wing of government, although it was assumed that, under the new system, coloureds and Indians would be admitted as MPs as well. Whether MPs from the three race groups should all sit in one chamber or whether there should be three separate chambers was one of the main issues which the government subsequently addressed as it considered the proposals. The recommendations were also widely discussed by the major political parties, by the leaders of the Indian and coloured communities, and by the blacks.

One year after the President's Council had reported, the government presented to parliament its draft proposals for a new constitution. In July 1983 a parliamentary select committee considered evidence on the bill which was then debated in the full House. One of the key issues to be raised by the liberal opposition Progressive Federal Party was the exclusion from the new constitution of the blacks, who represent 73 per cent of the population. During its parliamentary passage the bill was assailed from left and right and variously described as a 'witches' brew', 'mad', 'deformed' and 'illegitimate'. The right-wing Conservative Party (comprising MPs who had broken with the National Party over the government's reform plans) attacked the new constitution because the 'germ' of racial integration had been introduced into South African politics. The PFP said the exclusion of the blacks was an irredeemable flaw. Opposition interjections about the inevitability of black majority rule were met with an outburst from Minister of Finance Owen Horwood, who declared: 'At this moment black rule cannot be done. For a long, long time it will not be possible to do it. It cannot be done in my time, not in the honourable members' time, not in our grandchildren's time.' Some MPs recalled that Rhodesia's last white prime minister, Ian Smith, had once ruled out black majority rule – 'not in a thousand years' he had said.

With MPs from all sides attacking the bill, the government clearly saw the need to move quickly by cutting back on the debating time and taking the new constitution out of the chamber and directly to the people. On 31 August 1983 Minister of Constitutional Development and Planning Chris Heunis, whose department was responsible for the proposed reform, guillotined further discussion on the bill and three weeks later the *Republic of South Africa Constitution Act* was given the assent of the state president.

Given the rifts that had occurred among his own Afrikaner people and also the clear opposition to the reform by the liberal opposition, Botha obviously believed a clear mandate was required from the white population as a whole. The prime minister needed to demonstrate to his own people and to the world at large that he was carrying the whites of South Africa with him. So, after months of deliberation, the date for a whites-only referendum on the proposed reform was fixed for 2 November 1983. One of the most perplexing aspects of the announcement of the referendum was this: what would happen if the whites rejected the reform, given that it had already been passed by parliament? Would a rejection mean the parliamentary decision was null and void? Would the government have to rethink its strategy if there was a substantial majority against its constitutional plans? Would Mr Botha press ahead with his reform even if he was defeated by a narrow margin? Given these imponderables, Botha clearly felt confident that he would win the vote.

Gradually the details of the referendum were unveiled. The country was to be divided up into fifteen regional constituencies, and an estimated total of 2,675,000 whites would be eligible to vote. The problem was that the new constitution was such a formidable piece of legislation that few among the whites actually understood it. Indeed, as referendum day approached, there were several derisive comments as to whether there was anybody, bar those in the highest echelons of government, who had any grasp of what the new deal amounted to. It was in order to assist the white voters that an independent summary, ninety pages long, was published, entitled 'A simple guide to the new constitution – the book to read before you vote'. It was sold at newspaper stands and bookshops all over the country and did a roaring trade. Mr Botha's proposals were, after all, the most important constitutional change in South Africa since the country had left the Commonwealth: it divided white opinion; it unleashed a furious reaction among blacks; it aroused both encouraging and hostile responses overseas; more importantly, the subsequent implementation of the reform provided the political backcloth against which the turmoil of the past two years in South Africa has been enacted.

South Africa's new constitution represents a move away from the style of politics inherited from the mother of parliaments to one which, the government believes, is more suited to a country where there are several different races, each of which is pressing for the fulfilment of its particular aspirations, and where the passionate expression of demands can, if unchecked, lead to the political system becoming overheated and explosive. The government wanted to ditch the cut-and-thrust style of Westminster politics where MPs of various parties exchange often bitter tirades across the floor of the house; this robust style of parliamentary debate was all very well for a country like Britain with 900 years of parliamentary tradition to fall back on, the government concluded, but was most unsuited to a country like South Africa where the need to embrace the views of so many different sections of the population required a legislative and executive system where opinions, demands and the general input from the body politic could be contained and directed away from potential flashpoints.

Thus the key phrase 'consensus politics' slipped into South Africa's political vocabulary. Few people are absolutely certain what this expression means, but it is generally taken to imply that everyone tries to agree with everyone else and the good, old-fashioned parliamentary rows that are the life-blood of most democracies are conducted behind closed parliamentary doors out of the public's (not to mention the media's) eye. The consensus theme was reflected in the changes which the new constitution, if accepted, would mean for the various arms of government.

The legislature. The new constitution provided for the old single-chamber parliament to be turned into a tricameral legislature with one chamber each for whites, coloureds, and Indians. The white chamber would continue, as before, with 178 members.

The coloured chamber would be known as the House of Representatives and would comprise eighty-five members.

The Indian chamber, to be called the House of Delegates, would have forty-five members.

Whites, coloureds and Indians would be elected on separate voters' lists and members of one race group would not be allowed to vote or stand for election in the house of another race group. The number of MPs in each chamber was worked out on a 4:2:1 (whites, coloureds, Indians) proportion, reflecting the size of each race group in the country. This percentage distribution of seats is entrenched in the constitution so that, even if the whites were one day outnumbered by the other two race groups, they would still retain ultimate control in parliament.

As for the workings of the new three-chamber body, the duties of government were divided into so-called 'own affairs' (areas of legislation which affected each race group individually and could therefore be dealt with by the group's particular chamber on its own) and 'general affairs' (areas of legislation which affected all three race groups and which would therefore have to be discussed by all three chambers). The constitution spelled out which matters were 'own affairs' and which fell under the 'general affairs' category. The former, those affecting one race group only, were deemed to be areas like social welfare, education at all levels, health matters including hospitals, clinics, medical services at schools, also housing, community development, rent control, local government, water supplies and the appointment of marriage officers.

To administer these 'own affairs', each of the three chambers would have its own 'mini-cabinet' known as Ministers' Councils.

'General affairs' (those matters that affected everyone, regardless of which population group they belonged to) included defence, finance, foreign affairs, justice, transport, commerce and industry, manpower and internal affairs. Quite clearly there were all sorts of possibilities for some matters to be both 'own affairs' and 'general affairs'. To avoid any confusion on this, the constitution laid down that the state president would have the final say on which category of affairs a particular issue should come under.

Although the three houses would meet separately (except for special ceremonial occasions when they would all squeeze into the white chamber) arrangements were made for joint committees comprising members from all three houses to meet to discuss those issues of joint concern to all race groups. This is where the idea of 'consensus' came in; the hope was that all the contentious points concerning joint affairs could be thrashed out at committee stage so that by the time proposed legislation came to the floor of the respective houses, it would have been agreed upon in advance, thereby avoiding the need for heated parliamentary debates.

The constitution also provided for a multi-racial President's Council (again consisting of all three race groups on a 4:2:1 basis) which would serve as 'a body of last resort to overcome deadlocks and to prevent paralysis of government'.

The government. Under the new constitution, the powerful office of state president is created, referred to by some commentators as a 'Gaullist-style' presidency. The state president was to be elected by an electoral college of all three Houses of parliament on the same proportional basis as described above. The state president would hold office for the lifetime of a parliament. He would have the right to declare war and to proclaim and terminate martial law.

The state president would appoint the cabinet, on which it was expected that one or two coloured and Indian MPs would be invited to serve, making it South Africa's first multi-racial government. However, ministers would be required to swear an oath of secrecy with regard to cabinet decisions, a move that, in effect, gagged the non-white ministers from publicly criticizing any decision they did not agree with – another ingredient in the search for 'consensus politics'.

So that was South Africa's new constitution, one of the most complicated forms of government to have been designed. One newspaper correspondent, endeavouring to explain it all to his readers, advised them to take a stiff whisky before launching into his article, suggesting they should reward themselves with another tot if they managed to stagger through it. Political scientists and academics in South Africa had never had such a piece of work to pore over. But for the man in the street, the intricacies of how the constitution was to function – who would be appointed by whom, how many members would sit in which house, what were 'own affairs' and 'general affairs' – was not the subject of widespread interest. The only issue that mattered was that for the first time South Africa was to admit non-whites into its parliament: coloureds and Indians, but not blacks. The most intense public debate in over twenty years was about to commence among South Africa's white population. It took place at every level of society: among the political parties, of course, but also the churches, the universities, the business community and the country's press.

Launching its campaign for a 'yes' vote in the white referendum, the government sent its big guns out onto the hustings to convince the white community of the merit of the proposed change. On the one hand, they had to reassure those whites who feared the government was opening the door to eventual black majority rule; on the other hand, ministers had to win the support of those sections of the white community who believed South Africa was not doing enough to accommodate black political aspirations and that this neglect would become further entrenched with the new constitution which excluded the majority black population. Appealing to the former group Constitutional Development and Planning Minister Chris Heunis insisted that, far from paving the way towards black rule, the new constitution would eliminate the prospect of one race group dominating another; the blacks, he said, had their own constitutional path to follow in the black homelands. The reform was required, he declared, because South Africa was evolving on a 'plural' basis, i.e. different ethnic groups. Mr Heunis also suggested, however, that the plan did not mark the end of constitutional change in South Africa:

'it does not lay claim to solving all our constitutional problems and should not be evaluated on this basis'. Clearly there was a hint that further reforms, possibly affecting the blacks, might be considered in the future. During the campaign there was much debate over whether the government had a 'secret agenda' for further change, a reform package going further than what was currently on offer and which the government was keeping to itself. The government denied there was any such plan.

As for the liberal opposition, the Progressive Federal Party, it faced a dilemma. For years it had been campaigning for reforms which would break the mould of white-dominated politics and open the way to a system of government in which all race groups would have meaningful participation. How then should it confront the proposed constitution, which admitted coloureds and Indians but left the blacks out altogether? The party knew that many of the country's English-speaking whites, who were its traditional supporters, were much encouraged by Mr Botha's reform plans and would be likely to support him. But the party felt it had to keep faith with its aim of broadening the base of democracy to embrace all South Africans. The leader of the PFP, Dr Frederik van Zyl Slabbert (an Afrikaner) condemned the proposed reform in these words:

> The tragedy for South Africa is that at a time when the voters have come to acknowledge the need for such reform, the National Party has come forward with a plan that is so defective and ill-conceived that if implemented will set back the process of reform for at least a decade.
>
> What South Africa needs so urgently is not the National Party's apartheid policy dressed up in the form of a constitutional plan, but a constitution for South Africa which can bridge the divisions that exist in our country and bring our people together in a great cooperative effort that will guarantee the future of all South Africans.

Dr Slabbert called for a resounding 'no' in the referendum.

A similar call came from the opposing wing of white politics, but for different reasons.

'Political suicide' was how the right-wing Conservative Party described the new deal. The CP, which saw in the government's proposals nothing less than the beginnings of the slippery slope towards the extinction of the white man on the southern tip of

Africa, went so far as to recruit the Almighty in its campaign to mobilize the whites against a plan which would 'make representatives of other nations co-governors of whites.' The party leader, Dr Andries Treurnicht, addressing a rally in Johannesburg, suggested that there could not be unity among the Afrikaner volk if some people accepted the kingship of Christ, while others rejected it. The clear implication of his remarks was that those Afrikaners who voted in favour of the proposed constitution would be forsaking the principles of Christ's teaching. His remarks unleashed a furious row between the CP and the Nationalists. The government moved quickly to reassure simple, God-fearing Afrikaners that voting 'yes' to the government's plans would not condemn them to an afterlife in hell.

Undeterred, Dr Treurnicht ('Dr No', as he is nicknamed, because of his rejection of any reforms) went onto the offensive again a few days later at a CP rally in Potchefstroom in the heart of the Transvaal. This is solid Afrikaner country and the meeting was well attended. Talking to some of the Conservative Party members before the arrival of their leader, the message that came across in fairly blunt language was that 'Botha is selling us out to the blacks.' Dr Treurnicht, as he entered the auditorium, was given a triumphant welcome. He again took up the question of the voters' Christian convictions. He said he was not advocating a church state in South Africa but, he went on, one could not separate 'the way we live politically from the way we live religiously'. He spoke of upholding 'Christian decency'. It was not a rabble-rousing style, instead a nicely-judged appeal to the anxieties of the Afrikaners. All in all, it was a pretty vitriolic campaign among the major political parties.

For South Africa's business community, the proposed new constitution was seen, by many at least, as a successful weapon in the fight to head off possible economic sanctions against the country. Though viewed as inadequate, the planned reform was welcomed as a first step, they hoped, towards further liberalization measures. The major companies had been in the vanguard of those who, over the years, had been urging government to introduce significant reform, both because of the international pressure on South Africa and because many of these companies were themselves crippled by the multitude of laws stifling black advancement. Several business leaders representing the major banks, mining houses and supermarket chains came out in favour of a 'yes' vote. An exception was the former chairman of the giant Anglo American Corporation, and one of the country's most influential figures, Mr Harry Oppenheimer, who, no doubt as a result of his close connections with the PFP, announced that he intended voting 'no'. Writing in the *Rand Daily Mail* on 12 October 1983, Mr Oppenheimer acknowledged that the proposed representation of coloureds and Indians in parliament was 'certainly an important step forward in National Party thinking'. But, he said, the government had 'found it necessary to structure this reform in a way which entrenches the power of the white majority party . . . it should not surprise us that they [the blacks] bitterly resent and universally condemn the introduction of a new constitution entirely without reference to their opinions, their problems and their rights. . . . And therefore – with regret, certainly, but with no doubt in my mind – I have decided to vote "no".'

The debate within the principal churches mirrored that which was taking place at the political level. Despite the importance of the choice now facing the Afrikaner community, the main Dutch Reformed Churches were strangely reluctant to offer definitive guidance on which way to vote. Although traditionally regarded as the 'National Party at prayer', the Dutch Reformed Church was perhaps acutely aware that Afrikanerdom was no longer united, that it was torn between the National Party and the Conservatives, and that a firm recommendation on whether to vote 'yes' or 'no' would lead to a major political/ecclesiastical row. Over 200 ministers representing the three major Afrikaans churches met before the referendum to reject the constitution. They said that Christian values would be undermined because the planned reform was based on power-sharing with Hindus and Muslims who rejected the teachings of the Bible. But when it came to offering the final advice from the pulpit to church-going voters, the Dutch Reformed Church steered clear of taking sides. The Reverend Henno Cronje, scribe for the Northern Transvaal Synod of the Nederduitse Gereformeerde Kerk, said church members had been reminded of the necessity to act 'with Christian responsibility' and to keep in mind the importance of the referendum decision. Professor Bart Oberholzer, moderator of the Nederduitsch Hervormde Kerk (a smaller Dutch Reformed church), said his church would not advise members on how to vote. 'The idea is that members must assume their own responsibility for the referendum. They will have to vote according to their conscience and their view of what is best for the future of our country.'

Among the main English-speaking churches, there was no such

reluctance to offer guidance. A pastoral letter drawn up by the Southern African Catholic Bishops' Conference and signed by its president, Archbishop Denis Hurley of Durban, was read out in all Roman Catholic churches on 22 September 1983. It criticized the constitution because 'two-thirds of the population – the whole African section – is disregarded.' The letter described this omission as a 'serious moral failure' adding that the reform plan fell short of 'what is required in terms of truth, justice, love and freedom'. Bishop Desmond Tutu, the then general secretary of the South African Council of Churches, urged member bodies to reject the proposed changes, saying that they had been conceived and formulated without the participation of the authentic representatives of the people of South Africa. Methodist leaders rejected the proposed constitution because it was 'alien to the reconciling Gospel of Jesus Christ' and a recipe for 'further polarisation, unrest and violent conflict'.

While the debate was raging among the white community, outside the white laager opposition was mounting among those who were not included in the government's plans. The United Democratic Front was founded to lead the extra-parliamentary opposition to the constitution. Another important black figure who lent his voice to the anti-government campaign was Chief Mangosuthu Buthelezi, the chief minister of the KwaZulu homeland and also the political chief of the country's most numerous black tribe, the Zulus. Though an advocate of non-violent change in South Africa, Chief Buthelezi found little in the new constitution to indicate that the government was committed to meaningful reform. He stated that the establishment of separate parliaments for whites, coloureds and Indians, while excluding blacks, would 'close the door on negotiations'. He added that 'it would show blacks that whites are not interested in negotiating with them over the country's future'. A 'yes' vote, he suggested, would remove the justification for his moderate stance and for his opposition to economic sanctions against South Africa. During the campaign Buthelezi shared several platforms with PFP leaders, another factor which concerned whites who had traditionally voted for the party.

As referendum day grew closer so the nation's leading newspapers started offering editorial advice to their readers on which way to vote. Nearly all the Afrikaans papers supported the government while the English-language press was as divided as its readers. The *Sunday Times* and *The Citizen*, both Johannesburg newspapers, as well as the *Daily Despatch* of East London and *The Natal Mercury*, all came to the same general conclusion that Mr Botha's proposals betrayed serious shortcomings but that they were better than what existed at present. The influential *Financial Mail* said a 'yes' vote would hardly make the constitution bill any less of an 'abortion' but it would encourage business to support the government's 'experiment in improving race relations'. These newspapers all urged their readers to vote in favour of the deal.

On the other side of the argument, several papers lined up behind a 'no' vote, generally because of the exclusion of the blacks. These included the *Rand Daily Mail*, the *Cape Times*, the *Sunday Express* and the *Pretoria News*, the latter describing the plan as 'a Machiavellian design to place the National Party permanently in the driving seat with a multi-racial collection of passengers for cosmetic effect'. *The Star*, Johannesburg's evening paper, urged its readers to abstain, while the current affairs magazine *Frontline* suggested voters should spoil their papers.

Abroad, the result of the referendum was eagerly awaited. Among the major western powers there was a recognition that P.W. Botha was committed to reform, although it did not go far enough and was not moving quickly enough.

It was clearly understood that if the whites accepted the deal, Botha would feel confident to proceed with further reforming measures. A white rejection, however, could lead to Botha and his government retreating into their Afrikaner bunker, thereby setting back the cause of reform by a generation. Addressing a National Party congress in Pretoria, the Foreign Minister Pik Botha said that all South Africa's ambassadors believed a 'no' vote would have a terribly damaging effect on the country's image overseas. The referendum was the country's last chance to shape the future and was not just a vote for one political party but was a vote for South Africa, declared Botha.

The two months before the referendum were a torrid period in South African politics. Passions rose, insults were traded, communities were split. Essentially the whites were divided along the following lines.

Those in the 'yes' camp comprised two groups: Afrikaners who were traditional National Party voters who, although perhaps troubled by the notion of power-sharing with coloureds and Indians, had confidence in Mr Botha that he was leading them along the right path. This group also felt that South Africa had to do something to try to win back some international respect, although the idea of responding to overseas criticism was not paramount in their considerations. The 'yes' voters also included a sizeable proportion of English-speaking whites. Some of these had in any case been drifting towards the Nationalists in recent years. But they also included traditional PFP voters who were not happy with the party's out-and-out rejection of the planned reforms. These voters changed allegiance and went with Mr Botha because they believed that, however much the proposals failed to address the issue of real reform, they were nevertheless a 'step in the right direction'. They were prepared to give Botha the benefit of the doubt. The estimate was that something like 40 per cent of English-speaking voters eventually supported the government at the poll.

Those voting 'no' comprised two groups at opposite ends of the political spectrum. The Progressive Federal Party campaigned against the constitution because it saw it as being a face-lift on apartheid. The Conservative Party were in the 'no' camp because they saw it as the beginning of the end of white supremacy.

The problem was that if the 'no' camp won, the coloureds and the Indians, as well as international opinion, would read the result as a victory for those whites opposing change, rather than a victory for those who opposed the plan because it offered too little. Regardless of any voting analysis afterwards, the impression would be that South Africa's white population had again given the 'thumbs down' to reform. In the end, such considerations did not arise.

When the votes were counted in the fifteen regional constituencies it was clear that Mr Botha had won an overwhelming majority. In response to the question: 'Are you in favour of the implementation of the new constitution as approved by parliament?' the voting went like this:

Yes	No	Spoilt Papers
1,360,223	691,577	10,669
(65.95 per cent)	(33.53 per cent)	(0.52 per cent).

It was a two-to-one majority for Botha. Only one region went against him, Pietersburg in the northern Transvaal, the heartland of the Afrikaner hardliners. The turnout was 76 per cent, higher than that in the 1981 general election, but lower than the 91 per cent of whites who voted in the previous constitutional referendum in 1960 when they narrowly came out in favour of leaving the Commonwealth.

It was Hendrik Verwoerd who had gone to the Commonwealth conference in London in 1961 to take South Africa out of the organization. Since then no South African leader had visited the British capital. The years of increasing South African isolation over its apartheid policy made such a visit a political embarrassment for the host government. This pattern was to be broken by P.W. Botha.

With his power base at home secured through the referendum victory, and with a diplomatic triumph in his pocket in the shape of a peace accord with Mozambique, Mr Botha clearly felt it was time to try to win some international gratitude for his efforts in trying to move South Africa in a new direction, however slight the changes were in the eyes of many people. Diplomatic feelers were put out during the early part of 1984 and in May he departed on a tour of Europe which took in nine countries. South Africans were not naive enough to believe that the tour would lead to South Africa's 'pariah status' being ended. The best they could hope for was that the European leaders would gain a fuller understanding of Botha's reform programme and would subsequently temper their criticism of South Africa's domestic policies. For their part, the European leaders (particularly the British prime minister Margaret Thatcher) defied domestic pressure against the visit from the anti-apartheid lobby, insisting that the cause of reform and peace in southern Africa would be better served by maintaining a cautious dialogue instead of condemning the Pretoria government to a diplomatic Siberia. So, with both sides approaching the visit warily, Mr Botha began the most extensive tour of Europe to have been undertaken by a South African leader in four decades.

The most controversial part of the tour was always going to be the London leg. And so it proved. As Mr Botha was holding talks at Chequers with Mrs Thatcher, thousands of anti-apartheid demonstrators marched through central London to protest against the visit. The Chequers meeting itself ended with the two prime ministers posing briefly for photographs after a meeting which was described by South African correspondents accompanying Botha as 'fruitful, extremely frank but not acrimonious'. At one stage of the meeting, the British Foreign Secretary, Sir Geoffrey Howe, remarked to Botha that the British people found it difficult to accept the vast differences of prosperity and poverty which existed in his country. The remark prompted the response from Mrs Thatcher: 'Geoffrey, you are a Conservative, you should have no problem understanding that.' Botha then flew by helicopter to Heathrow Airport for a flight to Zurich; there was an unplanned delay at Heathrow when it was realized that all the South African security men had been left behind at Chequers, the prime minister's husband Denis having steered them into a side room to watch a rugby match on television, where they had been forgotten about.

By the time the South African party arrived in Switzerland, diplomatic correspondents for the British newspapers had clearly been 'nobbled' by their government contacts who, in an attempt to defuse any possible accusations at home that Thatcher had given her guest an easy time, put out the line that she had lambasted Botha with a series of demands about South African government policy. When the British Sunday newspapers reached Zurich on the following morning, the South Africans decided to go onto the offensive. Denying the charges that Thatcher had given his prime minister a dressing-down, the South African Foreign Minister Pik Botha said that their British host had spoken openly and critically of certain aspects of South Africa's internal policy but that she appeared to understand the complexities of South Africa's problems. 'If that's what she's like when she's taking you to task' said Botha, 'I'd like to see her when she's being friendly.' In fact, the meeting did establish something of a workmanlike relationship between the two leaders, with Thatcher telling P.W. Botha that there should be an 'open line' between them whenever bilateral problems arose. The relationship was to be severely tested later in the year when the two countries became embroiled in their most serious crisis for many years.

As well as Britain and Switzerland, Botha's trip to Europe took in Portugal, West Germany (including West Berlin), Belgium, France, Austria, Italy and the Vatican, where the prime minister met the Pope. Thirty-six hours before the meeting with the Pontiff, the security forces in South West Africa/Namibia swooped on the grounds of a Roman Catholic church near Windhoek, the territory's capital, and arrested thirty-seven leading members of SWAPO, the Namibian liberation movement, who were attending a barbecue. This affront to the Catholic church was another striking example of the bad timing which the South African security forces so often demonstrate.

Reviewing the tour, Pik Botha referred to several of the points of difference which had cropped up. South Africa had pressed the British government to close the office in London of the African National Congress, from where, South African security sources believe, most of the organization's political and many of its guerrilla activities are masterminded. Pik Botha said he had received no satisfaction on this matter and that pressure would continue to be applied upon the British government to have the office closed. As for the European leaders' criticisms of South Africa's international policies, Botha said he had not been given a satisfactory reason why 1.5 million migrant labourers from South Africa's neighbouring black states streamed into his country if it was, as alleged, such a 'racial hellpot'. As far as sporting ties were concerned Botha said he had asked why those sports which no longer practised racial discrimination could not be removed from the sports boycott list. Botha told newsmen: 'They just answered "Gleneagles". That was the only answer they had and it was not satisfactory.' (The Gleneagles agreement of 1977 commits Commonwealth countries to discourage sporting links with South Africa.)

The tour was followed avidly in South Africa itself. The state-run broadcasting service, as well as the Afrikaans press, described the trip as 'triumphant'. Mr Botha, they said, had broken his country's isolation, had received a sympathetic hearing wherever he went, and had won more understanding for the government's policies. The English press in South Africa reacted more cautiously, concentrating their reports on the demands for further reforms made by the European leaders and concluding that, at the end of the day, it was still apartheid which was preventing South Africa's readmission into the international community.

Both interpretations of the visit had an element of truth. Botha was certainly commended for his courage in introducing the reform programme, in beginning the process of dismantling apartheid. But it was made abundantly clear to him that the reforms would need to go a long way further and to bring about political representation for all South Africans, before the West would be able to offer its seal of approval. These explicit views left a marked impression upon Botha, a realization of just how far South Africa was out on a limb, although publicly he would not have admitted it. Nevertheless he came home feeling he had bought some time for South Africa abroad. But did he have enough time left at home?

Having won his overwhelming victory in the referendum for whites, Botha now had to win over the support of the coloured and Indian communities for his new constitution; after all, if they rejected it, the already limited legitimacy of the reform would be further tarnished. Within both population groups a heated and occasionally violent campaign began, involving those who favoured joining the Botha plans, because they marked the beginning of reform, and those who held that the two groups should boycott the whole deal and pledge themselves to continue to fight for political rights for all people, including the blacks.

The debate within the coloured community had already been sparked off by a decision made in January 1983 by the Labour Party (the dominant political party for coloured people) to co-operate in the government's plans. Meeting at Eshowe in Natal, only nine of the 300 delegates voted against taking part in the new constitution as a step towards achieving one man, one vote in South Africa. The decision shattered the Black Alliance of black, coloured and Indian groups opposed to apartheid, especially as the Labour Party had been instrumental in the downfall two years previously of another 'sham' body, the Coloured Representative Council.

The party's leader, the Reverend Allan Hendrickse, was firmly convinced that the time of boycott politics should come to an end and that the National Party (which he believed had undergone a change of heart) should be given a chance to prove its good intentions. This was despite the suffering which he had experienced in the past at the hands of National Party governments. Hendrickse was the son of a prominent minister in the United Congregational Church who built a small church in the centre of the town of Uitenhage in the eastern Cape. For fifty years his father served there as preacher and then principal. One day, though, the government ordered the closure of the church, having declared the area white under the terms of the *Group Areas Act*. His son, Allan, had to conduct the deconsecration of the church ('the saddest ceremony of my life' he once told an interviewer) and eighteen months later his father died, heartbroken, after the church had been destroyed by bulldozers. In October 1976, with the country experiencing widespread black unrest, Allan Hendrickse was put in prison for sixty days for his political activities against the government. And yet he was prepared to put these bitter experiences behind him by supporting Botha's plans, justifying his position, in an interview with the Johannesburg *Financial Mail*, by quoting Oliver Wendell Holmes: 'The great thing in this world is not so much where we stand but the direction in which we are moving.'

The direction in which the Indian community wanted to move was hard to judge. A survey conducted by the state-funded Human Sciences Research Council in September 1983 had found that a substantial majority favoured participation, but that many were anxious about the exclusion of the blacks. The South African Indian Council, a government-created body, had until then been the Indians' only representative forum but this too carried the label 'stooge' around its neck because it was seen as an instrument of the government. Added to this, the old Indian congress movement, which had struggled alongside the black nationalist movements in the fight against apartheid, gained a new lease of life in mobilizing opposition to the constitutional proposals.

The leader of the SAIC was Amichand Rajbansi who lives in the Indian suburb of Chatsworth in Durban. He owns a spacious house with black guards outside. On the wall of his lounge there is a picture of Rajbansi with former prime minister John Vorster. Rejecting the accusation that he was 'selling out' by supporting Botha's plans, Rajbansi used the phrase that 'it is better to fight through the ballot than through the bullet.' The tensions within the Indian community came to a climax twelve days after the white referendum when, in order to muster Indian support for the reform plans, Botha undertook an historic first meeting with members of the Indian community at the city hall in Durban.

Outside the building an anti-Botha demonstration was held by members of the Natal Indian Congress. Forty-four of them were arrested and charged under the Internal Security Act in connection with the staging of an illegal gathering and were released on R200 bail. Later that day several thousand NIC supporters held a meeting elsewhere in Durban to attack the constitution and Botha's visit to the city. Rajbansi was described as Botha's 'junior partner'. Eighteen thousand leaflets advertising the NIC meeting were allegedly confiscated by the police while they were being printed.

As the in-fighting grew within both the coloured and Indian communities, one of the most crucial problems facing the proconstitutionalists within each group and also the prime minister was whether the coloureds and Indians should also be allowed to vote on the new deal in referenda or whether they should move straight to elections for the two new chambers. The government's objection to holding referenda lay in the possibility that both groups would reject the proposals. Despite enjoying the support of the whites, would Botha then press ahead with the reform if the very people it was designed to help gave it the cold shoulder? Not surprisingly, therefore, it was eventually decided to skip the referenda and proceed directly with coloured and Indian elections.

The weeks prior to the elections were dominated by an intense struggle between those favouring participation and those calling for a boycott of the polls. The boycott campaign was organized by the recently-formed United Democratic Front opposition grouping as well as other anti-apartheid groups. The election days themselves saw considerable unrest; indeed the widescale violence which gripped South Africa throughout much of 1984 and 1985 began to shift into top gear at about the time of the elections.

The coloureds went to the polls on 22 August 1984, the Indians one week later. Clearly the turnout figure was going to be the most crucial indicator of whether the two groups were behind the new power-sharing parliament. In the coloured election, there were wide variations in the turnout level. In the Orange Free State there were constituencies where 50 per cent of the voters cast their ballot; but in the Cape, the most populous coloured area, some constituencies recorded turnout levels as low as 4 or 5 per cent.

When all the votes were in, the overall turnout figure proved to be about 30 per cent, a figure which looked even more dismal when it was taken into account that only two-thirds of the potential voters bothered to register to vote in the first place. Government opponents announced that the result was a victory for those who had campaigned for a boycott. The result meant that the government could hardly claim widespread acceptance of its plans among the coloured people. On the other hand, the vote was up on that for the old Coloured Representative Council; also the parties may have been hampered in getting out the vote by their own inexperience in fighting a fully-fledged parliamentary election. In general, the vote could have been a lot worse for the government. They could just about live with it. The turnout had been low, certainly, but not farcically so. Government ministers blamed the poor response on intimidation, a charge which was repeated when the Indians went to the polls, recording an even worse turnout – just 20 per cent.

Botha described the low turnouts as a 'minor obstacle' on 'the road to the future'. 'I don't say the new constitution is perfect, nor is it the total solution to our problems. But what is the alternative?' The leader of the white opposition, Dr Slabbert, said the overall impression was that the election had not been an inspiring or convincing mandate for the new constitution. He said that the parliament was starting off with a 'credibility problem' and that it was going to demand all the ingenuity and resources of those who served in it to demonstrate that South Africa was constitutionally better off than before and that the three-chamber parliament was 'a step in the right direction,' as its supporters claimed.

Clearly, in the eyes of many coloureds and Indians, the new MPs were going to have to achieve something fairly remarkable to justify their enormous salaries and allowances, especially as some of them had been elected by no more than a handful of votes and many of those were cast by their own family and friends.

When the new parliament began its first full working session in January 1985 the new non-white MPs were anxious to prove they were not 'Uncle Toms'. In the House of Representatives (the coloured chamber) MPs were out to demonstrate that they were there not to feather their own nests but to fight for meaningful reforms in South Africa. 'We're not here simply to decorate the furniture', declared one of the new arrivals. The historical irony was that the coloured chamber was the former Senate – the very house which had voted to deprive the coloureds of the vote back in the 1950s. The leader of the coloured MPs, Allan Hendrickse, sat in his new office beneath a picture of the former Minister of Justice Jimmy Kruger who had jailed him in 1976. Outside the House of Representatives the statue of Queen Victoria stood defiantly, even though the British parliamentary system of democracy which had blossomed during her reign was being consigned to history as far as South Africa was concerned.

Thus was South Africa's new power-sharing constitution born. A break with the past it certainly marked. But how big a break? Coloureds and Indians had been brought into the white man's laager; but were they there to help repel assailants or to start the process of widening the political circle so that blacks could join in as well – and if the blacks were to be allowed in, on what basis?

But these were questions for the future. P.W. Botha's prototype parliament had been run off the assembly line and appeared to be running smoothly. Talk of later modifications was a little premature. After all, the whites would need a few years to grow accustomed to the idea of having coloureds and Indians in government before there could be a further constitutional remodelling.

But that was before the wave of unrest and the mounting international pressure upon South Africa to move faster down the reform path. Changes which Botha perhaps had in store for a few years hence were quickly brought forward for consideration. And these proposed reforms would start eroding the pillars of the whole apartheid structure.

CHAPTER 4

The Wastelands
The changing face of apartheid

> Whereas we are, and always have been, prepared to play host to the MCC, we are not prepared to receive a team thrust upon us by people whose interests are not the game, but to gain political objectives which they do not even attempt to hide. The team, as it stands, is not the team of the MCC selection committee but of the political opponents of South Africa.

With these words, delivered at a meeting in Bloemfontein on 18 September 1968, the then prime minister John Vorster effectively vetoed a proposed cricket tour to his country by England's Marylebone Cricket Club scheduled for the following summer. The ban had become inevitable the previous month after the émigré South African coloured cricketer, Basil d'Oliviera, had notched up an innings of 158 runs for England in the final test against Australia at the Oval, thereby virtually ensuring himself a place on the forthcoming tour to South Africa. When he was selected Vorster told the MCC the team would not be acceptable and the MCC replied by cancelling the tour. The sports boycott of South Africa then took off.

Almost two decades later, an English team of eleven non-white cricketers would be welcomed by the South Africans with open arms, such has been the effect of this country's sporting isolation, coupled with a growing realization that apartheid has got to bend to take account of the world as it is. Such has been the change in the attitude of many South Africans that in November 1983 there was undisguised embarrassment in the government and sports bodies when a

West Indian cricketer became the victim of one of the apartheid laws.

Fast-bowler Colin Croft got into a whites-only railway compart-ment and asked whether it was all right to sit down. A white passenger said it was and they started chatting. Then a ticket collector reminded Croft that, despite who he was, if he wished to sit in a whites-only compartment, permission had to be sought before-hand from the railway manager. Eventually the white passenger led Croft into a non-whites compartment where they carried on talking.

The two incidents – the d'Oliviera affair and the Croft encounter with officialdom fifteen years later – indicate how South Africa is moving away from hard-line apartheid. It could invite a black West Indian team to play against whites and give the visitors red-carpet treatment in contrast to the cold shoulder turned to d'Oliviera. The Croft incident also demonstrated how difficult it is for the byzantine apparatus of apartheid to adapt or be adapted to the demands of everyday life, notwithstanding the good intentions of administrators genuinely trying to eradicate its more glaring absurdities.

But apartheid is not just about which races can sit in which train compartments, who can visit which cinema, who can use which lavatory. It is about the way a whole society is organized. What has happened in South Africa since 1948 represents some of the most formidable social engineering that the twentieth century has wit-nessed, a system that has set in progress vast movements of popula-tion, that has led to hundreds of thousands of people being uprooted, that has created an army of functionaries whose task it is to enforce the whole order. It is a system of government founded upon a master-plan which, because it is based on colour, has aroused the opprobrium of the world, even though many countries who are in the vanguard of the anti-South African lobby practise far more brutal discrimination towards certain sections of their populations. But it is because the South African system divides people by race and because this is legislated racism that the country earns the world's hostility. The protestations by the Pretoria government that its black population enjoys equal, although separate, freedoms to those of the whites, cut little ice. The rest of the world wants to see apartheid dismantled. But that is no easy matter. The policy was devised to ensure the survival of the whites whose entire thinking is directed towards the concept of separateness, and of different racial and tribal traditions. In addition, the whole monolithic system would be a nightmare to try to unwind. The house of cards is not going to come tumbling down overnight but rather piece-by-piece over a long period and with some of the more crucial supports remaining in place around which a new construction can be erected.

What is apartheid? What are its origins, philosophical justification, its major laws and, perhaps most important of all, how has the policy affected the everyday lives of the millions of people to whom it applies?

Legislated racial discrimination did not begin in South Africa in 1948; it dates back to the days when the British had ultimate responsibility for the dominion and when there was a British-appointed governor-general who oversaw the implementation of several race acts. The *South Africa Act* passed by the British parliament in 1909 establishing the Union of South Africa removed the right of blacks to sit in parliament; the *Natives Land Act* of 1913 set aside certain areas of the country as native reserves. Other laws passed in the 1920s established segregated black areas in the cities, controlled the number of blacks allowed to work in urban areas and allowed their removal if they were surplus to requirements. The governor-general could also introduce curfew measures. In the 1930s and 1940s the colour question began to assume prominence in the white politics of the country. Under Prime Minister Hertzog a number of acts were passed in 1926 concerning black representation and land tenure which clearly guarded the political and territorial exclusivity of the white population. Three years later Hertzog delivered his famous 'black manifesto' speech aimed at maintaining South Africa as a 'white man's land'. In 1936, the blacks were deprived of their common-roll franchise, their political representation being reduced to the election of three white MPs and to an advisory Natives' Representative Council. A similar procedure awaited the coloureds in the 1950s.

But these measures were only the beginning. Before the 1948 election a National Party commission, chaired by Mr P.O. Sauer MP, produced a report on future racial policy which first used the word 'apartheid'. The report spelled out for the first time the philosophical tenets of the policy. It was designed, said Sauer, to protect the white race 'against any policy, philosophy, or attack which might endanger or undermine its [the white race's] continued existence'. But the commission said this did not imply discrimination towards or exploitation of non-whites. 'National policy must be so designed that it advances the ideal of ultimate separation on a natural basis.' Thus was the policy of geographically separating whites and blacks first justified. The report recommended that there should be 'reserved areas' which would become the 'true fatherland' of the African population.

The Sauer Commission also tackled the question of blacks who would have to be in white areas as part of the labour force. Here the thinking was absolute. These mainly urban blacks would simply be visitors to white South Africa. They would have no permanent rights and their numbers would be subject to a strict system of 'influx control'. In addition, there would have to be separate residential areas for them while they lived in the big cities. Black trade unionism was opposed; education had to be oriented towards the native traditions of the Africans. Political representation had to be further reduced and confined to powerless urban councils, with the political life of the blacks confined to the tribal reserves even though a vast percentage of the black population was not living in them.

Most of the policy outlines recommended by the Sauer Commission were incorporated into the National Party's election manifesto of 1948. 'Apartheid and guardianship' was the theme, and in the slogan was captured the dominant idea of how the white man saw his future: separation to ensure his own survival and a paternalistic Christian concern to do the best that was possible for the blacks as they developed within their own political, economic and social framework.

It was a doctrine which was immensely appealing to the whites, a guarantee against their extinction at the hands of the black hordes, while assuaging their Christian consciences. The National Party election was followed within two years by the first of the many acts of parliament under which the theory was translated into practice.

Before any policy based on race could be introduced there had to be some mechanism to determine which race an individual belonged to and to keep a register of the entire population. The result was the *Population Registration Act (1950)* which set out the guidelines for deciding a person's race. Thus a coloured person was one 'who is not a white person or a native'; a native was 'in fact, or is generally accepted as, a member of any aboriginal race or tribe of Africa'; a white was described as a person who 'in appearance obviously is, or is generally accepted as, a white person, but does not include a

person who, although in appearance obviously a white person, is
generally accepted as a coloured person'. The last description was
clearly aimed at tying up some of the loose ends of racial classification; the demarcation line between who is white and who is coloured
in South Africa is often very blurred and indeed there are many
coloureds who to all intents and purposes appear white. In general,
though, this particular act was a reflection of the Afrikaner view that
there was a pure Aryan bloodstock which he represented.

The act was amended several times. In 1959 the coloured population was divided into sub-groups: Cape Coloured, Cape Malay,
Griqua, Indian, Chinese, other Asian and other Indian. In 1967
'appearance' or 'general appearance' were no longer the determining
guidelines for racial classification but 'descent'. In 1969 a further
amendment said that anyone wishing to belong to another race
group must assume the burden of proof himself.

The implementation of the *Population Registration Act* caused
heartbreak and suffering to many families which suddenly found
they were split along racial lines. The fact that in 1983, as an
example, 1,189 people went before registration boards to try to
change their racial classification indicates the distress. The figures
for successful applications were:

Indian to White	1
White to Cape Coloured	3
Cape Coloured to White	722
Cape Coloured to Chinese	4
White to Chinese	15
Chinese to White	7
White to Malay	1
Malay to White	4
White to Indian	1
Indian to Cape Coloured	34
Cape Coloured to Indian	39
Indian to Malay	19
Malay to Indian	16
Other Asian to Cape Coloured	3
Cape Coloured to Other Asian	1
African to Cape Coloured	109
Cape Coloured to African	11
African to Other Asian	3

African to Indian	1
African to Griqua	3
TOTAL	997

It is astounding that an entire government agency is tied up determining the racial group of each of the country's citizens. But without that, the rest of the system would collapse. An individual racial classification is a deciding factor in nearly every area of his or her everyday life. It has to be entered on post office forms, marriage certificates, hospital entry forms, census forms. It determines where one can live and swim, on which bus one can travel, where one can urinate. It stays with all South Africans from the cradle to the grave.

Or, rather, before the cradle: certainly in the case of Lize Venter, a baby abandoned by her mother when only a few hours old. After she was found and taken to hospital, baby Lize was subjected to an extraordinary series of tests carried out on strands of her hair which were taken away to a laboratory for examination. The system could not accommodate even an infant remaining unclassified. Lize was classified 'coloured' although there was severe criticism of the test within South Africa and abroad on both moral and scientific grounds.

So with the *Population Registration Act*, the architects of apartheid put beyond question the fact there were now several different 'blood groups' in South Africa, determined not by the more normal factors but by race. It was now the task of the government to ensure that there were no 'transfusions' of blood which would result in the pure Aryan variety becoming diluted. Marriage and sexual intercourse between the races were therefore the next target. The *Prohibition of Mixed Marriages Act (1949)* made marriages between whites and non-whites illegal even though there had never been more than 100 such weddings per year. A year later the *Immorality Amendment Act (1950)* extended the existing prohibition on sex between whites and Africans to include sex between whites and all non-whites.

Stories about the implementation of the acts are legendary and occasionally worthy of the best Feydeau farce, if their consequences were not so tragic. Policemen responsible for enforcing the acts burst into rooms where couples of different races were suspected of having sexual intercourse and tested the temperature of the bedclothes or searched for traces of semen. They set up hidden cameras to record couples in bed together. Once a young constable in the town of Brits in the Transvaal came across a white man and a half-naked black woman having sex; he made them pose for photographs in the position he had discovered them. Incidents like that accounted for the suicides of those afflicted by the laws and for the emigration of couples who could no longer endure the stigma of being from different races.

In 1971 the anguish which the two acts caused was brought home to the South African public. In the town of Excelsior in the Orange Free State, five white men and fifteen black women were prosecuted under the *Immorality Act*. The case was withdrawn minutes before the trial was about to start because a number of important prosecution witnesses decided they would not testify. But this came too late to prevent one of the accused committing suicide, the fifth such case that year. In the late 1970s a white man and his black girlfriend took their own lives following their conviction under the *Immorality Act*. In 1982 a farmer was sentenced to death for murdering his black servant who, he discovered, was pregnant with his child. Despite the tragedies, the search for the perfect order went on.

The year 1950 also saw the passage through parliament of the *Group Areas Act*, regarded by many Afrikaners as the cornerstone of apartheid. It legislates for the complete residential separation of the races. It had long been the tradition that whites and blacks lived in separate areas but this act extended residential separation to coloureds and Indians as well. The law came to be used to prevent non-whites from using whites' sports facilities, cinemas and so on.

Linked to the *Group Areas Act* was the *Resettlement of Natives Act (1954)* which gave the government the authority to remove 100,000 squatters living in the western suburbs of Johannesburg to improved housing in Meadowlands. The laws made possible the removal of entire communities: Indians were resettled in the Durban area and in Johannesburg, coloureds in Cape Town and Johannesburg, and Africans in the same cities. Established communities were simply uprooted and moved. A thriving Indian community in Pageview within easy reach of Johannesburg city centre was forced to move out to the new township of Lenasia some 25 miles away, adding time and money to their daily commuting, and forcing many business owners to start all over again.

In Cape Town, there was the notorious case of District Six which over the years had become a coloured area. It was a vibrant community, a favoured location of artists. Crime and squalor certainly existed but that was not uppermost in the minds of the 'master-builders'. Rejecting appeals to redevelop the area, the planners' main concern was the proximity of District Six to the white areas of the city. Consequently 60,000 to 70,000 coloured people were moved several miles further out of town to the sandy wilderness of the Cape Flats. Today, what was District Six is a flattened area, apart from two rows of Chelsea-style townhouses and housing units for the police. Because of the stigma attached to the area, companies will not risk the hostile political reaction from the coloured community to any attempt to establish themselves there. District Six is now a wasteland: a monument to the pursuit of the ordered society.

By the end of 1983, 878 group areas had been declared although some of the harsher aspects of the policy were being softened. In 1982 the Supreme Court ruled that nobody should be evicted from a group area where he was residing illegally unless alternative accommodation was available. In 1984 the first moves were made to open up the central business districts in the major cities to merchants of all races. Generally there has been a fall in the number of prosecutions under the acts. Indeed, in the Hillbrow district of Johannesburg (a white group area) there is now a black hospital, Hillbrow being a bustling, multi-racial community which the government so far has ignored along with other 'grey' residential areas. Despite these relaxations the *Group Areas Act* remains on the statute book; it is still a principal cornerstone of apartheid.

But despite this residential compartmentalization, the races could not remain separate twenty-four hours a day. There had to be some degree of social interaction as a matter of everyday life. So the next step was to lessen the extent to which the races had to mix. The *Reservation of Separate Amenities Act (1953)* was the answer. Separate facilities for whites and blacks in public places had long been the custom in South Africa. Years before the National Party came to power there had been separate park benches, separate buses and railway carriages, separate queues at the post office and so on. But this was not hard and fast enough for the apartheid planners. The separation of the races at this level had to be written into law. The act provided that, when the owner or person in charge of any property (a park, a train, a swimming pool, etc.) provided separate facilities for the different races, it would be a punishable offence to allow these to become mixed.

Of all the apartheid laws which were passed during the 1950s the *Separate Amenities Act* is the one which has undergone the most dilution as an increasing number of people have come to realize the absurdity, not to mention the cost, of providing separate facilities for the individual races. In some major cities where the city fathers were more liberally disposed, laws enforcing 'petty apartheid' gradually started being ignored or dismantled. In 1974 the mayor of Cape Town removed all discriminatory ordinances not required by law. In the same year Johannesburg municipal council desegregated its libraries, park benches, and lifts in official buildings. As more and more modern shopping precincts sprang up, lavatory facilities became non-racial. Theatres were gradually opened up to all races with the Market Theatre in Johannesburg actively encouraging black drama and black actors. In 1983 two theatres in the Orange Free State (not normally known for its liberal attitudes) were integrated. Also that year, drive-in movies were opened to all races at the discretion of local authorities. But most cinemas, like hotels and other public venues, still need permission to admit non-whites. Indeed there is a special telephone number (Pretoria 285500 ext. 103), manned twenty-four hours a day, which the owners of such premises can ring if in doubt about admitting a non-white. Many of the larger hotels in the major cities have been granted 'international status', a neat device which allows visiting non-white business people, black diplomats, tourists and sports teams to stay in decent hotels in the city centre instead of being consigned to establishments of inferior quality in a non-white area. The fear that these hotels would be swamped by the blacks was unfounded of course, because very few blacks in South Africa can afford the prices they charge.

In 1983 the Department of Community Development approved eleven of fifteen applications for multi-racial cinemas. One year later parks in Pretoria were allowed to remain open to all races despite efforts by the conservative-controlled city council to have them resegregated. Later in the same year some buffet and restaurant carriages on South African railways were opened to passengers of all races. Throughout the 1980s black taxi drivers began appearing in Johannesburg city centre. In 1980 all taxis had white drivers. Now taxi companies employ black and white drivers and all of them can pick up passengers of any race.

But the drive to rid South Africa of 'petty apartheid' has not been entirely smooth. There are a few white preserves which are still cherished, not least the country's beaches. Durban, for example, has a string of racially-segregated beaches – white, coloured, Indian and black – along its Indian Ocean coastline, although in 1982 a multi-racial beach was opened. In November 1985 the liberal-controlled city council voted to desegregate four more beaches as well as two pools while leaving each race group with at least one beach of its own. The move was made despite hostility towards creeping integration by conservative whites, especially those living in the Transvaal who travel to Durban for their annual holidays.

Opposition to opening up the beaches also occurred in Cape Town, but from a surprising quarter. Beach segregation had often been ignored in Cape Town; the city council doubted the legality of 'whites only' signs, and with non-white MPs now sitting in the national parliament in Cape Town it seemed to be something of an insult if their host city continued banning coloureds and Indians from using all the beaches. In January 1985 the beach police, the majority of whom are coloured, refused to implement the discriminatory laws and the city council subsequently agreed to open up the majority of its swimming pools to all races. The ensuing howls of protest came from sections of the white population who are generally regarded as the most enlightened. The liberals of Cape Town deluged the newspapers with letters of complaint. Allegations about blacks urinating in public, fouling toilet facilities, running around semi-naked, poured in. It all came as quite a shock to those whites who are supposed to be in the vanguard of the struggle for black rights.

So almost a quarter of a century after the Separate Amenities Act was passed the picture is varied. In some of the more liberal cities like Johannesburg one can walk around for hours and not notice any 'whites only' signs. The interplay between the races on the whole appears normal and relaxed. But take a trip out into the hard-line areas, and into some of the more conservative towns, and one would find the signs are still there. Clearly not all whites in South Africa are ready for all the barriers to come tumbling down at once and the government is alert to this. Speaking in parliament on 17 April 1985, Minister of Transport Hendrik Schoeman said he had no intention of doing away with separate facilities on suburban and main-line trains. 'The separate equivalent accommodation which is provided for passengers is essential to prevent friction and to maintain harmonious relations among the different race groups,' he said. However in June 1985 he announced that certain carriages were to be opened to all races although some would still be reserved for whites.

Having racially classified the population, forbidden whites and non-whites to cross the colour line in the most intimate areas, having created separate facilities for them in those situations where they inevitably had to come together, the government now took steps to regulate the number of blacks allowed to live on the outskirts of the white cities. Blacks were, after all, temporary sojourners, allowed to live in white areas only so long as their labour was required. Otherwise they had to remain in the black homelands. The whole system of 'influx control' was the answer. Moves towards controlling the flow of Africans from the tribal areas to the big cities began during the 1920s partly out of concern to protect the 'white man's land' and also to shelter white labour from black competition. This was when 'poor whites' became a contentious political issue. The *Native (Urban Areas) Act* of 1923 followed by the *Native Laws Amendment Act* of 1937 set up the mechanism to control the influx of Africans into the urban areas. But these laws proved largely ineffective because the wave of urbanization could not be held back. The big cities, with their prosperity and employment opportunities, were an inevitable attraction for the black population. In addition, the demands of the wartime economy meant that employers very often ignored the regulations on employing blacks.

In a bid to tighten up the laws the *Blacks (Urban Areas) Consolidation Act (1945)* was passed (and later amended) followed, after the Nationalists' victory in 1948, by the *Abolition of Passes and Coordination of Documents Act (1952)*, a piece of legislation which belied its liberal-sounding title by imposing the hated pass book system.

The main result of the influx control legislation was that no black could remain in a white area (including satellite townships like Soweto) for more than seventy-two hours unless, under Section 10(1) of the 1945 Act, he or she:

a) had resided there continuously since birth
    or
b) had worked there continuously for one employer for not less

than ten years, or had resided there lawfully and continuously for not less than fifteen years and was employed there

or

c) was the wife, unmarried daughter, or son under eighteen years of age of a black in one of the above categories who, after lawful entry, resides with him

or

d) had been granted special permission to be in the area.

The legislation immediately created two classes of black person, the 'insiders' who enjoyed 'Section 10 rights' (which soon slipped into the terminology of apartheid), and the 'outsiders' who did not. The laws were plainly discriminatory; similar restrictions did not apply to the movements of the whites. But then, of course, that was not the issue. It was to protect the whites that the legislation had been introduced.

The right to remain in the cities was stamped into each black's pass book, another creation of the legislation which has for the average black person become the symbol of apartheid. The pass book must be carried by him or her at all times and must be produced on demand.

The pass book contains details of the holder and information on his place of work and his employer's name and signature. No black can get a job unless he can produce his pass book, nor can he move from one job to another unless his previous employer has signed the pass book confirming the black employee is no longer working for him. It was an instrument of complete control over the movements of the blacks, aimed at restricting the flood of Africans from the tribal reserves.

During 1983, 262,904 people were arrested for pass law offences and filtered through special courts, some cases taking just thirty seconds to deal with. Usually those convicted end up paying a fine; at worst they can be 'endorsed out' of 'white South Africa'. The system is universally hated by blacks: it allows for police to make pass raids at any hour of the day or night and it means that some black workers can live in urban areas but rarely their families.

In 1983 black engineering worker Mr Mehlolo Rikhoto severely dented the pass laws when he contested a ruling by his local municipal labour office that he could not live and work permanently in a white area even though he enjoyed Section 10(b) rights because he had worked for one employer continuously for ten years. The labour office argued that because Rikhoto renewed his contract every year, his employment and residence were not 'continuous'. They refused to stamp his pass book. A Supreme Court ruling against the labour office decision was historic and up to 400,000 black workers may benefit from it.

The pass laws were designed to ensure that blacks, other than those required as workers, would remain in tribal homelands, regardless of how ill-equipped the infrastructure of the bantustans was to support millions of unemployed Africans. The creation of the black homelands is at the heart of the apartheid system, the point where the plans of the master-builders and the vision of the ideologues came together in one massive political mosaic.

The outline of the plan was drawn up shortly after the Nationalists came to power in a sixty-four volume report of a commission under Professor F.R. Tomlinson which investigated the development of 'bantu areas' to make them going concerns. Tomlinson's conclusions were dramatic. He recommended that the existing 260 scattered tribal areas should be consolidated into a small number of homelands each populated by one particular black tribe: Zulus, Xhosas, Tswana and so on. These homelands were to become mini-states with their own governments and would eventually form a kind of black commonwealth possibly linking up with the former British protectorates of Swaziland, Basutoland (now Lesotho) and Bechuanaland (now Botswana).

In 1963 Transkei, the homeland of most of the Xhosa-speaking blacks, obtained internal self-government. Thirteen years later it became a 'national state', as South Africa calls those homelands which are nominally independent under the apartheid policy. Bophuthatswana (the home of the Tswanas) followed suit in 1977, Venda in 1979 and Ciskei (where the remainder of the Xhosas live) in 1981. The population of these four 'states' is now over 5.8 million. The other homelands – Lebowa, KwaNdebele, Qwaqwa, Gazankulu, KwaZulu, and KaNgwane – have all reached the stage of 'self-government', the half-way house en route to 'independence'. The population of these areas is close to 7.3 million. The decision on whether to accept 'independence' rests with the homeland governments. Several have determinedly refused to accept it, notably KwaZulu, whose chief minister, Mangosuthu Buthelezi, rejects the homelands being used as political dumping grounds for blacks.

But what are the homelands like? Bophuthatswana, supposedly a fully-independent 'national state', consists of seven separate pieces of territory dispersed among three of South Africa's provinces. Transkei has three separated areas, although Ciskei is in one lump. But the component parts of KwaZulu are scattered all over Natal. Also, despite attempts to appear independent and self-governing they are not convincing as authentic sovereign states. The only one which does have an air of self-assurance about it is Bophuthatswana, despite being geographically divided. Its president, Chief Lucas Mangope, has achieved the same degree of stability in his country as exists in Botswana, the country which borders one of Bophuthatswana's areas.

Mangope has abolished 400 of over 600 security laws inherited from South Africa on the grounds that they infringe human rights or are racist. Bophuthatswana also has a bill of rights which does not incorporate detention without trial. Mangope has said he would be prepared to rejoin South Africa as part of some kind of federal structure but only when South Africa becomes non-racist.

The independence of Bophuthatswana, like that of the other three 'national states', is largely notional. South Africa controls the purse-strings and it would be unthinkable for any of the homelands to embark on a policy in any way hostile towards Pretoria. Before Bophuthatswana launched its own television service, known as 'Bop TV', an agreement signed by President Mangope and South African Foreign Minister Pik Botha bound both countries to ensure their reporting on current affairs would be conducted 'clearly, unambiguously, factually, impartially and without distortion'. There were a number of other clauses to the agreement, to ensure that Bop TV did not become a vehicle for pornography.

South Africa, however, has proved incapable of stopping the other homelands turning into what many people regard as classic 'banana republics'. Some cynics argue that many in Pretoria are not unhappy that these independent states slip into chaos and anarchy, thereby showing the world what happens when the blacks are granted self-government and what would happen if the same system were applied to South Africa as a whole.

The focus of concern for many has been Ciskei, which on occasions has come close to resembling Papa Doc's Haiti. A commission in the late 1970s found that a majority of the Ciskeian people were against independence, but the territory's leader Chief Lennox Sebe decided to accept it. Independence did not get off to a promising start, however. On 'independence day' in 1981 the flagpole fell over as the flag of the new state was being raised.

Indications that there was something rotten in the state of Ciskei grew during 1983. President-for-life Sebe rushed back from a visit to Israel to dismiss and then arrest his brother, General Charles Sebe, for allegedly plotting a coup. Another Sebe brother, Namba, who held the transport portfolio, was also detained along with other members of the Sebe clan. Until then naked nepotism had been the rule within the Ciskeian government. Lennox Sebe's family controlled the Ciskei Intelligence Service (modelled on the former South African Bureau of State Security – BOSS) and the implementation of tough security laws, under which several trade unions have been banned and government opponents detained.

But Sebe faced discontent on another front – from his ordinary subjects. On 18 July a bus boycott began in Mdantsane township on the fringe of Ciskei close to the job market in the 'white' city of East London. The protest was over an 11 per cent fare increase on buses which took the Mdantsane residents to work. Ciskei immediately tried to break the boycott, sending in the police, the army and party vigilantes. The security forces allegedly assaulted the boycotters. The vigilantes were accused of hauling residents out of taxis and forcing them to use buses while the police and army stood by and watched. On 4 August the security forces fired on dozens of workers who were boarding a train in support of the bus boycott. Five people were killed and over forty injured. The police claimed they were defending themselves after they had come under attack. Eye-witnesses told reporters that the police had continued to fire on those attempting to flee. More deaths followed as a security clampdown widened.

In October Nicholas Haysom, a researcher for the Centre for Applied Legal Studies at the University of the Witwatersrand in Johannesburg, compiled a report on human rights violations in the Ciskei which spoke of Sebe resorting to 'desperate measures' to control his subjects. It said that law and the administration of justice had almost ceased to operate in Mdantsane.

By 17 September 1983 the situation in Ciskei had deteriorated to such an extent that the United States government advised its citizens to stay out of the homeland 'because of unsafe conditions'. A State Department announcement added that the US government was 'deeply disturbed' by events in Ciskei which looked 'like fulfilling our worst expectations.' There was an angry response to this from South African Foreign Minister Pik Botha who said that Ciskei was an independent state and the situation did not warrant the American statement. However, seven months later Botha himself issued a thinly-disguised warning to Sebe to clean up his affairs, coupled with an equally transparent reminder that Pretoria was footing the bill and keeping Ciskei afloat. Sebe was reported to be planning grandiose 'white elephant' schemes including construction of a huge international airport which hardly any airlines would use and training twenty Ciskeian pilots in Israel even though they would have no planes to fly when they returned home. One official source was quoted as describing Sebe as 'difficult to handle'. Opposition MP Helen Suzman called him a 'vicious tyrant'.

Haysom's report on the bus boycott placed the confrontation in a wider context, suggesting that it was the whole separate development policy which gave rise to conflicts between the homeland governments and the people who live in these areas. Because the homelands are catchment areas for blacks who cannot find work in 'white South Africa' considerable stresses in the political and economic system build up. The grievances of blacks at being dumped by the thousand are channelled towards their only contact with the authorities, i.e. the homeland governments which are in general not equipped to sustain the hundreds of thousands of people who live there without work. Here is the most controversial aspect of the whole homelands policy and of 'grand apartheid' – the programme of relocating entire black communities from 'white South Africa' to the black homelands. The government calls it 'orderly resettlement'; opponents call it 'forced removals'.

In June 1983 a national research programme on resettlement undertaken by the Surplus People Project concluded, on the basis of three years' investigations, that 3.5 million people had been removed from their homes in South Africa since 1960. More than three-quarters of these were Africans, the report said, some of whom had been moved three or four times. The majority were those made redundant on white-owned farms, those who had been living in so-called 'black spots' in designated white areas, and those moved from the white cities to the bantustans and relocated as part of the process of consolidating the territory of the homelands. The Surplus People Project report calculated that a further 1.9 million removals were still threatened. Almost one year later, South Africa's then black affairs Minister, the controversial Dr Piet Koornhof, made an unprecedented confession that almost two million blacks had been relocated but that only 456,860 of these were for 'ideological reasons'. Dr Koornhof did not explain exactly what he meant by 'ideological' removals; but presumably these were people who had been moved in the pursuit of apartheid, whereas the rest were resettled in order to achieve a better life. The minister dismissed the report by the Surplus People Project as propaganda which was full of 'half-truths, quarter-truths and ten-per-cent truths'.

The homelands policy has had a devastating effect on the economic infrastructure of these areas. Rapid population growth has aggravated already impoverished areas. In the recent book *Up Against the Fences*, a study of black rural poverty, Jill Nattrass, Professor of Development Studies at the University of Natal, drew attention to the amount of agricultural land available to blacks in the homelands compared to that available to whites. Professor Nattrass pointed out that African ownership of farm land is restricted by the 1913 *Natives Land Act*, and subsequent amendments, to 14 per cent of South Africa's land area and to some 22 per cent of the available arable land.

Compared with an average of 78 hectares of land available to the average white man, the figure for every homeland black varied from 37 hectares in Bophuthatswana to just 5.1 hectares in Qwaqwa. When it came to arable land the figures dropped from 3.8 hectares per man in Bophuthatswana to 1.3 hectares in Ciskei.

The human consequences of forced removal can be shattering. What is it like to be forced out of a home where forefathers may have lived for generations and be carted off to a strange land where life must start all over again? Two examples.

Midnight. 28 December 1983. A hillside overlooking the Mogopa valley, a couple of hours drive south-west from Johannesburg. It is pouring with rain and the night chill is setting in. We are warming ourselves around an open fire on which supper is cooking. We are there to report on the expected arrival of the police to remove the people in the valley below us who constitute a 'black spot'. Bishop Tutu is there and also the Reverend Allan Boesak, president of the World Alliance of Reformed Churches. Both have come to Mogopa to comfort the villagers of the Bakwena tribe which has lived in the valley since 1911. The tribal chiefs possess title deeds signed by a government minister. They bought the land just in time; two years later the government passed the *Natives Land Act* forbidding the sale of white-owned land to blacks. Since 1911 the tribespeople have developed the valley into a thriving community, building homes and a church, and sinking boreholes for water. But neither their deeds nor their civic achievements will help them now. The authorities have decreed that they are to be moved many miles away to Pachsdraai, a spot soon to be incorporated into Bophuthatswana where, say the villagers, there are just tin shacks and limited water supplies.

In fact, the police do not arrive that night, just a few government officials who try to encourage the villagers to leave without the use of force. Some of the people pack up their belongings, bowing to the inevitable. The plight of the Mogopa people is reported in the world's newspapers. The impact in the United States is profound; an outcry begins over their removal. Hope is rekindled that they can remain.

But almost two months later, and out of the blue, the police move in to clear out the remnants of the tribe. The village is sealed off and news reporters are prevented from entering. Civil rights workers report people being handcuffed and placed under arrest. The last of the Bakwenas have been sent on their way. The government states that their new home will offer considerably improved facilities and that the reluctance of some of the people to move had been due to clan rivalries.

31 May 1984. P.W. Botha has just embarked on his tour of Europe. The leader of a community in the eastern Transvaal threatened with forced removal writes to the Queen and to Mrs Thatcher:

> Please intercede with our prime minister, Mr P.W. Botha, to leave us to continue our peaceful, productive life at KwaNgema and to stop all the forced removals of black people from their homes.

The letter addressed to the Queen adds:

> We live in a farm situated in the eastern Transvaal in South Africa. It was given to us in 1904 by the Lieutenant Governor of the Transvaal, in the name of King Edward VII, your late great-

grandfather. We believed this land was ours forever. We love this land of ours. Since England gave us this land, how can South Africa take it away? We fear that if we are to be moved . . . we will suffer great hardship and loss. What will happen to the houses we have built over the years? Where will our cattle graze in these places?

The letters were brilliant public relations and they worked. When Botha met Thatcher at Chequers she read the letter to him and explained the serious view she took of forcibly removing settled communities. In December 1984 the people of KwaNgema won a temporary reprieve though whether this is the final decision on their fate is at the time of writing uncertain.

Mogopa and KwaNgema between them arguably brought South Africa more international hostility during the early part of 1984 than any other aspect of apartheid. They appeared to many to epitomize the inhumanity of such removals and portrayed a picture of an unbending bureaucracy, enslaved by ideology, for whom the fate of individuals was of little concern. Another advertisement for the harshness of the system was the plight of 'commuter victims' of apartheid, blacks forced to live in homelands and travel many miles to and from work in white areas. One newspaper said some of the people of KwaNdebele had to get up at 2.30 in the morning to reach work, returning late at night to snatch a few hours sleep. One woman said: 'I leave Pretoria to return home at 5.30 each night and get home after 8pm. In the morning I leave home at 4am. My children get ready for school alone, eat supper alone, and if the bus is late go to bed without seeing me.' This is what the homelands policy means to thousands of people like her.

In a devastating critique of the homelands, opposition leader Dr Frederik van Zyl Slabbert told parliament in 1984 that the policy was nothing but 'a multiplication of bureaucratic disaster areas, consuming vast amounts of capital, that serve no other purpose but to service the wants and needs of small, privileged bureaucratic elites in seas of poverty and underdevelopment'. For thirty years, he said, South Africa had been pouring money into these areas. Slabbert warned that the single most important cause of instability in Africa was not revolutions or coups but the creation of self-perpetuating, bureaucratic, privileged classes which destroyed the economies of countries. The warning signals were now flashing in South Africa, he declared.

Of course, the warning lights were flashing long ago. The homelands policy, the separation of the races, all the apartheid laws which have been enforced over the past four decades may have satisfied the ideologues, but the politicians who have the task of carrying through these policies have come to recognize their shortcomings. This was reflected in two speeches by President Botha to parliament in 1985. The speeches amounted to a radical re-think, an acknowledgment that some of the old structures were no longer acceptable.

Botha effectively ordered the bureaucracy to improve its treatment of black people 'by giving searching attention to attitudes and relations in their daily human context'. He outlined the kind of reforms he had in mind:

- Blacks were to be given freehold land rights, subject to certain qualifications. Previously most blacks only had leasehold rights.
- 'Steps to promote urbanization and to eliminate negative and discriminatory aspects of influx control are receiving urgent consideration', said Botha. 'It is also the government's firm intention that problems relating to the resettlement of communities will be given attention and be solved to the greater satisfaction of all those concerned.' In other words, a softening of the policy of forced removals.
- Botha announced that the government did not intend forcing independence on the black homelands, even though independence remained the government's goal. This was hardly a great change of policy, but the fact that Botha mentioned it implied that the policy of creating a 'constellation' of black homeland states around South Africa's borders was no longer sacrosanct.
- 'The government accepts the permanence in the Republic of South Africa in large numbers of members of the black population communities who find themselves outside the national states.' In other words the blacks living in white areas were there to stay; they could not be treated as *gastarbeiter*. Some form of enhanced political representation would therefore have to be found 'up to the highest level', as Botha put it.
- As a result of this, Botha went on, clarification had to be

reached on the question of citizenship for the blacks. Under the apartheid policy all blacks lose their South African citizenship once their respective homeland becomes independent, another profound grievance.

– To study how political rights for the blacks could be furthered, Botha announced the establishment of an informal non-statutory forum. Blacks would be invited to negotiate on their political rights, another break with the past, although most black leaders were extremely sceptical.

In the weeks which followed, Botha and other cabinet ministers fleshed out the principles which he had outlined. There was no suggestion that white control was about to be relinquished. The principle that one race group should not be in a position to dominate another remained entrenched (i.e. one man, one vote was not on the cards). However, it was the strongest signal yet that, in terms of ideology, the South African government was retreating from hardline, Verwoerd-style apartheid. Until then the debate in South Africa had been about how to keep the blacks out. Now it was about how to bring them in. Botha later invited members of other political parties to join a special cabinet committee to examine black political rights. Slabbert and the leader of the small New Republic Party immediately accepted. The problem was: which black leaders would be willing to negotiate with the government?

Botha announced that full property rights were to be granted to blacks who at present qualified for leasehold rights – a step which would permanently improve the security of some five million urban blacks. He said the government no longer accepted that blacks should lose their South African citizenship once the homelands became independent. This issue was followed up three days later in a remarkable daily commentary by the South African Broadcasting Corporation, which generally reflects government thinking. On the morning of 23 April 1985 listeners were startled to hear that:

> The approach which has been followed up to now has been unsatisfactory in a number of areas. The lack of recognition by any state other than South Africa of the independence of the national states has placed their people in an awkward position in international dealings . . . The incongruity of the approach has become intolerable. It is simply not possible to justify, logically or humanely, a policy that would strip of his citizenship a person

who has always lived in the country and always will live here, as will his children and their children.

The broadcast was clearly preparing the whites for a fundamental change of policy. Sure enough, in September Botha told a party congress that his government was prepared to restore South African citizenship to blacks belonging to the 'independent' homelands, a decision which was to affect almost ten million black people. As recently as 1978 the Minister of Plural Relations (black affairs) Connie Mulder had looked forward to the day when there would be 'no more black South Africans'.

But what progress has been made on some of the other reforms hinted at by Botha?

Each year when parliament begins its new session, cabinet ministers brief foreign correspondents on the background to government policy. On 22 January 1985 the Minister of Co-operation and Development Dr Gerrit Viljoen suddenly announced during his briefing that all forced removals were to be suspended pending a review of the whole system. The news was welcomed by civil rights workers and threatened communities alike, although some adopted a more cautious 'wait and see' attitude. They were wise to be wary. By April government ministers were admitting that removals could still take place 'with the agreement, that is in consultation with, residents'. According to the Black Sash civil rights organization 'consultation' can often involve finding a member of the tribe to consult who is prepared to be relocated but who is not representative of the community as a whole.

But while a question mark hung over the government's genuine commitment to reforming the forced removals policy, there was no doubt about its desire to get rid of two key apartheid laws, the *Prohibition of Mixed Marriages Act* and Section 16 of the *Immorality Act*. Moves towards scrapping these 'sex across the colour line' laws had been gathering momentum before parliament began its new session. Among many appeals for the repeal of the laws, those from certain sections of the Dutch Reformed Church were highly significant. Ironically the Dutch Reformed Church had been one of the principal forces behind the government's decision to introduce the laws in the first place. In 1936 the Cape Synod of the church moved the following resolution:

Convinced of the unwholesome results of marriages between

whites and coloureds, this honourable Synod urges the
Committee for the Combating of Social Evils to urge the
government, in the name of the Synod, to introduce legislation in
this matter.

But the Afrikaans churches, though still a bulwark of conservative
thinking, have been reconsidering many of their doctrines, led by one
or two more liberal church leaders.

One such is Professor Johan Heyns who in September 1983 was
elected moderator of the influential Northern Transvaal Synod. One
afternoon, sitting in his Pretoria study, he explained how he had
adopted a position opposed to many aspects of apartheid, including
the sex laws. Perhaps the most important influence on his life had
been his experiences while working and studying abroad, particularly in Amsterdam and Basle where he had studied under the famous
theologian, Karl Barth, a strong opponent of Nazism. In the European environment Professor Heyns, who had grown up under a
system where blacks were discriminated against, suddenly discovered that the colour of a man's skin was not a symbol of inferiority.
Similar ideas were gaining ground among members of the Cape
Synod which in October 1983 issued a twenty-page report admitting
for the first time that the church 'apparently exceeded the boundaries
of its prophetic witness with its representations to the authorities to
set up these laws.' The report outlined four reasons why the acts
should be repealed:

- they could not be justified by scripture.
- the church had condemned racism yet the law prohibited on
  the basis of race alone the choice of a marriage partner.
- the laws were worded to prohibit relations between 'whites'
  and 'non-whites', terms which applied to no definable nation
  or ethnic group.
- they were designed to protect the Afrikaner in the 1930s and
  conditions had 'drastically changed'.

For years the church had preached the doctrine that the separateness
of man was created by God deliberately and it was therefore the duty
of man to maintain this diversity. At last the church had realized that
such thinking was politically-motivated humbug.

A few months after the Cape Synod decision a further boost for the
abolitionist cause came from a group of liberal academics at the

University of Stellenbosch, regarded as the 'cradle of Afrikanerdom', who published a booklet arguing that after twenty-five years there were no visible signs that the two laws were necessary to maintain the biological or cultural purity of the whites, they were contrary to the principles of human dignity, they conflicted with biblical teaching and the concept of brotherly love, and they were motivated by racial prejudice.

Set against calls for the laws to be repealed were the findings of a survey carried out by the Human Sciences Research Council in March 1984. This discovered that around 61 per cent of whites were in favour of both acts. (Interestingly about a quarter of the coloureds and Indians who were polled were also in favour of them.)

The then Internal Affairs Minister F.W. de Klerk told parliament in April that the laws would disappear from the statute book. The repeal was seen more as a symbolic gesture, another sign that Afrikaners, or some of them, were retreating from the old hard-line doctrines. There was a general recognition that 'people of different races aren't suddenly going to start rushing into each other's beds' as Helen Suzman MP put it. Moreover, there was some disappointment that the government had not shown any willingness to repeal other apartheid legislation like the *Group Areas Act*.

This was the 'front line' of the reform programme. In the past, government race policies had reflected the political ideology of the time. Thus, when the homelands were being hived off, when the total political separation of the races was the aim, complete segregation at every level had to apply, otherwise the policy itself had no philosophical justification. Policy remains the servant of ideology. Complete separation of the races has now been replaced by a new approach under which the various race groups may in time return to 'one South Africa' but within the framework of separate political structures for each race group (or 'own affairs' as the new constitution puts it). Thus, in terms of the new ideology, it is acceptable to allow the sex laws to fall away and let people of different races mingle on a day-to-day basis. It is also possible for the government to announce, as it did in May 1985, the repeal of the *Prohibition of Political Interference Act (1968)* which forbids multi-racial political parties while insisting that the racially-segregated basis of the new parliament would remain.

Without jeaopardizing its overall policy, the government could also feel free to consider the recommendations of a top constitutional committee (September 1985) advocating abolition of the influx control system of pass laws so long as the eradication of such legislation is not seen as heralding a breakdown of racially separate political structures as well. In the same month P.W. Botha was even prepared to announce the proposed inclusion of blacks on the advisory President's Council, though insisting at the same time that the principle of group rights would remain. But should the *Group Areas Act* be dispensed with, the entire justification for the new constitution would fall away. After all, if everybody was thrown in together, what, for example, would the Indian minister of education do; would there still be a job for the coloured minister of housing? The main thrust of government policy remains one of 'group rights' with no individual group achieving dominance over the others. Within that context reform is possible; beyond it, it is not. Government critics argue such terminology is a device for maintaining the essentials of white rule.

That is not to say, however, that pressure on these pillars of apartheid will not mount and that there will not be reforms to such laws. The government has modified the *Group Areas Act* to allow for multi-racial trading in the central business districts of the major white cities. The pace of reform is often guided by what people will accept rather than what party policy determines. For example, if the government is encouraging the emergence of a black middle class to give blacks an interest in not trying to overthrow the system is it possible that such up-and-coming blacks can be excluded for ever from living in the plusher white areas? If unrest in the black townships continues, will not more prosperous blacks, who could easily become the targets of the underprivileged, look to the government for assistance, which in many cases would mean the right to live in the relative safety of the white suburbs?

The problems facing the South African government is how to manage reform without letting it run out of control. The French Revolution, the 1905 uprising in czarist Russia and the downfall of the Shah of Iran in 1979 all demonstrate how, once the tap has been turned on to allow the 'drip-drip' of reform, the floodgates can quickly be forced open to permit the waters of violent revolution to break through. Botha knows he can only move as fast as the white voters will let him, even if he has written off the ultra-rightists. Counterbalancing this, however, is the rising tide of black expectations.

So are the developments in South Africa over the past couple of years cosmetic changes or genuine reform? Those who hold the former view contend that the new constitution is simply a mechanism for entrenching white power, with the coloureds and Indians co-opted for moral support while the blacks are fobbed off with dubious forms of local representation. Any offer to the blacks of a share in central government, argue the critics, will be on the government's terms and will involve puppet status only. Changes to sex laws and the like may appear dramatic to the outside world, but in terms of how apartheid affects the blacks they are of little significance. Such changes do not tackle the central issue of black political rights.

The contrary view was summed up by Mr Harry Oppenheimer, the former chairman of the giant Anglo American industrial empire, in an address to the governors of the Foreign Policy Association in New York on 11 October 1984. Although an opponent of the new constitution at the time of the referendum, Oppenheimer seemed to have decided to make the best of a bad job. He told the association:

> . . . the government's willingness to share power with people of other races – even though this involved a split in their own party – is something quite new in South Africa and was undoubtedly intended as a step forward. It was because matters were generally perceived in this way that the government was supported in the referendum by an overwhelming white majority. It is quite wrong to think of the new constitution as a sham, or as a device to entrench apartheid in a new form, even though the division of parliament into separate, racially-constituted chambers is a clumsy device which reflects the prejudices of the past.

Recent changes do mark a genuine attempt at reform as the government realizes that undiluted white power cannot exist for ever. But the government's main problem is that the reforms are seen by many blacks as the white man dispensing his grace and favours, of all races together deciding the country's future. Negotiating forums are all very well except that those invited to sit down and discuss with the government are not the real black leaders (like Nelson Mandela or the United Democratic Front) but quislings. Black anger over their second-class status was to explode across the country. But what about P.W. Botha's own white supporters? How have they reacted to this rush of reforms to the old order? Botha once told them they had to 'adapt or die'. How willing are they to change?

CHAPTER 5

Broedertwis
Dissent within the white man's laager

On 30 April 1985 some 2,000, mainly Afrikaner, white South Africans gathered in Pretoria city hall. They belonged to the Afrikaner Weerstandsbeweging (Afrikaner Resistance Movement), a body pledged to keep South Africa white. Their leader, Eugene Terre' Blanche, delivered a rousing speech, calling for the establishment of a white fatherland in South Africa to be created out of the old Boer republics in the Transvaal and in the Free State. Also in attendance at the meeting were members of the youth wing of the AWB, the Storm Falcons, wearing their traditional fascist-style, blackshirt uniforms with Nazi-like insignia.

After the rally some of the crowd marched on the central police station in Pretoria to hand in a letter to South Africa's police commissioner, General Johan Coetzee, to thank him for the splendid work his men were doing trying to quell black unrest in the townships. The letter added: 'We are always at your disposal to help maintain law and order.'

And they were not joking. Over the previous two years several of the AWB's leading members had appeared in court and been sentenced on a number of charges relating to right-wing terrorism. In June 1983 Jacob Viljoen and Hendrik Jabocsz were sent to jail for fifteen years after the Pretoria Supreme Court heard they had illegally possessed arms and ammunition; had planned to assassinate the prime minister (presumably because of his reform plans), as well as Bishop Desmond Tutu and the coloured anti-apartheid leader, Dr Allan Boesak; and had planned to blow up a multi-racial hotel, and also Sun City ('Satan's City,' as the accused called it, because blacks and whites can relax there together without any race bars) and to infest Sun City with syphilis germs. One month after being sentenced Viljoen appeared in court again, along with Terre' Blanche, on charges of unlawful possession of arms, and later terrorism.

The accused were found not guilty of terrorism but guilty of unlawful possession of firearms. Terre' Blanche was sentenced to two years' imprisonment and another accused, Jan Groenewald, to three years, both suspended for five years. The AWB leader was carried shoulder-high from the court building by his supporters and then in a fiery speech and while waving the flag of the old Transvaal Boer republic, he announced: 'the battle for the survival of a white Christian nation will continue.'

In sentencing the accused, Mr Justice van Dyk said: 'The accused are civilized and decent people. The fact that they were in possession of these articles was an unfortunate concurrence of events. The community would certainly not expect me to send them to jail.'

Some time later a black man whose tea mug was found to be engraved with ANC slogans was sentenced to three years' imprisonment. His sentence was not suspended.

If the unrest in black townships ever seriously threatens white suburbs, the AWB will be the first to organize white vigilante groups; if and when the black revolution comes they will be the first to man the barricades. But for the moment, they do not threaten Botha's government. One must look at the mainstream white political parties to see whether Botha's reforms will be tolerated or whether there will be a 'right-wing backlash'.

Since the *South Africa Act* establishing the modern South Africa in 1910 the shape of white politics in South Africa has almost entirely been determined by the Afrikaners. South Africans of English descent have played a largely secondary role in the country's political life. Within the Afrikaner-dominated political structure there have generally been two quite distinct political threads: on the one hand, parties which have pursued the total defence and promotion of Afrikanerdom; and on the other those which have attempted to build some kind of bridge towards the English-speaking community.

Immediately after Union the largest political party was the South Africa Party (SAP) led by the two Boer generals, Louis Botha and Jan Smuts, who aimed at uniting Afrikaner and English as one white nation within the British Empire. The SAP's policies slowly alienated a large section of the Afrikaner population who feared that they would lead to the virtual demise of the Afrikaner at the hands of British capitalist interests. The result was the emergence of the National Party of Hertzog which broke with Botha and Smuts. Interestingly, though, the Afrikaner-oriented National Party was also supported by many of the poorer English-speakers who saw the NP as their defence against big business and competition from blacks for their jobs. By 1929 the National Party had become the majority party in parliament.

By 1933, however, Hertzog's position had weakened, mostly because of economic factors linked to the Great Depression. This, coupled with Hertzog's feeling that the identity of the Afrikaner had now been secured and that Afrikaners and British should join forces to protect themselves against the Africans, led to the fusing of the NP with the South Africa Party in 1934, with Hertzog as prime minister and Smuts as his deputy. It called itself the United Party. But, unconvinced that the Afrikaners were being protected and concerned that they should not lose their racial purity to British influences, some of the NP members formed a second Nationalist Party led by D.F. Malan which overturned Smuts' majority in the 1948 election on a straight apartheid ticket. Since then the National Party has gradually consolidated its position and is now the strongest party by far.

The National Party victory marked the end of an era. No longer would the erstwhile Boer War enemies try to bury their differences and forge a new South Africa using the talents of both sections of the white community. Now a new breed of Afrikaner was at the helm, dedicated to an 'Afrikaner first' philosophy. The new breed were to exert their influence immediately, appointing Afrikaners (especially members of the Broederbond – a secret Afrikaner brotherhood) to leading positions in the civil service, judiciary, and public services. English-speakers who stood on the verge of promotion to senior positions suddenly had the carpet pulled from under them.

Following Malan's retirement in 1954, the prime ministership fell to J.G. Strijdom who unashamedly espoused the policy of white 'baasskap' (domination). Under both Malan and Strijdom apartheid amounted to straightforward segregation. But by 1958, when the National Party had increased its representation in the 156-seat parliament from 70 seats (in the 1948 election) to 103, the man who would implement the grander design had arrived on the scene.

Hendrik Frensch Verwoerd was born in Holland in 1901. He moved to South Africa while still a child, later graduating at the University of Stellenbosch. One of his earliest political actions was to lead a deputation to Prime Minister Hertzog to urge that the government refuse to permit the immigration to South Africa of Jewish refugees from Nazi Europe. In 1937, following in the tradition which links many Nationalist politicians with the Afrikaans press, Verwoerd became the first editor of *Die Transvaler* which was to become the mouthpiece of the National Party. In this capacity he gave strong backing to the cause of Afrikaner nationalism as well as to Nazi Germany during the Second World War. In 1949 he dismissed his paper's news coverage of the tour of South Africa by King George VI in a paragraph, referring to 'some visitors from Britain'. He survived a first assassination attempt in 1960, but not the second in 1966.

Apart from his identification with the implementation of apartheid, Verwoerd is also remembered for presiding over the final break with Britain. The elders of the National Party had long looked forward to the day when the Afrikaner state would no longer be beholden to the crown. But they doubted whether they could carry all the whites with them in a decision to sever the link finally with Britain. A substantial proportion of the population were English-speakers, whose numbers were being increased by the swelling post-war emigration of the British to South Africa. Some Afrikaners, too, retained Smuts' vision of a united Afrikaner/English South Africa developing within the framework of the British Commonwealth. Verwoerd, though, trusted his fellow Afrikaners to support him and two events boosted the republican cause.

In early 1960 British Prime Minister Harold Macmillan arrived in South Africa at the end of a tour of several African states. On 2 February, addressing a joint sitting of both Houses of Parliament in Cape Town, Macmillan delivered his famous 'wind of change' speech, in which he made it clear that the rise of African nationalism across the continent could not be halted even by South Africa. The speech stunned white South Africans and was guaranteed to raise the hackles of the Afrikaners. Here again was the old colonial power, they thought, laying down the law to South Africa as though it were still an outpost of the empire.

A few weeks later, police gunned down sixty-nine blacks in the

Sharpeville massacre and another spate of anti-South Africa criticism was sweeping Britain and elsewhere. A kind of 'fortress South
Africa' mentality gripped many whites, with the result that when
Verwoerd called a referendum the following October on whether
whites wished South Africa to become a republic, the prime minister
won a majority, albeit a narrow one, of 74,000 votes out of a 1.63
million turnout. The following March Verwoerd went to London to
attend the Commonwealth Prime Ministers' Conference and on 15
March 1961, in the face of a concerted attack on his government's
policies by several of the assembled leaders, announced that he was
withdrawing South Africa from the Commonwealth. Verwoerd
returned home to a hero's welcome. It was the fulfilment of a dream.
Everything that had been fought for in the Boer War, the Afrikaner's
struggle to survive for over three centuries, had now been rewarded.
At last he had his own country.

Verwoerd then attempted to broaden the base of his party's
support through an appeal to English-speakers. Two English-
speaking members of the National Party were appointed to the
cabinet. The policy clearly had some success as in the general election
of 1966 the National Party increased its representation, winning 126
of the 166 seats. But the overtures to the English community were
not to the liking of the old guard. As had happened in the past
whenever Afrikaner dominance was challenged, a new faction arose
to preserve the conservative order. It was at this stage that the
struggle between the 'verligtes' (enlightened ones) and the 'ver-
kramptes' (narrow-minded ones) began within Afrikanerdom. John
Vorster, who succeeded Verwoerd in 1966, faced something of a
right-wing revolt. Dr Albert Hertzog, son of General Hertzog, told
parliament that English-speaking South Africans were too liberal
and should not be given an important role in the country's political
life. Hertzog was also responsible, as Minister of Posts and Tele-
graphs, for delaying the arrival of television in South Africa, describing it as evil, degenerate and subversive. Vorster sacked Hertzog
from his cabinet in February 1969. The struggle between the two
came to a head the following September at the Transvaal congress of
the National Party when the breakaway politicians refused to support a vote of confidence in the leadership and its policy and either
resigned from the party or were expelled. One month later the
dissidents founded a new party – the Herstigte (reconstituted)
Nasionale Party (HNP) which throughout the early 1970s attracted

right-wing Afrikaners fearful that the government's more moderate policies would lead to the downfall of Afrikanerdom. The party has had varying success at the polls. In 1981 over 13 per cent of white voters supported it. But the party has only ever gained one parliamentary seat. Vorster tried desperately to avoid the breach, but the HNP having departed, he had more important issues to turn his mind to.

Balthazar Johannes Vorster, another student of the University of Stellenbosch where Verwoerd was one of his lecturers, was an ardent Afrikaner nationalist. He stood for parliament in 1948 and was defeated, but was elected five years later. Vorster's reputation was made during 1961–6 when he was Minister of Justice. This was a time which saw the emergence of the first really organized opposition by black nationalist groups to the government's policy; it also saw the implementation of some of the toughest security legislation any western country has experienced. As prime minister after 1966, Vorster presided over the 1976 riots in Soweto and elsewhere; began edging towards a liberalization of hard-line apartheid in certain areas; applied South Africa's considerable leverage upon Ian Smith's régime to end the Rhodesian crisis; and entered into several contacts – overt and covert – with a number of black African leaders. Under Vorster's leadership the National Party won the greatest electoral victory in the history of South Africa when, in 1977, it won 134 seats in parliament, attracting substantial support among English-speakers.

But within a year Vorster had retired, effectively 'kicked upstairs' into what was then the largely ceremonial position of state president, the most important political casualty of the 'Muldergate' scandal, named after the Minister of Information of the time, Connie Mulder, whose department was caught siphoning off vast amounts of secret funds to mount a South African propaganda offensive abroad. Vorster took responsibility for the secret funding but said he deplored the irregularities in the way the money had been spent, as revealed in the findings of an inquiry by the auditor-general. But his case appeared increasingly flimsy following the report of the official commission of inquiry (under Mr Justice Erasmus) which concluded that Vorster had been aware of the irregularities and had covered them up. He immediately resigned as state president, his career finished in ignominy.

With the succession of P.W. Botha those associated with the

Muldergate scandal were swept away and further liberalization of apartheid was set in motion. The National Party had a convincing victory in the 1981 general election although it lost half a dozen seats largely because conservative Afrikaners expressed disapproval of the reformist trend by voting for the HNP or by abstaining. The Botha reform moves since 1978 have placed a severe strain on the Nationalists. Some left the party to form a new mainly Afrikaner party. But those who have stayed have generally supported Botha all along the line. There has also been a shift in the base of National Party support, away from miners and farmers towards more sophisticated urban middle classes willing to give reform a chance.

The left of the party, those regarded as enlightened, comprises many younger MPs who believe that reform is possible, provided one race group does not dominate another. That means one man, one vote is out but it does not exclude a system of government in which the blacks would be a majority, with checks and balances to protect the position of whites. MP Wynand Malan says this:

> My views are based on Christianity. I want a just society:
> participation in an effective way for everybody. I can foresee for
> the future a situation where a black could be at the head of
> government. But I do not foresee a situation where blacks are
> ruling whites, in the same way that I do not see a situation where
> whites would be ruling blacks.

Malan represents the school of Nationalists who want to see structural changes to government policy, not just face-lifts, but still within the framework of separate group rights.

Further to the left of Afrikaner thinking are the so-called 'oorbeligtes' (over-enlightened) consisting principally of liberal academics and journalists. One such is Hermann Giliomee, Professor of Political Studies at the University of Cape Town, who is wary of P.W. Botha's plans for a forum to discuss blacks' rights. He said in early 1985:

> I really think it is far too late in South Africa's history to still
> create a black forum by invitation. I would certainly have insisted
> on this black forum being constituted by virtue of elections . . .
> that the time is ripe to un-ban the ANC but very clearly spelling
> out that there are very stringent laws against any kind of
> undermining activity. Once you have un-banned the ANC, once
> you have made the elections for the black forum open and free,

then you can get genuine representatives of the black population to come together with whites and start talking about an alternative political situation. I think the government will find out pretty soon that very few credible black leaders will come forward and be prepared to serve on that black council.

What were Giliomee's views on releasing imprisoned black nationalist leader Nelson Mandela to serve on such a forum?

I would certainly try to find, do everything in my power to find, a formula in terms of which I could release Mandela and I would certainly allow him to play a role in any kind of constitutional debate about South Africa's future.

Such opinions may be voiced on the enlightened fringe of Nationalist thinking, but the rump of the party is not yet ready for them. There is a group of pragmatic party leaders: P.W. Botha himself, constitutional affairs Minister Chris Heunis, Foreign Minister Pik Botha and possible future contender for the leadership, black affairs Minister Dr Gerrit Viljoen, a former head of the Broederbond who, insiders say, is becoming 'more liberal by the day'. This group want to push the reform train along but they realize they can only move as fast as white public opinion, or at least that section supporting the National Party, will tolerate. The right wing of the party is very wary of the current pace of liberalization. They take their complaints to the Minister of National Education F.W. de Klerk, another possible challenger for the leadership after Botha if only because he is the leader of the party in the Transvaal, the NP's power base. He and his fellow-MPs from that province are right in the firing line of the new Conservative Party which has emerged as the voice of the right-wing Afrikaner, of those who believe that Botha has gone too far and that now is the time to halt reform before black rule becomes inevitable. The Conservative Party has established itself as a force to be reckoned with, especially in the Transvaal, and it threatens to eat into some of the traditional NP strongholds elsewhere in the country.

The split within the National Party which led to the formation of the breakaway Conservative Party was one of the most severe schisms to have occurred within Afrikanerdom. Throughout 1980 and 1981 there had been increasing friction between Botha and the more conservative elements in the party whose views were expressed most vociferously by Andries Treurnicht, then Transvaal leader of the party. The tensions burst into the open on 23 February 1982 when twenty-two members of the party abstained on or voted against a motion supporting the prime minister and the way he was interpreting party policy on power-sharing with coloureds and Indians. Botha was livid. Reporters were summoned to the cabinet room in parliament where Botha laid it on the line: the rebels were given one week to sign a motion expressing their full confidence in him, or else . . . During the next few days, six of the MPs returned to the fold leaving sixteen others who either resigned or were expelled from the party. They included Treurnicht, who was Minister of State Administration, and one other minister, both of whom resigned from the cabinet within a week.

The dissidents were quick to organize. Less than a month after the showdown with Botha, some 8,000 supporters gathered in Pretoria to form the new Conservative Party and to elect Treurnicht unanimously as the party's leader. The CP mopped up the support of several right-wing fringe groups. In parliament it is the second largest opposition party after the liberal Progressive Federal Party.

But the struggle was not confined to parliamentary seats. It extended into the furthest corners of Afrikaner cultural and social life. It set in motion an earthquake within the organization which since the early part of the century had virtually controlled the political life of South Africa, which had helped organize the victory of the National Party in 1948, which had assisted it to remain in office, and which over five decades had proved itself to be one of the most successful secret organizations in the world – the Afrikaner Broederbond.

During the first two decades following its formation in 1918, the Broederbond helped rebuild self-confidence among Afrikaners after the defeat in the Boer War and after bitter internecine fighting over whether South Africa should support Britain in the First World War, a period known as 'Broedertwis' (brother taking up arms against brother). But the Broederbond slowly began to expand its horizons and during the early 1930s started to assume its secretive, more sinister role. It became an exclusive brethren, organized in tightly-controlled cells which met after midnight. Members were required to swear an oath, address each other in prescribed ways and greet each other with a secret handshake. Vetting of potential members was as rigorous as for the intelligence services of the major western nations – probably more stringent. The Broederbond was more secretive than South Africa's own security services. Every area of the applicant's (males only) life was investigated – usually without his knowledge – before he would be considered for membership. An aspiring member had to be an Afrikaner, of course, Protestant and committed to maintaining his and South Africa's Afrikaner identity. To be married to an English-speaking woman, or to have been educated at an English school, were sufficient to be rejected. The Broederbond worked incessantly behind the scenes for a National Party victory in 1948 by seeking to undermine Smuts and Hertzog, although the government had Broederbond meetings bugged and tapped members' telephones.

After 1948 the Broederbond ardently set to work to establish itself as the controlling influence in the country's political and economic life. At the height of its power in the 1950s and 1960s few senior appointments went to non-broeders in the cabinet (Malan, Strijdom, Verwoerd, and Vorster were all members, as is Botha), the National Party parliamentary caucus, provincial councils, the South African Broadcasting Corporation, the Dutch Reformed Church, the civil and public services, the police and the defence force, the sports governing bodies, universities and colleges, the boards of Afrikaans newspapers, and so on. It was one of the most remarkable networks of nepotism the world had seen, or rather not seen, as it was all undertaken behind closed doors. The result was that within fifty years white political power and a substantial slice of economic power was in the hands of the Afrikaners and was controlled by the Broederbond through the ruling National Party.

But the Broederbond was not immune to the wider political ructions. When Treurnicht led the rebel MPs out of the National Party in 1982 he also took them out of the Broederbond, a move seen as a call to all Conservative Party members to quit the organization. It was estimated that out of a Broederbond membership of 13,000 around 3,000 were likely to withdraw. Among the defectors was the chairman of the Broederbond, Professor Carel Boshoff, who in the following months became the driving force behind the formation of a new, more right-wing organization, pledged like the Conservative Party to fight Botha's reform plans all the way. Boshoff was also chairman of a Broederbond front organization called the South African Bureau of Racial Affairs (SABRA) which, contrary to the

Broederbond's pro-National Party line, had come out against the new constitutional proposals. In July 1983 Boshoff, in the name of SABRA, said the proposed reforms would stimulate rather than appease racial conflict because they did not 'conform to the requirements of exclusiveness and equality'. Every race group, he said, should have its 'own geographical sphere in which it can exercise authority'. Thus was the die cast. Boshoff resigned from the Broederbond and was replaced by a more verligte figure. But it left the Broederbond in turmoil.

Boshoff and fellow-conservatives began making inroads into a number of Afrikaner cultural organizations. Two days before the whites-only referendum on 2 November 1983 he announced he was setting up a new right-wing organization to uphold as non-negotiable the principle of a white state. The new organization, the Afrikaner Volkswag ('People's Guard'), was formed at a rally in Pretoria in May 1984. Among those who attended was Mrs Elizabeth Verwoerd, widow of the former prime minister.

Boshoff, married to Verwoerd's daughter, is not a wild-eyed racist fanatic. His supporters do not dress up in Ku Klux Klan outfits. They do not go on the rampage killing and maiming blacks. Boshoff is a quiet, hospitable, and extremely courteous theology professor who explains his views calmly and without rhetoric. He told me in February 1985 that Botha's plans for a better political deal for blacks within 'white South Africa' would set the nation on a road which led to black majority rule and disaster. 'We have got ten different nations, black nations, and they are also not willing to accept one of them as the ruling nation or the ruling power in South Africa', he said. 'So it's not only a matter of providing for white and black separate determination, it is also a matter of determination for the different black nations of South Africa.' But why such concern about Botha's plans? After all, one man, one vote was certainly not on his agenda and, while allowing for greater integration, Botha's policies still enshrined the principle of separate political representation for the blacks. Boshoff explained: 'I think that's lip service. I don't think it's possible to accommodate two different ideologies. You have separate development or you have integration and we are now on the way towards integration, there is no question about it. This effort [by Botha] to work towards integration with some sort of separate development is not possible.'

The formation of the Afrikaner Volkswag was a serious blow to the Broederbond which in recent years has been losing some of its influence. With P.W. Botha very much his own man, the Broederbond's influence will possibly shrink further. But it is unlikely to become extinct.

The founding of the Volkswag completed the split in Afrikanerdom: on one side, the ruling National Party supported by the Broederbond and, on the other, the Conservative Party and the Volkswag. The new right-wing force in white/politics still had to be put to an electoral test. This came in a string of by-elections which followed the CP defection. The first, in November 1982, were inconclusive. But in May 1983, the 'Battle of the Berge' by-elections in Soutpansberg and Waterberg, both in the rural northern Transvaal stronghold of right-wing support, clarified the trend. The two elections were precipitated by an extraordinary challenge thrown down in parliament early in 1983. Manpower Minister Fanie Botha offered to resign his seat and fight a by-election provided CP leader Treurnicht and a fellow CP member did the same. The challenge was accepted. Botha defeated the CP candidate in Soutpansberg, although his majority was slashed from 3,467 in the previous general election to just 612; in Waterberg, Treurnicht won a sweeping victory with 46.9 per cent of the vote compared to 31.4 per cent for the NP. The Nationalists held onto a third seat in another by-election that day where there was no CP candidate.

The right wing had arrived and the National Party could no longer claim to be the sole representative of Afrikaner aspirations. The elections were also memorable for a different reason: a cartoon in a black newspaper showed a black woman walking with her small grandchild past election advertisements saying 'Vote Nationalist' or 'Vote Conservative'. The girl asks: 'Granny, what is a vote?'

In November 1984 the CP's standing among urban whites was put to the test for the first time in the constituency of Primrose near Johannesburg, comprising mainly middle-class and lower middle-class Afrikaners. Voting experts maintained that if the CP took Primrose, the party would have achieved an 'urban breakthrough' and that forty other similar seats held by the Nationalists could become vulnerable. In the event, the NP held onto the seat but with a greatly reduced majority. The next crucial test came in five by-elections in October 1985 when the National Party lost the seat of Sasolburg, an industrial town in the Orange Free State, to the ultra-right Herstigte Nasionale Party. The result suggested that the right wing were at last eating into the traditional urban strongholds of the National Party. In three of the other seats contested on the same day the Conservative Party succeeded in cutting back the Nationalists' majority.

Support for the right wing came primarily from those worried about power-sharing with non-whites but also from poorer whites beginning to feel the effects of the deepening recession. Blue-collar workers saw their pay eaten away by inflation and saw their jobs threatened by black competition. Once again in Afrikaner history the spectre of 'poor whites' began to loom large although not to the same extent as in the 1920s. As a result of by-elections since the CP's formation, the state of the parties in the white House of Assembly as at October 1985, looked like this:

National Party	127
Progressive Federal Party	27
Conservative Party	18
New Republic Party	5
Herstigte Nasionale Party	1

The Conservative Party represented a right-wing backlash against the government's policies but the question was: how big? The CP was picking up the votes of whites who were determinedly set against Botha's reforms but also those registering opposition to the government's economic policies. The latter was likely to be a temporary 'protest' vote. The conclusion was, therefore, that the CP was possibly reaching the limits of its support, given current political circumstances. Nevertheless, some political commentators calculated that on the basis of the October 1985 by-elections a total of fifty-four seats could be won by the right wing in a general election (the next one is scheduled for 1989) which could of course provide a springboard for a more significant surge if events go really badly for Botha. Before 1989 though, constituency boundaries are likely to be redrawn which could make it risky to predict the outcome of the election. Also, the CP and the HNP have so far failed to join forces and fight the Nationalists on a single platform. If this remains so, the right-wing vote is clearly going to be split in the National Party's favour. At the very least, the Conservative Party stood poised to become the main opposition party in the white chamber, with the possibility of further defections by Nationalist MPs. But where would that leave the traditional opposition, the Progressive Federal Party, representing the liberal wing of white politics?

The Nationalists' victory in 1948 caused the centrist United Party (formed by the fusion of Smuts and Hertzog) to rock back on its heels. The party began to founder, unable to present a definable policy, outvoted by a party whose policy of racial separation found favour with the electorate. Attempts to oppose the 'new politics' were disastrous. Smuts died in 1950 a demoralized man, his ambition of uniting Afrikaner and English killed off by the NP success. First under the leadership of J.G.N. Strauss and then under Sir de Villiers Graaff, the United Party gradually lost parliamentary seats, some members crossing the house to join the NP. Attempts were made to launch more effective parties to oppose the Nationalists, most notably the Liberal Party of South Africa which was established just after the 1953 election. A founder member was the author of *Cry, The Beloved Country*, Alan Paton. The party decided to disband in 1968 after the passing of the *Prohibition of Political Interference Act* which barred multi-racial parties, rather than remain a 'whites-only' party.

The most important defection from the UP was in 1959 when twelve MPs split to form the Progressive Party. In the first three general elections after its formation only one of the party's parliamentary candidates was elected – Helen Suzman, MP for the Houghton constituency in Johannesburg. By 1977 the United Party, weakened by defections and decreasing support, dissolved itself, the majority of its remaining members forming the New Republic Party, which now has a narrow base largely confined to Natal and which struggles to keep a separate identity to that of the Nationalists. This left the field clear for the Progressives to mop up the liberal English-speaking voters. In 1974 the party's representation rose to seventeen, and in 1981 (when it had changed its name again to the Progressive Federal Party) it could claim twenty-six MPs.

Support for the PFP derives largely from upper-class, fairly affluent, English-speaking voters, although a substantial number of its MPs (including the leader Dr Slabbert) are Afrikaners. The party is also supported by many leading businessmen, the most important of whom has been Mr Harry Oppenheimer who backs the PFP's call for a free market economy devoid of racial restrictions. The party programme calls for the introduction of universal franchise in South

Africa linked, as its name suggests, to some kind of devolved legislative structure to ensure that one race group does not dominate another. The party has fought strenuously against the plethora of security laws introduced by successive National Party governments. The PFP is supported by much of the English press, though the demise of the strongly anti-apartheid *Rand Daily Mail* newspaper early in 1985 was a serious blow to the party.

But the real threat to the PFP lies not in the possibility of the CP taking over as the official opposition; indeed, such a scenario could work in the PFP's favour as moderate whites might rush to the party's side to counter the threat of a right-wing takeover. A bigger threat is that with so many new parties and factions – both intra- and extra-parliamentary – the PFP stands to be squeezed between them all. The days when liberal whites could stand up in the white House of Assembly to expound what the 'blacks really think' are long gone. The blacks have their own organizations now, like the United Democratic Front. As for the coloured and Indian electorates, they now have their own parties in parliament, while those who boycotted the elections under the new constitution because they objected to 'stooge' MPs would be no more likely to vote for the PFP now than they were in the past.

Another threat to the PFP vote comes from the emergence of a new centrist constituency in white politics. The constitutional referendum and subsequent parliamentary elections showed that around 40 per cent of English-speakers supported Botha and his policy of measured reform. The gap between National Party policies and those the PFP have advocated for twenty-five years is narrowing. Botha says the kind of things and is introducing the kind of measures which PFP MPs acknowledge privately as a genuine break with the past. If Botha's English-speaking support holds up, it is unlikely that the PFP can make further inroads into parliament. But the party has never seen its effectiveness entirely as a matter of how many seats it holds. If that were the case the party would have folded during the thirteen lonely years when Helen Suzman was its only MP. Rather it sees its importance in being the liberal conscience of white South Africans, the party which is continually knocking on the doors of government ministries to discover how many blacks have died in police detention, how many people are being forcibly removed from their homes, how damaging the apartheid policy has been to the black homelands, and so on. The party is there to spell out an alternative way ahead. As the National Party embraces further reforms to apartheid, the PFP will be judged on how effectively it can continue to set out the arguments for more far-reaching change in South Africa; to what extent it can ensure that the debate is not solely on the government's terms; that there is a goal for reform ahead of that proposed by the government. In other words a party which will not allow the government to rest on its laurels.

It is, though, the schism between the National Party and the Conservative Party which currently provides the focus of white politics. It is not the first time that Afrikanerdom has been divided. This time, though, there is a difference. Previous splits occurred within the Afrikaner camp and were contained within the laager. What P.W. Botha has brought about is of a different order. For the first time an Afrikaner leader has sent part of Afrikanerdom (the right wing) on its way and waved farewell to them at the laager gates, while through the back door he has admitted a substantial proportion of the English population. There is the possibility that the right wing will one day return to the fold, but not for the moment. P.W. Botha has achieved what Smuts and Louis Botha failed to bring about, something of a common identity between Afrikaner and English. This is arguably the most important development in South African politics in the past few years: that, and the rise of the first organized black opposition to apartheid in twenty-five years.

CHAPTER 6

'Only Free Men can Negotiate'
The struggle for black freedom

The ANC's struggle is a truly national one. It is a struggle of the African people, inspired by their own suffering and their own experience. It is a struggle for the right to live. During my lifetime I have fought against white domination and I have fought against black domination. I have cherished the ideal of a democratic and free society in which all persons will live together in harmony and with equal opportunities. It is an ideal which I hope to live for and to achieve. But, if need be, it is an ideal for which I am prepared to die.

These are the words of the man who is without question the commanding figure in the black nationalist struggle in South Africa. His reputation has been enhanced by the many years spent behind bars. Most blacks recognize him as their true leader; even those who do not share his particular brand of black nationalism acknowledge his stature. The government knows it, hence its long-standing reluctance to free him; the rest of the world knows it, which is why streets in foreign cities are named after him and why the United Nations honours him. He is the symbol of the struggle against apartheid.

Nelson Rolihlahla Mandela was born into the Xhosa tribe in the Transkei in 1918, the son of a royal chief. He studied at Fort Hare University near King William's Town where he became involved in student politics and later worked in Johannesburg, first in the mines and then for a firm of white lawyers. He later set up his own legal partnership with now-exiled leader of the African National Congress, Oliver Tambo. Mandela joined the ANC in 1944 and established its youth wing. In 1952 he led over 8,000 people in a campaign of defiance for which he was given a suspended prison sentence and banned, a unique South African method of silencing dissidents by curtailing their political and social activities and prohibiting any public statements. After the ban expired Mandela reappeared in public life. In June 1955 at the Congress of the People in Kliptown he supported the formation of a Congress Alliance which was to unite all the principal organizations fighting apartheid. The organization adopted a 'Freedom Charter' which, ever since, has remained the political lighthouse of the anti-apartheid struggle, the doctrine which many of the opposition groups see as their blueprint for a free South Africa.

The 1955 Freedom Charter began with the words:

We, the People of South Africa, declare for all our country and the world to know:

- that South Africa belongs to all who live in it, black and white, and that no government can justly claim authority unless it is based on the will of the people.
- that our people have been robbed of their birthright to land, liberty and peace by a form of government founded on injustice and inequality.
- that our country will never be prosperous or free until all our people live in brotherhood, enjoying equal rights and opportunities.
- that only a democratic state, based on the will of all the people, can secure to all their birthright without distinction of colour, race, sex or belief.
- And, therefore, we, the People of South Africa, black and white together – equals, countrymen and brothers – adopt this Freedom Charter. And we pledge ourselves to strive together, sparing neither strength nor courage, until the democratic changes here set out have been won.

The charter spelled out the principles upon which a democratic state should be established: the right of every man and woman to vote and the right to stand as candidate for all bodies which make laws; equal rights for all national groups; the people to share in the country's wealth; the land to be shared among those who work it; all to be equal before the law; all to enjoy equal human rights, and so on. Essentially it came down to a call for a multi-racial society in South Africa in which each would have full democratic rights regardless of colour, a country where there would be no domination by one group over another. The blacks saw it as the framework for a peaceful and just South Africa in which all races would live side by side in a spirit of friendship and goodwill. The whites saw it as a recipe for black Marxist rule and the driving of whites into the sea.

The charter has remained the credo of Nelson Mandela since it was drawn up. The following year he and 155 other Congress Alliance leaders appeared in a treason trial which ended with all the accused acquitted. He then went underground to set up Umkhonto we Sizwe (Spear of the Nation), the military wing of the ANC, with the aim of sabotaging public buildings though not attacking civilian targets. A year later Mandela was arrested and charged with inciting strikes and leaving the country without a permit. He was jailed for five years but while serving his sentence was brought to court in Pretoria to join other leaders of Umkhonto (six Africans, two whites, and one Indian) on charges of sabotage, high treason and conspiracy to overthrow the government. The new charges followed a police raid on the ANC's underground headquarters in the northern Johannesburg suburb of Rivonia on 11 June 1963. The words quoted at the start of this chapter were the climax to a 4½-hour statement by Mandela which opened his defence. He admitted planning sabotage to combat oppression but denied the campaign was communist-inspired. The seven-month-long non-jury trial ended in June 1964 when eight of the defendants – Nelson Mandela, Walter Sisulu, Govan Mbeki, Dennis Goldberg, Ahmed Kathrada, Elias Matsoaledi, Andrew Mlangeni and Raymond Mhlaba – were found guilty of sabotage and conspiracy and sentenced to life imprisonment. Mandela spent the first period of his sentence on Robben Island, breaking bricks and working in the lime quarries. On 1 April 1982 he was transferred to Pollsmoor Prison on the mainland just south of Cape Town, ostensibly for administrative reasons, though it was suggested that the move was the result of the strong influence Mandela was exerting over the prison island inmates, for whom he had organized an educational programme.

The imprisonment of Nelson Mandela, together with the banning of his organization and other anti-apartheid bodies, left a vacuum in the black nationalist struggle which no single figure has been able to fill. The power of the state to detain activists without trial or to ban them, and thereby neutralize them politically, has contributed in no small measure to the comparative lack of organized opposition over the past twenty-five years to the gradual implementation of apartheid. But the struggle has also been hindered by divisions among the blacks themselves, divisions which exist at two levels but which often overlap.

At one level is the historical animosity between the rival black tribes, especially between the two largest, the Zulus and the Xhosas. This animosity is reflected in the fierce faction-fighting which often breaks out in mining compounds and in townships like Soweto during times of unrest when emotions are running high. Even among the clans within one particular tribe, particularly the Zulus, traditional rivalries can frequently spill over into waves of murderous violence. In June 1984, seventy people were killed and thousands fled their homes during an outbreak of Zulu clan-fighting in Natal. According to black newspapers horrific atrocities were committed and local hospitals had difficulty in matching up the various parts of the bodies which had been discovered.

Such hostility between rival black families is compounded by the divisions among the blacks at a political level. The divisions derive from a number of issues central to the black liberation cause in South Africa: to what extent violence should be used to further the anti-apartheid struggle; whether whites should be allowed to participate in the black man's fight for freedom; whether the blacks should compromise on demands like that for one man, one vote as a way of resolving the country's political problems. That these divisions cut across each other is evident in, for example, the bitter hostility which exists between the ANC, which has been dominated by Xhosas, and the large number of Zulus who are loyal to Chief Mangosuthu Buthelezi.

The most important event in black politics in recent years took place on 20 August 1983 with the launch of the United Democratic Front. Some 10,000 people gathered at Mitchells Plain near Cape Town to form the organization, the broadest alliance of anti-apartheid bodies since the congress movement. Moves towards forming such an organization had been taking place all year, inspired by Allan Boesak, and encouraged by the success of the Anti-South African Indian Council Campaign against what its supporters regarded as the 'puppet' representative body for Indians, one of the most effective such boycotts that the anti-apartheid movement had mounted. Further impetus came in January 1983 when the old Transvaal Indian Congress, a member of the Congress Alliance and a signatory to the Freedom Charter, decided to revive itself to mobilize resistance to the participation of coloureds and Indians in the new constitution. Calling for a united front, Boesak declared: 'There is . . . no reason why the churches, civic associations, trade unions, student organizations and sports bodies should not unite on this issue, pool our resources, inform people of the fraud that is about to be perpetrated in their name and, on the day of the election, expose their [the government's] plans for what they are.' Gradually the new front was taking shape.

The Mitchells Plain launch was attended by some 1,000 representatives of about 575 anti-apartheid organizations. Each had its own policies; the United Democratic Front was to be an umbrella body co-ordinating the activities of the member groups. In other words, it was a loose coalition of anti-apartheid forces which, in the absence of a unified black struggle, had come together to fight Botha's reforms.

The UDF did not take the Freedom Charter as its manifesto, largely because the organization insisted that it did not 'purport to be a substitute movement to accredited peoples' liberation movements'. Also some UDF groups had reservations about the socialist slant of many of the charter's economic clauses. Nevertheless the UDF's inaugural declaration bore a strong echo of the 1955 programme:

> Freedom-loving people of South Africa say with one voice to the whole world that we cherish the vision of a united democratic South Africa based on the will of the people, and will strive for the unity of all our people through united action against the evils of apartheid and economic and all other forms of exploitation, and in our march to a free and just South Africa we are going to be guided by these noble ideals. We stand for the creation of a true democracy in which all South Africans will participate in the government of our country. We stand for a single, non-racial, unfragmented South Africa, free of bantustans and group areas . . .

Boesak was appointed a patron of the organization along with others whose names appeared like a 'who's who' of the liberation movement, including Nelson Mandela and Walter Sisulu. Three national presidents were elected: Archie Gumede, a veteran of the Congress Alliance, Albertina Sisulu, wife of the imprisoned black nationalist, and Oscar Mpetha, a Cape trade union leader. Boesak caught the spirit of the occasion when he declared to the gathering: 'We want all our rights. We want them here and we want them now.'

From Mitchells Plain the delegates returned to their respective areas to begin mobilizing for the campaign against the coloured and Indian elections. The aim was to achieve as widespread a boycott as possible in order to deprive the new power-sharing parliament of its credibility. Here again, it was not a matter of the UDF laying down the strategy but rather of co-ordinating the various political campaigns. Many of the affiliated organizations had, after all, been party to boycott campaigns in the past; the tradition was already long established, especially in the coloured community in the Cape.

But the UDF's success created a problem: how to maintain the momentum when the government was not going to be deterred from pressing ahead with implementation of the new constitution. What should become the focus of the UDF's campaign? What were to be the political goals of the movement? How easy would it be to provide leadership with the security authorities rounding up many of the key figures? How to maintain unity in a movement which reflected many different threads of political thinking? The evidence suggests that since the election boycott campaign the UDF has experienced difficulty in defining a clear concept of the way forward, for a number of reasons.

First, there is no doubt that the UDF leadership has been weakened. There is not one powerful figure who would be acceptable to all the affiliated groups or to the various schools within the movement (especially since Allan Boesak was alleged in early 1985 to have had a personal relationship with a white female churchworker which, in the eyes of many, cast doubt on his authority as both a political and a religious leader). It was therefore left to inexperienced political figures to steer the UDF: African clergymen, black trade unionists, members of the black intelligentsia and radical whites. Second, there is a question as to whether the UDF controls the situation on the ground, to what extent events are running ahead of the organization. Some of those orchestrating the unrest are now so radicalized that even the UDF – despite its pivotal role in the anti-apartheid struggle – is seen by many as too conservative. The

true ideology of the movement is not yet clear. Within the UDF a
struggle is taking place between those who represent three different
political schools of thought. First, there are those who subscribe to
the theory – supported by the ANC and the also-exiled South African
Communist Party – of a two-stage revolution, i.e. a period of
national democratic government followed by a socialist takeover. A
second school places greater emphasis on the working class being in
the vanguard of the struggle. A third school favours a much broader
struggle embracing not only front-line political groups, but also the
churches and civil rights organizations. Until now the UDF has
admitted people of all races to its membership and leadership. The
UDF parts company on this issue with the organization which
represents the other principal stream of black politics, the Black
Consciousness movement of the late Steve Biko.

This division in black nationalist ranks dates back to 1959 when
young leaders of the African National Congress broke away from the
organization to form the Pan-Africanist Congress. They considered
themselves to be 'Africanists' first and were deeply suspicious of the
role played by white radicals in the freedom struggle. These ideas
were taken further with the emergence of Biko's Black Consciousness (BC). Biko's contribution to the history of black nationalist
thought was to emphasize the role of the black man in leading the
liberation movement and to urge the blacks to establish and preserve
their identity. Though not anti-white, Biko's doctrine sought to
lessen the dependence of the black man on the social and cultural
environment of the ruling white class. It had a strong echo of the
Black Power movement in the United States. During the late 1960s
and early 1970s the Black Consciousness ideology found wide
appeal among the more literate class of blacks which was beginning
to emerge despite the blacks' inferior educational opportunities
compared to those of the whites. The intelligentsia in the black
townships were attracted to the BC doctrine and helped spread its
message among politically-conscious blacks. Although it filtered
through to many levels of black society beyond the urban intelligentsia, it never gained as much support as the charterist movement
of the ANC.
    The first overt BC grouping was the Black People's Convention in
1972, nine of whose student leaders were found guilty of terrorism in
1976 and sent to prison. The movement was practically extinguished

in 1977 when the BC organizations were banned and Steve Biko died while in police custody. Biko had been a popular young leader among certain sections of the black community but it was the circumstances of his death which ensured that his name would live on as one of the principal figures in the black liberation struggle.

The organization which emerged from the ashes of the 1977 clampdown called itself the Azanian People's Organization (AZAPO) and it has now become the heir to the Black Consciousness tradition within black politics. It is therefore the main rival to the United Democratic Front, which favours all races playing a part in the fight against apartheid, in the struggle for influence among South Africa's urban blacks. The term 'Azania' was first coined by the ancient Greeks as the name for the unknown land mass south of Egypt and was revived by the Pan-Africanist Congress in the 1960s as the black nationalist name for South Africa. The name is generally assumed to be the one which will replace 'South Africa' in the event of a black majority government, in the same way that Rhodesia became Zimbabwe upon independence.

In the early 1980s AZAPO was the only liberation movement not to be made illegal, probably because its effectiveness was marginal. But then it received an important injection of new thinking with the release of several of its leaders who had been in detention or banned. One of these was Dr Neville Alexander who had spent ten years on Robben Island and a further five years under a banning order which expired in 1979. Alexander introduced into Black Consciousness thought the notion of what at first was called 'racial capitalism', a class-based analysis of society which concluded that the apartheid state maintained its economic hegemony by means of racial suppression. AZAPO was further reinvigorated when the 1976 detainees were freed in 1982, among them Saths Cooper who was elected the organization's vice-president shortly after his release. While in the other camp Boesak was formulating the proposed United Democratic Front, Alexander, Cooper and other BC leaders just released from the Island were planning their own broadly-based organization to fight the constitution. It called itself the National Forum and it met at Hammanskraal near Pretoria in June 1983, just a couple of months before the UDF launch.

The forum was an attempt to bring together all those groups which shared the black exclusivist position. There were strong attacks on the Freedom Charter, notably from Saths Cooper who drew attention to those parts of it which refer to preservation of group rights and recognition of minority rights. This was at odds with AZAPO's vision of an entirely reconstructed society based on a one-nation, socialist system with the working class playing a dominant role, and with all traces of the former oppressors, far from being protected, eradicated altogether. AZAPO also attacked the UDF (and the ANC) for, in its view, perceiving the liberation movement in South Africa simply as an anti-apartheid struggle or as a civil rights campaign – a reformist ideology, as AZAPO saw it, not a revolutionary doctrine aimed at the total overthrow of the established 'racist/capitalist' order. The forum was also confronted by the problem of what role white radicals should play in the struggle. The final manifesto spoke of 'non-collaboration with the oppressor and his political instruments' and Alexander told the conference that whites who wanted to contribute to the struggle had their place, but that the black working class had to be acknowledged by all as the leaders. Despite Alexander's statement that white activists would have to be accommodated in the struggle, many delegates left with the impression that there was no place for whites. The shift to a more left-wing stance, emphasizing the role of the black working class, took the theory beyond Black Consciousness and was not entirely acceptable to all the groups represented. The forum made little impact upon the constitutional debate, but AZAPO has since emerged as an intellectual force in black politics. Its base of support is not as wide as that enjoyed by the UDF but it is popular among important opinionformers within the black community – journalists, writers and teachers – because of its mixture of African nationalism and its socialist analysis of South African society.

The divisions between the two organizations – the UDF and AZAPO – were highlighted soon after both organizations got off the ground. Zindzi Mandela, the daughter of Nelson Mandela, attacked AZAPO for being 'ideologically-lost bandits' and demanded adherence to the Freedom Charter. But the rivalry was for the most part set aside during the campaign against Botha's reform plans. Behind the scenes however, and especially since the release of the BC leaders, a fight for influence was beginning within the black townships. Bishop Tutu at a very early stage had called for ideological differences to be set aside. He was soon to find himself actively trying to stem not only ideological differences but an outbreak of violence between the two bodies which threatened to turn into a black civil war.

It erupted during the early part of 1985, first of all at the (black) University of the North at Turfloop in the northern Transvaal where there were clashes between supporters of the rival organizations. Then began a wave of petrol-bombings in the townships with the homes of political rivals being burned down. In one incident two young children were burned to death when a petrol bomb was hurled into the house of an AZAPO member in the eastern Cape. Sinister killings took place which activists blamed on government agents trying to fuel the inter-black war. Suspected police collaborators were burned alive – and all this on top of the more general violence which was taking place.

As the situation deteriorated, the respected black journalist Percy Qoboza of the black Johannesburg newspaper *City Press* wrote a despairing article pleading with black leaders to get a grip on the situation:

> There must be something immensely wrong with our communities if black-on-black violence continues unabated without any of us raising a finger . . . The time has surely come for supporters of the United Democratic Front and the Azanian People's Organization to come together and reassess their values and project in their strategies the fundamental issues of what they want to achieve. Even more importantly, they must identify who the real enemy is.

Bishop Tutu stepped in to try to stem the escalating violence. He called the rival factions together and tried to halt the fighting but there was little response.

But if the struggle between the UDF and AZAPO was not damaging enough to the black cause, there was also the running battle which both were waging against the Zulu-dominated organization called Inkatha led by Chief Mangosuthu Buthelezi.

There is little love lost between the ANC and Mangosuthu Buthelezi. The ANC label the Zulu chief a 'puppet' because he heads a black homeland set up by the apartheid government. He, in turn, refers to the ANC as the 'external mission' of the black nationalist struggle, the suggestion being that he, at least, is in South Africa fighting for the black man, whereas the ANC leaders are waging their struggle on the diplomatic cocktail circuit in several of the world's capitals. The two sides held talks in London in 1979 to try to heal the rift but they came to nothing. Buthelezi attacked the ANC as 'opponents of the black people' while, in the ANC's eyes, Buthelezi was an 'obstacle to liberation'.

Mangosuthu Buthelezi is the chief minister of KwaZulu, a jigsaw puzzle empire whose pieces are scattered all over northern Natal. He has not accepted 'independence' from South Africa for his home-land, much as Pretoria would like him to, because he opposes the bantustan policy. He once told the *Rand Daily Mail* that: 'My opposition to apartheid in preventing six million black South Afri-cans [the Zulu population] from being taken up the primrose path to independence was a major achievement.' It is likely that, but for Buthelezi's opposition to 'independence', other homeland leaders would have caved in to Pretoria and taken their territory out of 'white South Africa'. But KwaZulu is self-governing, if not fully independent, and Buthelezi is head of it. He is sensitive to charges from his critics that 'he wants it both ways' by espousing opposition to apartheid, yet accepting the leadership of a government-created homeland. His response is that the Zulu national home predates apartheid and that he, as Zulu leader, derives his authority from his Zulu ancestors and not from the South African government.

The one million-strong Inkatha movement is to all intents and purposes a Zulu version of the Afrikaner Broederbond, although the organization insists its membership is open to non-Zulu blacks and it is considering allowing all races to join. It is described as a 'cultural liberation organization', but clearly, were South Africa to be handed over to black majority rule, Inkatha would be a formidable political force. It is not surprising that Inkatha is engaged in a vitriolic struggle for power with the United Democratic Front, which despises Buthelezi. This is not only because of the chief's position as home-land leader but also because of the suspicion among many black activists that, despite his avowed opposition to apartheid and despite his condemnation of the new constitution, Buthelezi is the black leader who might be prepared to do a deal with the South African government and, in effect, hijack the revolution. Such suspicions are based on the chief's declared opposition to international economic sanctions against South Africa and because he has diluted the demand for one man, one vote to give the whites some reassurance about their future in the country. This is anathema to black national-ist organizations like the United Democratic Front. His opposition to violence is also noted by those who believe the peaceful struggle for black rights should, whenever necessary, be supplemented by the use of violence. Perhaps also the spectre of another Shaka, a Zulu giant who might one day try to dominate other tribes, haunts non-Zulus.

Serious violence between Inkatha and the UDF broke out in November 1983 at the University of Zululand, whose chancellor is Mangosuthu Buthelezi. During 1983 the UDF became active among the students of the university, many of whom clearly had their doubts about Buthelezi's style of leadership and the tribal exclusiveness of Inkatha. The latter is a sensitive issue for Buthelezi who, as a potential black leader of South Africa in the event of the whites surrendering power, is clearly anxious to overcome any suggestion that his power base is limited to the Zulus. The views of some of the students at the University of Zululand, which is open to blacks from all over South Africa and elsewhere, were summed up by one student leader who told a local newspaper:

> Most students are anti-Inkatha because they know how to read and analyse things. At the apex of the Inkatha triangle is the rule that to be president of Inkatha you must be chief minister of KwaZulu. To be head of the KwaZulu government you must be a chief and a Zulu. With that information you do not hesitate to believe Inkatha is tribally-oriented. It is a party which mobilizes people to keep the government of KwaZulu alive. We look at some of the courses offered in the schools – they are tribally-oriented and tribalism has evil consequences. There is a belief that Inkatha wants to keep the university Zulu-oriented.

Such attacks undoubtedly sting Buthelezi because they imply that he is helping to keep apartheid alive, as well as supporting its philosophical justification, by maintaining the separate tribal identities of the blacks. His critics maintain that tribally-based organizations like Inkatha play into the government's hands by helping to keep alive the concept that South Africa's blacks are formed by different nations which should be treated separately.

Tensions within the university boiled over after some of the students issued a call to Buthelezi to resign as chancellor. Pamphlets which were distributed on the campus accused the chief of being 'a sell-out, a traitor, and a Pretoria puppet'. This was too much for the Inkatha leaders, one of whom described the students' move as a 'highly provocative insult'. By breakfast-time the following morning six students were dead and dozens more were in hospital with split heads and broken bones. According to the students, Zulu warriors dressed either in khaki uniforms or leopard skins had gone on the rampage throughout the campus with spears, battle-axes and pangas (bush-knives). The insult to Buthelezi had been avenged.

Violence like this provides the whites with their greatest ammunition and fuels their fears about the consequences of handing the country over to the blacks. They look north into black Africa and recall the Belgian Congo, the Nigerian civil war, Idi Amin, and, more recently, Zimbabwe, where tribal rivalries between the Shona tribe of Prime Minister Robert Mugabe and the Ndebele of opposition leader Joshua Nkomo have led to atrocities in Zimbabwe's south-western province of Matabeleland. The whites look at the tribal make-up of their own country and firmly believe that what happened in the rest of Africa once the blacks were given power would pale into insignificance compared to the tribal war which would be unleashed in South Africa if the blacks took over: a power struggle in which they, the whites, would inevitably be involved, besieged once again inside their white laager in the midst of menacing black hordes. Events like the slayings at the University of Zululand and the often violent rivalry between the UDF and AZAPO convince the whites that the tribal and political differences between the blacks run so deep that they are bound to explode if the whites ever lose their grip on the country.

At the end of the day, as the whites see it, it boils down to this: the history of Africa has been about one black tribe dominating another. It has been about who is going to be the strong man, who is to be the tribal chief who will reign supreme over the others. And here we come back to Mandela.

In a curious way there is admiration for Mandela among more enlightened Afrikaners. They will insist he is a terrorist, imprisoned not for his beliefs but for sabotage, and will say that there are other black leaders who are just as representative of black opinion. But in their heart of hearts there is a grudging recognition of the integrity of a man willing to spend over two decades in prison in the service of his beliefs. Such a sacrifice can be acknowledged by the Afrikaner because his own history has been one of sacrifice and commitment to an ideal. And being an African tribe themselves, the Afrikaners, like the blacks, tend to respect the concept of the strong leader. Some government ministers have acknowledged privately that Mandela should have been freed years ago, a conviction which grew during

1984 and 1985. They realized that nothing would look worse for South Africa than if Nelson Mandela died a martyr in prison.

The disclosure in November 1985 that Mandela had undergone an operation for the removal of a prostate gland obviously heightened the government's concern on the issue, although it raised the possibility that ill-health might be the excuse for the authorities to release him without losing face. But the government faced several problems in releasing Mandela. He could not be free unless the government had a shrewd idea beforehand what his role would be after his release, in other words, how it would handle him. Would he become the focus of a surge of popular revolutionary fervour, or would he slip quietly into the background? Would he return to plotting acts of violence? Or would he be the man the government could sit down and talk to about the future of South Africa? How would whites react to his release?

The government had on several occasions in recent years offered him his release but on condition that he would agree to settle in the Transkei, which as a Xhosa is his designated homeland. This he always refused, insisting he was a South African and not a Transkeian. For many of South Africa's critics abroad the continued imprisonment of Nelson Mandela became the symbol of what they saw as the oppressive system in the country. Until recently the government remained fairly impervious to these attacks. As recently as September 1983 Prime Minister Botha, asked about Mandela's imprisonment, said the black nationalist leader had been found guilty in an independent court, that he was serving his sentence and that was all he wished to say on the matter. But less than eighteen months later the approach had mellowed. Mandela was allowed a prison visit from the British Euro-MP, Lord Nicholas Bethell, a visit arranged by Helen Suzman. During the course of his interview with Lord Bethell, Mandela reportedly indicated that he would be prepared to call a truce in the ANC's campaign of violence if the outlawed organization were legalized which would, of course, open the way for direct negotiations between the ANC and the South African government. Writing in a British newspaper about his interview with Mandela, Bethell called upon Pretoria to order Mandela's release.

No sooner had the interview been published than the state president stole the initiative by in effect offering Mandela his freedom. Botha's move was not universally welcomed by the National Party but waving the protests aside, P.W. Botha rose in parliament on 31 January 1985 to announce for the first time in public that his government was willing to consider Mandela's release. Botha declared:

> The government is not insensitive to the fact that Mr Mandela and others have spent a very long time in prison, even though they were convicted in open court. The government is willing to consider Mr Mandela's release in the Republic of South Africa on condition that Mr Mandela gives a commitment that he will not make himself guilty of planning, instigating or committing acts of violence for the furtherance of political objectives, but will conduct himself in such a way that he will not again have to be arrested.

Botha's statement concluded: 'It is therefore not the South African government which now stands in the way of Mr Mandela's freedom.' The announcement meant the government had dropped its earlier offer of releasing Mandela to a tribal homeland – he could now be freed in South Africa itself. In return, they wanted him to renounce the use of violence.

Why did the government make the offer after all that time? First, Botha knew all along that Mandela would reject the offer as it would almost certainly have meant an irreparable loss to his credibility within the ANC, despite the many years dedicated to the cause. Indeed one of those nationalists who did accept Botha's offer, Dennis Goldberg, was given a noticeably less than heroic welcome by his fellow-freedom-fighters after his release. From the government's point of view, the Mandela release offer was worth trying. If he accepted he would either be politically neutralized or else, if he were welcomed back into the ranks of the ANC, his presence would mean a reinjection of the nationalist element within the movement to counter the communist influence within the ANC.

And if he refused, nothing would have been lost. The offer would win South Africa some political mileage internationally at a time when its policies were under increasing attack and the campaign for economic sanctions was gaining ground in the United States. Also, a refusal could be used to 'wrong-foot' the ANC by showing, as South Africa saw it, that this was an organization which was irrevocably committed to violence. Interestingly, the ban on quoting the ANC leader Oliver Tambo in South African newspapers was relaxed one

Prime Minister, later President, P. W. Botha addressing a National Party congress in 1983 about his plans for power-sharing with coloureds and Indians but not blacks

Dr Andries Treurnicht, leader of the right-wing Conservative Party which represents whites opposing the reform of apartheid

South African Foreign Minister Pik Botha leaves Vienna after talks with US officials about apartheid reforms (9 August 1985)

Veteran anti-apartheid campaigner Helen Suzman MP, meeting eye-witnesses of the Uitenhage police shootings (22 March 1985)

Zindzi Mandela relays to the people of Soweto her father's response to P. W. Botha's conditional release offer (10 February 1985)

Dr Allan Boesak, president of the World Alliance of Reformed Churches, coloured anti-apartheid leader and a founder of the United Democratic Front

Bishop Desmond Tutu is welcomed by parishioners in Soweto after winning
the Nobel peace prize 1984 (21 October 1984)

Mangosuthu Buthelezi, chief minister of the KwaZulu homeland and head of
the predominantly Zulu Inkatha movement

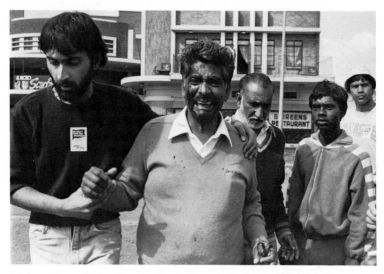

Violence flares during elections for Indians under P. W. Botha's new constitution (29 August 1984)

The end of the anti-apartheid sit-in at the British consulate, Durban. Billy Nair, the only one of the 'Durban Six' not to be rearrested, is carried shoulder-high from the consulate by his supporters (12 December 1984)

Kwanobuhle black township near Uitenhage, 25 March 1985. A black town council official, accused of 'co-operating' with the white authorities, is attacked by a hostile crowd and set on fire

Crossroads squatter camp, Cape Town, 19 February 1985. Police wearing gas masks move in to break up rioters. Behind them, a screen of smoke from burning tyres. The Crossroads violence left eighteen people dead

Those killed by the police at Uitenhage are buried along with other unrest victims (13 April 1985)

Three senior churchmen lead a march through Cape Town (26 March 1985) to protest against the Uitenhage police shootings. From left to right: Methodist minister Rev. Abel Hendrickse; president of the World Alliance of Reformed Churches; Dr Allan Boesak, general secretary of the South African Council of Churches, Dr Beyers Naudé. All three were arrested with dozens more and spent the night in prison

Palls of smoke drift across Inanda black township near Durban during clashes
involving blacks and Indians (9 August 1985)

King William's Town, 11 August 1985. The burning body of a Ciskei
homeland security officer, stoned and set on fire after the funeral of leading
anti-apartheid lawyer Victoria Mxenge

Cape Town, 11 September 1985. The body of a policeman beaten to death by crowds angry over the police killing of a local leader

Cape Town, 28 August 1985. Police with whips break up anti-government demonstrators to thwart a march to the city's Pollsmoor Prison to demand the release of black nationalist leader Nelson Mandela

Cape Town, 11 September 1985. A man is carried away after being shot by a policeman who had allegedly been under attack from mourners attending the funeral of an unrest victim. The policeman is later killed by the crowd

President Samora Machel of Mozambique and South African Prime Minister P. W. Botha meet to sign the Nkomati peace accord between their two countries (16 March 1984)

US Democratic senator Edward Kennedy greets squatters at Crossroads shanty town near Cape Town (10 January 1985) during his controversial visit to South Africa

From left to right: British Foreign Secretary Sir Geoffrey Howe; South African Prime Minister P. W. Botha; British Prime Minister Margaret Thatcher; South African Foreign Minister Pik Botha, meeting at Chequers on 2 June 1984

week after the release offer to allow the publication of an interview with Tambo, originally published by a newspaper in Zimbabwe, in which he said that the ANC would continue the armed struggle and that Mandela would reject the government's approach. In terms of its own position, the South African government was able to turn round and say: 'We told you so.'

Mandela's formal reply to the offer came a few days later. His wife, Winnie, had travelled to Pollsmoor Prison from the town of Brandfort in the Orange Free State to which she was banished, for her regular monthly visit to her husband. Mandela also discussed the release offer with his fellow long-term prisoners but the discussion simply concerned the terms in which a response should be couched. Although Mandela's supporters knew what the answer would be, his formal response was awaited expectantly. On the morning of Sunday 10 February 1985 several thousand UDF supporters attended a mass rally at Jabulani Stadium in Soweto. Bishop Tutu was there and also Mandela's daughter, Zindzi, who was borne shoulder-high into the stadium. It was to her that Mandela had entrusted the task of revealing his response to the outside world. He wanted the reply to be read directly to his people. It was the first time in a quarter of a century that he had been able to communicate with them, albeit through a third party. As a testimony to Nelson Mandela's faith in the justice of his struggle and as a measure of the man's commitment to that struggle, the address at Jabulani amphitheatre stands comparison with his defence from the dock at the Rivonia trial. These are the words his daughter read out:

> On Friday my mother and our attorney saw my father at Pollsmoor Prison to obtain his answer to Botha's offer of conditional release. The prison authorities attempted to stop this statement being made but he would have none of this and made it clear that he would make the statement to you, the people.
>
> Strangers like Bethell from England . . . have in recent weeks been authorised by Pretoria to see my father without restriction yet Pretoria cannot allow you, the people, to hear what he has to say directly. He should be here himself to tell you what he thinks of this statement by Botha. He is not allowed to do so. My mother who also heard his words is also not allowed to speak to you today.
>
> My father and his comrades at Pollsmoor Prison send their

greetings to you, the freedom-loving people of this our tragic land, in the full confidence that you will carry on the struggle for freedom. . . .

My father and his comrades wish to make this statement to you, the people, first. They are clear that they are accountable to you and to you alone, and that you should hear their views directly and not through others.

My father speaks not only for himself and for his comrades at Pollsmoor Prison but he hopes he speaks for all those in jail for their opposition to apartheid, for all those who are banished, for all those who are in exile, for all those who suffer under apartheid, for all those who are opponents of apartheid and for all those who are oppressed and exploited.

Throughout our struggle there have been puppets who have claimed to speak to you. They have made this claim, both here and abroad. They are of no consequence. My father and his colleagues will not be like them.

My father says 'I am a member of the African National Congress. I have always been a member of the African National Congress and I will remain a member of the African National Congress until the day I die. Oliver Tambo is much more than a brother to me. He is my greatest friend and comrade for nearly fifty years. If there is any one amongst you who cherishes my freedom, Oliver Tambo cherishes it more and I know that he would give his life to see me free.

'There is no difference between his views and mine.'

My father says 'I am surprised at the conditions the government wants to impose on me. I am not a violent man. My colleagues and I wrote in 1952 to Malan asking for a round-table conference to find a solution to the problems of our country but that was ignored. When Strijdom was in power, we made the same offer. Again it was ignored. When Verwoerd was in power we asked for a national convention for all the people in South Africa to decide on their future. This, too, was in vain.

'It was only when all other forms of resistance were no longer open to us that we turned to armed struggle.

'Let Botha show that he is different to Malan, Strijdom and Verwoerd.

'Let him renounce violence.

'Let him say that he will dismantle apartheid.

'Let him unban the people's organization, the African National Congress.

'Let him free all who have been imprisoned, banished or exiled for their opposition to apartheid.

'Let him guarantee free political activity so that the people may decide who will govern them.

'I cherish my own freedom dearly but I care even more for your freedom. Too many have died since I went to prison. Too many have suffered for their love of freedom. I owe it to their widows, to their orphans, to their mothers and to their fathers who have grieved and wept for them. Not only I have suffered during these long, lonely, wasted years. I am not less life-loving than you are. But I cannot sell my birthright, nor am I prepared to sell the birthright of the people, to be free. I am in prison as the representative of the people and of your organization, the African National Congress, which was banned. What freedom am I being offered whilst the organization of the people remains banned? What freedom am I being offered when I may be arrested on a pass offence? What freedom am I being offered to live my life as a family with my dear wife who remains in banishment in Brandfort? What freedom am I being offered when I must ask for permission to live in an urban area? What freedom am I being offered when I need a stamp in my pass to seek work? What freedom am I being offered when my very South African citizenship is not respected?

'Only free men can negotiate. Prisoners cannot enter into contracts . . .'

My father says 'I cannot and will not give any undertaking at a time when I and you, the people, are not free. Your freedom and mine cannot be separated. I will return.'

With this statement, Mandela recommitted himself to the anti-apartheid struggle in his country. He also turned the tables on Botha, declaring that it was up to the South African government, and not him, to renounce violence. He identified his fate with that of his people. Botha's reply came four days later. Referring to the decision of Mandela and his fellow prisoners to reject the conditions, the president stated: 'Their continued imprisonment must, of now, be attributed to their refusal to renounce their commitment to violence. We cannot order their release if they remain committed to violence, sabotage and terrorism.'

But the ice had been broken. . . . For his part, Botha had all but admitted that Mandela had served long enough behind bars and that the government wanted to release the man who, for twenty-five years, had been regarded as Public Enemy Number One by most whites. As for Mandela, he had refused to give any undertakings as the price of his freedom. On the other hand, his statement did not go out of its way to assert a commitment to the campaign of violence and sabotage. 'I am not a violent man', he stated.

A renewed flurry of speculation concerning a possible release came in November 1985 with Mandela's prostate gland operation. While he was in hospital, contacts were established between the government and the Mandela family to see if a face-saving formula could be agreed for setting him free. The government was looking for assurances about Mandela's future political activity, while Mandela himself was holding out for guarantees that his fellow-ANC prisoners would be freed with him, and that the ANC might be legalized and brought into political discussions on the future of the country. At the same time worldwide calls for Mandela's release intensified, notably from South Africa's overseas bank creditors, who indicated there would be no rescheduling of the country's short-term debts unless political prisoners, Mandela included, were released and major reforms enacted. By the end of November the government's search for a release deal had become increasingly frantic, despite its firm public denials that any negotiations were underway. Hopes were raised that the man who had been behind bars since 1962 would soon be set free, to be reunited with his exiled friend Oliver Tambo, to resume his work for the ANC, and to spend the last years of his life with his family, who for nearly a quarter of a century had mostly seen him only through a pane of glass in a prison visiting room.

But will Mandela's freedom settle the question of who is the strong man in the black nationalist struggle, the figure who would lead his people out of Egypt and become their leader in Israel? Probably not. Mandela would certainly have the most support among blacks, particularly in the highly-politicized black townships. But numbers don't necessarily count. Would the Zulus ever allow Mandela to become the unrivalled leader of the blacks in a free Azania? Would the Xhosas allow anyone but Mandela to assume the leadership?

Would Buthelezi allow Mandela to take over? Would Mandela sit back, after his years in prison, and let Buthelezi take control, a man who has criticized apartheid but from the safe distance of the chief minister's office in KwaZulu? Would either Mandela or Buthelezi tolerate the continuance of a different school of political thought (for example, that of the Black Consciousness movement) in the event of a black-ruled Azania? Would Bishop Tutu, who disclaims any political ambition, assume a leadership role?

These are the kinds of questions which have to be discussed in any assessment of the black struggle in South Africa. In the same way that the whites are divided, so are the blacks. The notion of a united black struggle in South Africa is appealing, but misleading. The search for basic human rights for the blacks is common to all black leaders, but the way to achieve them, and how those rights would be handled once acquired, are the source of much division. Such divisions hindered the fight against the new constitution. Unity might not have prevented its implementation, but a combined front of the UDF, AZAPO and Inkatha would have made a formidable political force instead of the fragmented opposition which did occur.

In any case, events ran ahead of the established black leaders. In townships in several parts of the country unrest was brewing. Discontent over local economic and social conditions was largely responsible; political activists were able to translate these grievances into a wider political setting by targeting on the new constitution. These tensions were about to explode and turn 1984 and 1985 into the most violent period in South Africa's post-1948 history.

CHAPTER 7

Sharpeville Again
The rise of black anger

It began as just another protest meeting, on a Monday morning in February 1984, but it was a turning-point. The death of a young black schoolgirl, Emma Sathekge, marked the moment when the unrest started to spread, when confrontation between the blacks and the white authorities would break out into the open at a more serious level.

The signs had been there for some time. After two fairly quiet years in the black schools, 1983 had seen a growing number of protests about educational facilities, the standard of teachers, the way in which black schools were administered and the nature of pupil representation. There had been schools boycotts affecting some 10,000 pupils and demonstrations had been broken up by police firing tear gas. A headmaster in Soweto had his house stoned by 1,000 pupils. School inspectors' cars were set alight and education officials were stoned. Already, student leaders were viewing the unrest in the schools against the wider political background in South Africa. Pule Monama, national organizer of the Azanian Students' Movement (the pupil wing of AZAPO) said that although the boycotts and protests were over specific issues they could not be seen in isolation from the political struggle. But despite the rumblings within the black school system it took the death of the black schoolgirl to bring the tensions to the surface.

The incident happened outside a black high school in drab Atteridgeville township near Pretoria. About 6,000 pupils at five high schools in Pretoria had been boycotting classes. On the day of the girl's death, the South African police said they were called to one of the schools to break up a demonstration and were stoned. They fired tear gas to try to restore order after which several pupils were taken to hospital. The fifteen-year-old girl died shortly after being admitted. It was later established that she had been run over by a police landrover. Her funeral a few days later was extremely tense. Young people, some wearing their school uniforms, sang ANC freedom songs and gave the black power salute. Here were tomorrow's freedom fighters. Today they were honouring a martyr; her fate would inspire them to intensify their commitment to the struggle. So the spiral of violence escalated.

The crisis in black education had been coming for some time, as shown by figures for black pupils' level of attainment. The results of matriculation examinations showed that the pass rate was 48.3 per cent in 1983, down from 53.2 per cent in 1980, which was itself a decrease from the period 1977–9 when the average pass rate was 73 per cent. Other statistics demonstrated the inferior position of black education in terms of financing and manpower.

The South African Institute of Race Relations said that during 1982–3 the per capita amount (including capital expenditure) spent in the education system was:

White	R1,385
Indian	R 871
Coloured	R 593
Black	R 192

Teacher–pupil ratios for the same year were as follows:

White	1:18
Indian	1:23
Coloured	1:26
Black	1:42

As for the proportion of the teaching staff in each race group who were underqualified, the figures for 1982–3 were:

White	3%
Indian	17%
Coloured	59%
Black	77%

In response the government attacked critics of the system for applying 'unrealistic criteria when comparing an education system [for blacks], which was still in an early growth phase, with well-established provincial education departments [catering for whites].' Doubts about the government's commitment to move away from separate, and therefore unequal, education systems were raised by its reaction to a major report on the nation's education by the Human Sciences Research Council. It was compiled by Professor J.P. de Lange, rector of the Rand Afrikaans University in Johannesburg and the man who was elected chairman of the Afrikaner Broederbond in July 1983 after Carel Boshoff had resigned. One of the principal recommendations of his report, published in October 1981, had been that there should be a single education ministry instead of the segregated education departments which had existed for almost three decades. The recommendation was seen by many educationalists as an important step; it would bring education for all race groups under one roof and this would go a long way towards levelling out the financing and the standards of education. However, after the government had studied the report the minister responsible, Gerrit Viljoen, declared that segregated education was a non-negotiable cornerstone of the ruling party's policy. The subsequent white paper, published in November 1983, recalled that the cardinal premise of the proposed new constitutional system was the distinction between 'own' and 'general' (common) affairs. Education at all levels was to be an 'own affair' of the white, coloured and Indian race groups and would therefore be administered within the context of the particular group's own culture and frame of reference. African education would be a 'general affair', the responsibility of a minister with his own department.

The rejection of the single-ministry proposal was a bitter disappointment for many working in education, whites as well as non-whites. To many black pupils it appeared that the government was finally closing the door on them and had no real interest in raising the level of black education to that of the whites. The discontent expressed itself in the classroom on a number of issues: pupils started demanding student representative councils along the lines of those in many universities; they wanted an end to what they called 'excessive corporal punishment'; they also demanded the readmission of pupils who wished to resit examinations even though they were over school age. The age limit which barred pupils over twenty from re-enrolling in school after they had left was aimed at trying to prevent the formation of a semi-permanent student agitator body. But it meant that students who had been unable to sit examinations because the schools were closed were unable to retake them. The minister then in charge of black education, Barend du Plessis, is a compassionate man, who was deeply concerned about tackling the causes of discontent among black school children without relinquishing the authority of the government in dealing with the schools' unrest. He took a sympathetic view of the age limit problem and tried to assist pupils wherever possible. As for black schoolteachers, they were demoralized and unwilling to carry out what many saw as 'apartheid education policies'.

Unrest in South Africa's black schools is an extremely sensitive issue. It was in the high schools of Soweto that the 1976 uprising began. On that occasion the issue was compulsory teaching in the Afrikaans language. By 1984 pupils' grievances had increased.

Pupils identified much more clearly with their parents' complaints about housing conditions and standards of living. The parents seemed less inclined to restrain their children. There was evidence of intimidation but it is unlikely that this was what fuelled the original discontent. Also the grievances of the pupils were being channelled by a nationwide pupils' representative organization which was proving itself highly effective in mobilizing pupil power and in placing their protests in a wider national context.

The Congress of South African Students (COSAS), formed in 1979, is an affiliate of the United Democratic Front and therefore believes in striving for a multi-racial, democratic South Africa. It identifies pupil grievances as being principally the result of an education system ('exploitative capitalism' as one COSAS leader described it) which seeks to educate blacks only up to the level required for them to service the white man's labour requirements. In that sense, says COSAS, the ills of the education system are directly linked to those of society as a whole. The UDF opposed the new constitution and government policies generally and COSAS carried the struggle to its own terrain by mobilizing the pupils, emphasizing that their grievances were part of what the activists declared to be the whole unjust system. The government attributed the unrest to 'agitators', and it would be naive to believe that organized agitation was not at work. Three COSAS members were convicted in April 1983 under the Internal Security Act of furthering the aims of the

ANC by making contact with the organization's members in Botswana and learning how to set up an ANC cell inside South Africa.
The general mood of discontent allowed the political organizations
to set to work. Time and time again in 1984 and 1985, as blacks
became more dissatisfied, localized grievances became transformed
into a rejection of the whole system. In this way the schools protest lit
the flame and became a fuse running permanently through the
months of discontent. It meant that by the time the campaign against
the new constitution was gathering pace the pupils and students of
the townships had been brought to a highly politicized state.

On the day of the coloured election (21 August 1984) around
60,000 coloured pupils boycotted their classes. A government
spokesman admitted that 80 per cent of the coloured pupils had
stayed away from school and that all eleven of the country's coloured
teacher-training colleges were at a standstill. Unrest flared up across
the country. At Parys in the Orange Free State pupils stormed a
school, smashing windows and breaking down doors and setting fire
to the principal's car and home. In the township of Tembisa near
Johannesburg attempts were made to set two schools on fire. In
black townships across the country pupils stepped up their boycott
action to protest against the exclusion of the blacks from Botha's
new constitution. As the polls closed a housing board office in the
coloured township of Eldorado Park near Johannesburg was petrol-
bombed. When Indians went to the polls the following week, the
campaign concentrated on deterring Indian voters from casting their
ballot.

Lenasia township near Johannesburg. 28 August 1984. We are
standing on top of a half-constructed building looking down from
our vantage point on the streets surrounding the civic hall which is
being used as one of the polling stations for the Indian election.
Hundreds of Indian youths are milling around. The police have set
up a heavy security cordon around the civic hall to protect candidates engaged in last-minute electioneering. A short distance away
numerous police vehicles are lined up; inside there are large numbers
of police reinforcements. The demonstrators start playing a cat-and-
mouse game with the police, first gathering as near as possible to the
polling station and shouting 'sell-out' at the trickle of Indian voters,
then running away when police units move in to disperse the crowd
using sjamboks (whips) and tear gas. Suddenly a policeman becomes

detached from his unit and is stoned, but manages to crawl into a shop doorway for safety. His colleagues reach him and he is taken to hospital unconscious. Several journalists standing close to the violence complain they are beaten by the police while covering the events. A press photographer says she was hit over the head and chest and has the marks to prove it. During the afternoon the situation deteriorates, with police firing 150 rubber bullets at the demonstrators. By evening there is a running battle in progress with protestors hurling petrol bombs at police. The air is thick with tear gas.

The government blamed the low turnout in the polls on intimidation and to an extent they were right. South Africa's Indians are mainly conservative people, not used to political violence on the streets. The sight of rubber bullets, tear gas and stoning close to the polling station undoubtedly deterred some of them from casting their vote. But had there been a substantial groundswell of support for the new tricameral parliament, such fears would probably have been overcome and they would have defied the demonstrators.

The violence which occurred during the elections, but which failed to halt the new constitution being introduced was, however, to be eclipsed by what followed. . . .

Cape Town. 3 September 1984. MPs are gathering on the day the new constitution comes into effect. Suddenly, the local South African Press Association news printers are flashing an urgent item: 'Four dead in unrest near Sharpeville.'

The word 'Sharpeville' is enough to cast the grand opening of the new parliament into the shadows as journalists pack their bags and catch the first flight to Johannesburg, the nearest airport to Sharpeville.

Sharpeville township. 23.30 hours. 3 September 1984. An uneasy calm has descended over the area after twelve hours of rioting. But the streets bear testimony to the ferocity of the violence. Huge boulders and rocks make entry into the township by car virtually impossible. Burned-out vehicles are everywhere. A government official, weary after a day of unrest, advises us not to venture in. 'It's quiet now', he tells us, 'but it could explode again at any time.' By the end of the day the full extent of the disturbances has become clearer. In rioting in Sharpeville and nearby Sebokeng at least nine people are

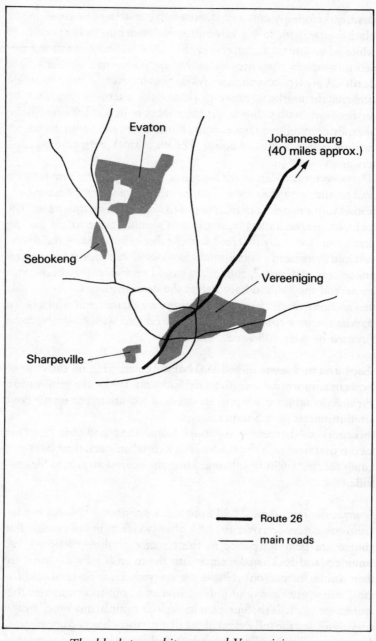

The black townships around Vereeniging

dead, most killed in confrontations with the police but some dying as blacks unleashed their anger on fellow-blacks associated with the white administration. Two blacks have been burned to death trapped in their cars. The deputy mayor of Sharpeville was hacked to death on his front doorstep. Widespread looting and arson has occurred throughout the day; private homes and businesses were set on fire and liquor stores and beer halls plundered. As we leave Sharpeville in the early hours of the morning ten armoured personnel carriers are lined up ready for further trouble; three military helicopters are also on standby.

Sharpeville. 4 September 1984. The number of dead rises to fourteen. More gruesome killings come to light: four people are found strangled behind a plundered garage; a man is discovered stabbed to death near the home of the deputy mayor whose body was found yesterday; a man is found burned to death in a liquor store. The police figure of thirty-five people injured appears to be on the conservative side; hospitals are said to be overflowing with casualties and providing extra beds. Around mid-morning I find myself standing on the main road past Sebokeng and Evaton townships. Fires are burning everywhere and police vehicles speed through the townships dispersing mobs. About twenty Indian families, their shops and businesses looted and burned to the ground, stand close by, watching from a safe distance the smouldering remains of their livelihoods. Why have they been singled out? No doubt because they are Indians and being Indian means being associated with the new constitution whether or not these particular individuals voted in favour of it – that, and the fact that well-stocked shops are a natural target for the ordinary criminal element among the rioters. By the end of the day the number of dead has almost doubled to twenty-six.

Sharpeville. 5 September 1984. An ugly confrontation is shaping up across the main road into the township. Several hundred black youths are taunting police to come and get them, chanting and waving placards. The police are there in strength; they have moved their armoured personnel carriers into position and the riot squad are loading live ammunition into their weapons. For a chilling moment it looks as though we are about to witness another 'Sharpeville', a repetition of the incident in 1960 when police shot dead sixty-nine blacks who were demonstrating against the pass laws outside the township police station. This time though, wisdom prevails on both sides. With a priest mediating between the police and demonstrators, the situation is defused and the crowds disperse without any serious unrest. But the violence continues elsewhere in Sharpeville and in the other nearby townships: an office complex is set on fire, also a garage, a private house, and a migrant workers' hostel; petrol bombs are thrown at private dwellings; the home of a black councillor who was killed in the first day's rioting is stoned. The unrest spreads to townships on the East Rand (the industrial area east of Johannesburg). At Tembisa a mob stones a primary school, a beer hall, a bus and a delivery van. Similar incidents occur in Vosloosrus. In Cape Town P.W. Botha is elected South Africa's first executive state president.

Sharpeville. 6 September 1984. A helicopter lands on an open field close to Sharpeville bringing three senior government ministers, including Law and Order Minister Louis le Grange, on a fact-finding tour of the troubled townships. The three ministers transfer to a police coach, which has its windows covered by steel netting and is accompanied by three armoured vehicles. The tour of Sharpeville is uneventful, but in Sebokeng the convoy turns back when several hundred blacks block the road. The ministers meet local council representatives but not the leaders of the protestors. The visit does nothing to ease the situation. The unrest continues. . . .

Why Sharpeville again? The township whose name was emblazoned across the world's headlines on 20 March 1960 and again on 3 September 1984 started its life in the 1950s with the hope of white authorities that it would develop into a model black township. It is a satellite of the nearby white town of Vereeniging with its huge local steel works. The plant was expanded during the Second World War as Vereeniging, 50 miles south of Johannesburg, became the site of the country's largest munitions factory.

Sharpeville 1960 marked a turning point in the history of the black struggle in South Africa in that it was the beginning of a move away from passive resistance to out-and-out protest and armed struggle against the apartheid government. Sharpeville 1984 marked a similar turning point, the moment when blacks turned their anger on those among their own people who were seen as collaborators with the white government, especially those blacks who had agreed to take part in the government-created black local councils. Many considered the councils were being offered as a 'second-best' form of representation, after blacks had been excluded from the new constitution. The violence in Sharpeville, Sebokeng and Evaton in the so-called Vaal Triangle during September 1984 was frightening at the time but unrest became even more horrifying when it spread the following year to the eastern Cape. Local councils were the target not only because of their association with the white government, but also because they had implemented steep rent increases in the Vereeniging townships. Again, what started out as discontent over local economic factors became a more general protest against the government's black administration and the entire constitutional system which offered the blacks nothing.

When the government established black local councils, they insisted they should be self-financing, an impossible task for most of them as black townships do not generate sufficient wealth to pay for themselves. Since December 1983 several rent increases had been introduced in the townships south of Johannesburg. These were an added financial burden on top of increases in general sales tax, food prices and transport costs. The burden became heavier when the town council for Sharpeville and Sebokeng, fearing that residents would accrue rent arrears, imposed a R50 deposit on some township dwellers, to be forfeited by anybody evicted for rent debts. The council naturally became the focus of the frustration of the residents, particularly as it had been elected on a 14 per cent turnout of registered voters or less than 9 per cent of the townships' entire population. Local protest movements were co-ordinated by the Vaal Civic Association, a community-based alternative to the local councils, which conducted a vigorous campaign against the government's plans. The government stated that intimidators were behind the violence and that the majority of people wanted to live their lives peaceably; the statement certainly contained some truth in that the radicals could not possibly hope to politicize entire communities and many people had little interest in taking their discontent onto the streets. It was no coincidence that Sharpeville should have exploded on the very day that the new constitution was taking effect. Nevertheless Botha's reforms were, at this stage, only a tangential issue in the protests. Within ten days, however, the campaign against the government's constitutional policies was to become the centre of domestic and international attention.

On Friday 7 September 1984 the Supreme Court in Pietermaritzburg, the provincial capital of Natal, ordered the release of seven
political detainees seized on the eve of the constitutional elections
apparently to curtail the election boycott call. Law and Order
Minister Louis le Grange immediately issued fresh detention orders,
but by then the former detainees had gone to ground.

Six of them surfaced a week later when they knocked on the door
of the British consulate in central Durban saying they had an
appointment to see the consul, Mr Simon Davey. Once inside, they
said they were staying . . . and Durban, Pretoria and London went
into a diplomatic paroxysm. The most serious crisis between Britain
and South Africa since the latter left the Commonwealth had begun
although it all had something of a Gilbert and Sullivan quality.

The 'Durban Six' affair came just a few weeks after the moderately
successful visit to London by P.W. Botha, although relations between the two countries were not exactly top-notch. Late in 1983
British Prime Minister Margaret Thatcher had made plain her
opposition to apartheid and South Africa's 'destabilization' policies.
In November the British Foreign Secretary Sir Geoffrey Howe
stressed that Britain was looking for progress towards a constitution
acceptable to all the people of South Africa. South African Foreign
Minister Pik Botha's response, stripped of its diplomatic niceties,
sounded remarkably like 'mind your own business!' In May 1984
Louis le Grange had attacked the needling presence of an ANC office
in London, asking how Britain would feel if there were an IRA office
in Pretoria. Relations were outwardly cordial when P.W. Botha and
Thatcher met at Chequers in June but old animosities ran deep. The
progress of the consulate sit-in became a diary of increasing hostility
between the two countries.

Durban. 13 September 1984. The corridor outside the British consulate on the seventh floor of the Barclays Bank building is crowded
with supporters of the six fugitives.

Who are the six? Eldest is Archie Gumede, 70, accused in the
mammoth 1956 treason trial, detained during the state of emergency
in the 1960s, a founder member of the Release Mandela Committee,
a key figure in the anti-election campaign; George Sewpersadh, an
executive member of the Natal wing of the UDF, who worked for the
Congress Alliance in the 1950s, a member of the Natal Indian

Congress, banned twice; Billy Nair, also a member of the NIC, sent to Robben Island in 1963, recently released: Mooroogiah Naidoo, also an NIC member; Mewa Ramgobin, NIC executive member whom I had met earlier at his home near Durban; and Paul David, banned for a total of seventeen years, NIC executive member. Between them they had comprised a major force in the UDF campaign against the new constitution. Their demands? A face-to-face meeting with le Grange to discuss their redetention orders, the British government to intercede with Pretoria to help arrange such a meeting, consulate telephones and telex to be available for the six to conduct their negotiations. The demands are refused by both le Grange and the British, although the Foreign Office in London rules that the six should not be expelled from the consulate against their will. The Durban Six plunge Britain into the midst of the volatile internal situation in South Africa and presents it with a highly embarrassing diplomatic wrangle. It also throws up a host of diplomatic and legal arguments which will keep students of international relations occupied for years.

Durban. 14 September 1984. The six have spent their first night in the consulate. Consul Simon Davey, true to the spirit of British sea captains, has remained on the bridge of his ship throughout the night, he and his staff bedding down on makeshift mattresses. The position of the two governments becomes clearer. Britain, having recently signed a European Economic Community declaration opposing political detentions, has to demonstrate sympathy with the six, but cannot allow the diplomatic status of the consulate to be infringed by allowing it to be used as a propaganda centre. Thus the six can stay, but will not be allowed contacts with outsiders except their lawyers (this was later relaxed to accommodate occasional family visits).

Durban. 16 September 1984. One of the group's lawyers, Zak Yacoob, leaves for Britain, Ireland and the United States to try to whip up support for the six. Yacoob, who is blind but darts energetically hither and thither through the corridors of court buildings guided by an aide, emerges as one of the most forceful negotiators on behalf of the six fugitives, launching scathing attacks on what he regards as Britain's moral failure in refusing to champion the case of the six in their bid to escape detention without trial.

Durban. 20 September 1984. Having originally expressed satisfaction with Britain's handling of the affair, describing it as 'diplomatically correct', Foreign Minister Pik Botha suddenly turns nasty, saying in effect that Britain has had long enough to persuade the six to leave. The change of tone seems strange. Is something else going on behind the scenes? Indeed there is. In London South African ambassador Dr Denis Worrall has tried to see Thatcher to offer her a deal: no prosecution of the Durban Six, when they emerge from the consulate, in return for the dropping of the case against four South Africans facing arms smuggling charges at a court in Coventry, England. A Coventry magistrate has earlier released the four on bail and allowed them to return to South Africa after Pretoria promised to send them back when their trial begins. Worrall and his government are furious when the British Foreign Office refuses to forward Worrall's request for an interview with Thatcher. In Pretoria's eyes the first test of the 'open line' relationship established the previous summer at Chequers has failed.

Cape Town. 24 September 1984. The bomb drops. Pik Botha announces that because of Britain's 'refusal' to evict the Durban Six, his government has decided that the four alleged South African arms runners will not be returning to Britain to stand trial. Botha says that Britain, by still harbouring the six fugitives in its consulate, is in breach of the Vienna convention on consular relations, hence South Africa's reprisal. So it is now the case of the 'Durban Six' and the 'Coventry Four'.

It is deadlock. Three weeks later the first break comes.

Durban. 6 October 1984. A crowd is gathered outside the consulate, word having got round that some of the fugitives have decided to end their sit-in. Three make a bid for freedom but are arrested. Mewa Ramgobin, George Sewpersadh and M.J. Naidoo are locked up in a police van and are driven away to prison.

Durban. 9 October 1984. A new row blows up between Britain and South Africa after the Southern Africa Correspondent for Independent Television News of London, Peter Sharp, secures a journalistic scoop by arranging for a two-way radio to be smuggled into the consulate. He records an interview conducted via the radio – the fugitives at a consulate window, Sharp talking to them from a nearby rooftop. Pretoria accuses Britain of 'a flagrant violation of international law' by allowing the consulate to be used for 'anti-South African propaganda'.

Jan Smuts Airport, Johannesburg. 14 October 1984. Donald Anderson, Southern Africa spokesman for the British opposition Labour Party and special emissary of Labour leader Neil Kinnock, arrives for a fact-finding mission to discover more about the consulate affair. The British allow Anderson into the consulate to conduct a prayer meeting, ostensibly to the annoyance of the South Africans. He appears to make a major play to end the sit-in, which would be a considerable coup for the Labour Party and an embarrassment for the British government which has been trying to evict its uninvited guests for weeks. But the three fugitives do not give up their struggle simply to afford a visiting MP a little kudos. It later emerges that Anderson had bent over backwards to try to get the three to leave, insisting that after his departure their case would lose publicity.

Coventry, England. 22 October 1984. The arms smuggling trial begins without the four South African accused. In Durban, Britain rules out further visits to the three remaining fugitives by wives and lawyers. The wives send a message to Thatcher saying: 'It is clear to all of us that it is your government's intention to create as many hardships as possible for our husbands.'

Durban. 12 December 1984. Hundreds of supporters of the three again gather outside the consulate. The three descend by lift to the lobby where the security police serve them with arrest warrants. It is chaos in the lobby as the police grab the men, fight through relatives and journalists and bundle two of the fugitives into waiting police vehicles. The only fugitive not arrested, Billy Nair, is carried shoulder-high by his supporters from the building. Security officials close the door behind him with a sigh of relief.

The consulate affair was over after almost thirteen weeks. It raised a serious question about whether South Africa could be relied on to maintain good faith in international agreements. The old idea that 'the Boer's word is his bond' no longer seemed to be true after the refusal to send back the Coventry Four. Pik Botha's comment to the effect that one couldn't have expected the four alleged smugglers to spend years in a British prison 'in that miserable climate' seemed to sum up the cynicism with which South Africa had acted. As for Anglo-South African relations, the lasting damage appeared to have been slight. Ambassador Worrall was called into the Foreign Office for a dressing-down when the Coventry trial began, minus the South African accused. But the Conservative government took no reprisal measures and continued to insist that punitive measures against Pretoria would hinder rather than help the search for peaceful change in South Africa. The fact, though, that Pretoria could get away with such a blatant contempt of court demonstrated clearly that those countries which set themselves against punishing South Africa are left with limited room for influencing the Pretoria government.

More importantly perhaps, the consulate affair gave the UDF and the Natal Indian Congress the best three months-worth of publicity that it could have hoped to enjoy, raising its profile internationally. The Durban sit-in propelled South Africa's internal turmoil onto a new plane. No longer was it simply a matter of boycotts and demonstrations. Suddenly it was about human rights, the freedom of individuals who in other societies might be seen as liberal activists rather than terrorists, to wage a campaign for political rights. Pretoria's attempts to put its side of the case were drowned as the international campaign against apartheid grew. Few people now were interested in hearing P.W. Botha explain that the government was introducing reform; the genuine moves away from apartheid which were taking place were largely ignored as the international community expressed its concern about the way developments were unfolding. An announcement from the Norwegian capital, Oslo, was to give that campaign a fresh impetus.

When the Nobel committee announced the name of the 1984 peace prize winner its recipient was in the United States, thousands of miles away from the country where he had performed the services which were now being honoured. But Bishop Desmond Tutu immediately left the American seminary where he was on sabbatical leave to return to South Africa. His homecoming was extremely emotional. Many of his relatives, friends and supporters were at Jan Smuts airport, Johannesburg, to meet him. As the bishop and his family emerged from the arrivals hall they were besieged by television cameras and journalists. He stood to attention and led the assembled gathering in the singing of 'Nkosi, sikelel' iAfrika' which resounded around the concourse drowning the airport announcements. From the airport he drove straight to the headquarters of the South African Council of Churches, of which he was then general secretary, to share the honour of the Nobel laureateship with his fellow church workers. Rebel Afrikaner churchman, Beyers Naude, formerly a member of the Broederbond but later banned for anti-apartheid activities, declared: 'I pray, Desmond, I pray, that my own people will come to understand the message you are bringing to us.' A few days later, Tutu and his family attended the regular Sunday morning service in their local Anglican church in Soweto which was filled with the sounds of hymn-singing in Xhosa and Zulu. Then it was back to the United States to resume his theological studies and to take the struggle against the South African government onto the television screens of America just at a time when apartheid was becoming an American political issue. For many Americans Tutu became the voice of the anti-apartheid movement. He scolded the Reagan administration for being 'too soft' on Pretoria and came perilously close to calling for economic sanctions against South Africa (had he made the call explicitly he said he would have risked prosecution when he returned home). In South Africa abuse was poured upon him by the government-controlled broadcasting media and the pro-government press. South African diplomats expressed the view privately that the awarding of the Nobel prize to Tutu was the last straw coming after the months of international hostility which Pretoria had had to endure. But the authorities had been trying to cut Tutu and the SACC down to size for some time. Tutu took all this in his stride, maintaining the impish sense of humour and infectious laugh for which he is famous, along with the distinctive voice and his unique manner of speaking as a result of which he starts each sentence slowly and ponderously and then gradually starts racing ahead like a steam engine gathering speed. On a radio phone-in programme he amused listeners by admitting that his name suggested he was a ballerina.

Desmond Tutu (formerly Dean of Johannesburg and Bishop of Lesotho) became leader of the SACC, an umbrella organization of most English-speaking churches in South Africa, in 1978 shortly after the jailing of the Black Consciousness leaders. His was one of the few anti-apartheid voices still heard. The government gave Tutu free rein but in February 1984 a government-appointed commission strongly criticized the activities of the SACC. The Eloff Commission said the council supported a campaign of economic sanctions against South Africa and recommended that a new offence of 'economic sabotage' should be created. The SACC, continued the report, had developed from an organization which spread the gospel to one which increasingly identified with the 'liberation struggle' in South Africa. Most organizations with which the SACC had ties favoured confrontation with the government, said the commission, which accused Tutu of disseminating liberation struggle propaganda through speeches at home and abroad. Tutu tended to become inflammatory when he addressed blacks, the report added. The commission was also extremely critical of the way in which the SACC finances were handled. The report was described by Tutu himself as a 'thinly-veiled part of the government's strategy to vilify and discredit the council'.

The reality of South Africa is that leaders of the main English-speaking churches, men like Bishop Tutu and the Roman Catholic leader Archbishop Hurley, and organizations like the SACC will inevitably come into conflict with the authorities. They believe that apartheid is an offence against Christian principles, against the ideal of the equality of man, and the English churches feel they must always be on the side of victims of apartheid laws – the pass-law offenders, those subjected to forced removals, the migrant workers who see their families once a year. I once asked Bishop Tutu whether he saw his ministry in political terms, whether he shared the views of the left-wing priests in Latin America who had developed the doctrine of 'liberation theology' much to the consternation of the Vatican. His response was most emphatically that he was not a politician, he was not going to become a party leader, largely because it was not necessary to develop a political philosophy in the struggle against apartheid. 'It is all there in the pages of the Bible', he declared. His crusade had not been a political one but a moral one, he said, and for that reason South Africa was the easiest place in the world to be a Christian.

His subsequent appointment as the first black Bishop of Johannesburg was not without its critics within the Anglican church. Several members of the church, mostly white, expressed outrage that such a political priest should be appointed to such an important ministry. A few announced that they were leaving the church. Tutu acknow-

ledged the doubts when he addressed the congregation at his en-
thronement, declaring:

> I would be grossly insensitive and blind not to know that a
> significant section of my diocese, being influenced by some
> strange newspaper, radio and television reporting, is at the very
> least apprehensive of the one they have got as father in God.
> Some may feel, like most whites in South Africa, that they have
> been given a horrid ogre, someone many white South Africans
> most love to hate. . . . It could just be that a miracle will happen
> and people will be a little surprised that I was perhaps not quite
> such a horrid ogre as they thought, that I might just be a slightly
> more loveable ogre than they had believed possible.

But Tutu did not soften his stand on apartheid to appease his white
flock, declaring that:

> I give notice that if in eighteen to twenty-four months from today
> [3 February, 1985] apartheid has not been dismantled, or is not
> being actively dismantled, then, for the first time, I will myself
> call for punitive economic sanctions whatever the legal
> consequences may be for doing so.

Rather than shying away from political issues now that he had
assumed a higher office, Bishop Tutu tackled them head-on, urging
whites to join him in his struggle and ending his address with a
ringing declaration which appeared to enshrine his most cherished
beliefs:

> The problem of our country . . . is right here in our midst – it is
> apartheid, it is injustice and oppression. . . . Please dear white
> fellow-South Africans hear the cri du cœur we utter. It is that we
> too are just ordinary human beings. We too love to be with our
> wives everyday. We too want our children to rush out to meet us
> as we come back from work. We too would like to live where we
> can afford it. We too want to be able to move freely everywhere
> in the land of our birth. We too want to have security of tenure.
> We too want to participate in the decisions which affect our lives.
> These are not extravagant demands. They are the expectation of
> any human being. We want to have a new kind of South Africa,
> where we all, black and white, can walk together, black and
> white, into the glorious future which God is opening up before
> us . . .

The campaign of protest which had begun in Atteridgeville among the schoolchildren in February and spread to the townships of Sharpeville, Sebokeng and around Johannesburg, which had been the focus of worldwide interest after the Durban consulate affair and the award of the Nobel peace prize to Bishop Tutu, now took a further turn. The final component in a formidable alliance of anti-apartheid groups decided now was the time for it, too, to make itself felt.

A two-day work stayaway by black labour in the Transvaal on 5–6 November 1984 differed from previous work stoppages in that several interest groups came together to organize the mass action: the pupils who had led the schools boycott campaign; the civic associations which co-ordinated the township protest actions; and, most importantly, the trade unions who in the past had rarely dipped their toes into the water of politically-inspired mass action. Previously the unions had been more concerned with building up their membership and becoming more established. It was only in 1979 that the government had legalized black and multi-racial trade unions. Until then, Nationalist governments had clamped down hard on any attempt to mobilize black labour power. The South African Congress of Trade Unions (SACTU) led a campaign of civil disobedience during the 1950s in support of the African National Congress. But the banning of the ANC in 1960 left the blacks without any form of political or labour leadership.

This was the picture until the late 1970s when the pressure for black trade unions grew once more. The blacks became more politicized as a result of the 1976 Soweto uprising and there was also a recognition on the part of some liberally-inclined employers that black unionization was bound to come and that it was better to legislate for it than to be forced to grant it grudgingly. Since the 1979 legislation the number of black unions, together with the size of their membership, has mushroomed. In 1969 there were no unions for blacks. By 1983 there were 469, and union membership was put at 1,545,824.

This figure did not include the expansion of union membership in the gold and coal mines, the former clearly being the more important as gold exports account for almost half of South Africa's foreign earnings. In the pre-union era, black worker representation had been negligible and ineffective. The giant mining houses, which were grouped together under the Chamber of Mines, used both paternalism and brute force to maintain a quiescent black workforce. Most of the half a million black miners are migrant workers from the black homelands or from other states in southern Africa, each of whom knows that in the event of his dismissal there are hundreds of other blacks queueing up for his job, an economic fact which gives the employers considerable leverage. When, in 1985, two mining companies, Anglo American and Anglo Vaal, between them sacked over 15,000 black miners, many observers detected a return to the less enlightened days of the 1950s, 1960s and early 1970s despite the two companies' protestations that unrest and intimidation had been rife in the mining compounds and that no employer could tolerate such activities.

The employee side of the industry's labour relations was dominated by the right-wing Mineworkers' Union (MWU) which represented some of the 70,000 white miners and which was determined to preserve its members' privileged position. The union's leader, Arrie Paulus, stated that he would never allow 'other race groups to do the work of white miners'. Although wage differentials between white and black miners had shrunk dramatically since the early 1970s, any real closing of the gap was hindered by the job reservation scheme under which only 'scheduled persons' (i.e. whites) were allowed to fill certain jobs. The most important of these categories was the right to undertake blasting at the pit face. The MWU had surrendered on some areas of job reservation but the granting of blasting certificates to blacks was an issue they were not prepared to concede. Industrial relations chiefs like Bobby Godsell of Anglo American insisted the companies wanted blacks to win the right to have blasting certificates and expressed the hope that the government would soon legislate for this. The government, in turn, passed the buck back to the Chamber of Mines saying the issue should be resolved in negotiation with the MWU. Pretoria was clearly haunted both by the fear of upsetting the MWU and sending many of its members into the camp of the Conservative Party and by the memory of the 1922 strike by white miners which was crushed when the army and the air force were sent in, a move which contributed to the downfall of General Smuts' government two years later.

The cosy relationship between the employers and the MWU was to be challenged by the emergence in August 1982 of the first black miners' union, the National Union of Mineworkers, led by a young and impressive lawyer, Cyril Ramaphosa. The NUM faced an uphill struggle in trying to mobilize the black mining force. Many miners are deeply conservative, wary of becoming involved in political protests, more concerned about earning as much as possible for their families back home for eleven months of the year and being able to return to them for a month at Christmas-time. Nevertheless by 1984 the NUM had made considerable inroads into recruiting members and had won recognition at a number of the mines.

But the granting of union rights did not mean that the employers were weakening on crucial issues like wage increases and conditions of labour. They were certainly ready to acknowledge trade union rights; many favoured them as a way of regulating industrial bargaining. But they were not about to cave in at the negotiating table. Eventually there was bound to be a confrontation between the new young union, which was anxious to flex its muscles, and the Chamber of Mines which seemed keen to demonstrate that things in the industry may have changed, but not that much. It came over the chamber's 1984 pay offer of 14 per cent, compared to the NUM's demand for 25 per cent. After painstaking negotiations and the use of legal disputes procedures, the union declared the first-ever legal strike by South Africa's black miners in September 1984. Workers on eight mines were called out after the chamber had gone ahead and implemented its 14 per cent offer. Eventually the dispute was settled before the strike gathered momentum but not before there had been considerable violence at the pits with a number of miners being killed. The unrest was not connected directly with the wider disturbances in the country but it obviously could not be divorced from the general mood of resistance among blacks.

But the difficulties of mobilizing the black mining force had been clearly demonstrated and were evident again the following year when, at the height of the country's political tension, the NUM called its members out on strike over a pay claim during the first week of September 1985. Lack of support among the miners coupled with some deft footwork by employers more experienced at brinkmanship caused the strike to crumble after two days with only a few thousand miners having downed tools.

The NUM's growth of membership and the threat to use its industrial muscle, although not forcing the employers to their knees, had nevertheless demonstrated the benefits of co-ordinated action. In the wider industrial field two predominantly black trade union federations had emerged since the 1979 legislation: the Federation of South African Trade Unions (FOSATU) which claimed 120,000 members including several white organizers and the Council of Unions of South Africa (CUSA) whose estimated membership of 250,000 was exclusively black. The division between them mirrored the ideological rift separating the UDF and AZAPO. FOSATU and CUSA had tried unsuccessfully to form an all-embracing trade union federation but, for the purposes of the industrial action planned for the Transvaal, they decided to bury their differences.

The initiative for the stayaway came from the pupils' organization COSAS which by October 1984 had become concerned that the schools' boycott campaign was beginning to lose momentum, partly because of the detention of over 500 of the organization's leaders, and partly because of the pupils' disillusionment that their grievances were not being listened to. A meeting on 10 October concluded that COSAS needed trade union support. Meetings followed; gradually union bodies were brought into the discussions; a Transvaal Regional Stayaway Committee was formed.

The committee issued a pamphlet outlining its demands and it reflected the grievances of the pupils, the township residents and the black unions. The demands were for democratically-elected students' representative councils; the abolition of any age limit on secondary education; the abolition of corporal punishment; an end to sexual harassment of pupils by teachers; the withdrawal of the security forces from the townships; the release of all detainees; no increase in bus fares, rents, or service charges and the reinstatement of workers dismissed in a previous industrial dispute. The strike proved to be outstandingly effective. There were allegations of intimidation but that could not possibly have accounted for the massive stayaway which occurred over the two days, involving up to 800,000 workers. The stayaway in Atteridgeville was almost total; migrant labourers (who often refuse to become involved in political action) joined the boycott in large numbers as did the township dwellers; some 400,000 school pupils stayed away from school with 300 schools closing down. In the Vaal Triangle townships around Vereeniging, on the East Rand and in Atteridgeville, schools were empty. Economic grievances, pupils' protests and the trade unions' awareness that they could not detach themselves from what was happening in the country at large had combined to produce the biggest mass political action South Africa had seen.

Employers reacted in various ways. The parastatal company
SASOL, which produces oil from coal, fired 6,000 workers. But
more enlightened employers were quick to read the message. Three
major employers' organizations, including the body representing
Afrikaner-controlled companies, warned le Grange after thirty leaders of the stayaway had been arrested that the detentions were
leading to an explosive situation. Le Grange gave them little ground.
The stoppage had shocked some employers; it was their first full
realization of what black labour muscle could achieve.

The boycott had also impressed the union leaders. Just over a year
later, in December 1985, the long-drawn-out talks on merging some
of the major unions into a giant federation eventually came to
fruition at a rally in Durban with the formation of the Congress of
South African Trade Unions (COSATU). Over thirty multi-racial,
though predominantly black, unions came together, including
FOSATU and the NUM, whose deputy leader Elijah Barayi was
elected president of the new body. Some half a million workers were
represented, many in key sectors of the economy. The black consciousness unions loyal to CUSA chose not to affiliate. COSATU's
launch meant the trade union movement in South Africa had come of
age, that the efforts of diffuse unions were now to be channelled in
one concerted drive on behalf of black workers, both on and off the
shop floor. The speeches at the Durban rally suggested the unions
had shed their doubts about engaging in political action, in the face
of growing protests from their members about the apartheid laws
and the security forces in the townships. Suddenly the unions were
laying down a timetable for the dismantling of apartheid. 'If they
don't abolish the pass laws within six months, we'll burn our pass
books', declared Barayi in his inaugural speech. The message was
clear: the unions would increasingly look to labour stoppages as a
political weapon. The Transvaal stayaway had provided a model for
possible future action.

The unions had chosen their weapon carefully and they had
judged its likely effects. The stayaway was not a weapon to be used at
the drop of a hat, only at critical moments, and it was a warning of
what could happen when the blacks chose to use their most powerful
weapon. The whites were uneasy, but there were more shocks to
come.

CHAPTER 8

'A Symbol of Anarchy and Chaos'
The tragedy of Crossroads

Rumours were spreading like wildfire. 'This is the big push', they said. 'Tomorrow the bulldozers will be in to knock down our homes and we will be taken away in government trucks. The time for action has come.'

It was mid-February 1985 and the black population of Crossroads squatter camp near Cape Town, who had resisted removal for almost a decade, were convinced the government meant business this time, that the shanty town would be demolished. About 5,000 black workers had arrived from the Transvaal and the squatters feared they were the demolition squads sent to pull down the shacks which had been home to some people for years. Squatter leaders decided to call a work stayaway the next day, Monday 18 February. When food delivery vans and government vehicles entered Crossroads that morning they were stoned; the police arrived in force and by midday there was a full-scale confrontation. By the end of it eighteen people were dead.

Crossroads squatter camp. 18 February 1985. By late afternoon the shanty town is sealed off. From a helicopter we see fires burning while groups of black youths roam in gangs. Several burned-out vehicles dot the squalid camp. Circumference roads are deserted. The police man road blocks at all entry points and journalists are admitted at their own risk. It is impossible to venture too far because all vehicles are stoned. As dusk falls, a huge barricade of fencing, boxes, tyres, etc. is built across the main access road – a defiant symbol to the authorities for whom Crossroads has become a virtual

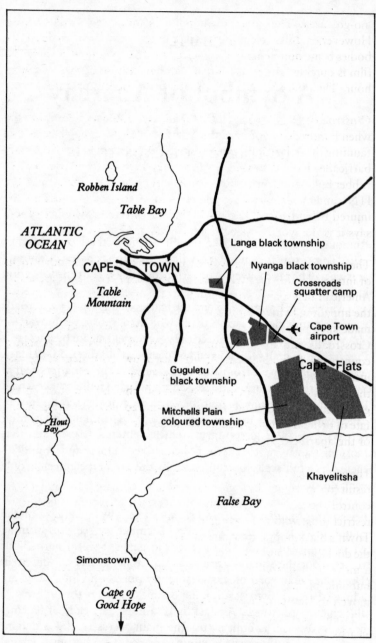

Cape Town and its townships

'no-go' area. The government puts the number killed at three. However, a BBC television news camera team films at least six bodies being dumped into the back of a police armoured carrier. The film is quickly sent by satellite to London and broadcast within an hour. The police soon revise their casualty figures upwards.

Crossroads. 19 February 1985. An uneasy calm overnight is broken when hundreds of youths gather on the street, stoning vehicles and taunting the police. Police line up some 300 yards in front of the main barricade. I stand behind them as they fire round after round of rubber bullets and birdshot. A truck is set on fire half a mile away. An ITN camera team reach a clinic inside Crossroads and film the injured being treated, many with hideous wounds. A police officer says it is the worst violence he has seen at Crossroads.

The two days of unrest provided for the outside world another focus of interest on the internal problems of South Africa. Despatches by American newspaper correspondents aroused anger in the US over the appalling living conditions at Crossroads and the system which made such places necessary. For years the world had known about Crossroads and the question had been asked: 'How is it that a country as rich as South Africa can allow such degrading and insanitary living conditions to continue?' For many, Crossroads was the ultimate advertisement for apartheid, the darkest stain on the government's reputation. Its history showed how, once again, the fate of ordinary human beings had taken second place to the dreams of the apartheid master-builders.

The emergence of the Crossroads squatter problem was an inevitable result of attempts by successive South African governments to control the flow of blacks into the western Cape Province and to restrict those who were living there. At the turn of the century, Cape Town's black population consisted of 1,500 people, mostly living in the docks areas, and a further 8,000 in District Six. In 1901 there was a move to relocate them further out of town after an outbreak of bubonic plague. Because they were a 'health hazard' they were moved to Uitvlugt, later renamed Ndabeni.

Twenty years on they were still there. A new settlement was built at nearby Langa (which along with Nyanga and Guguletu became the established black townships) but by 1939 the squatter community had risen to 50,000 and increased during the wartime boom. The government was anxious to reverse the process. Black labour would be needed from the pool of jobless in the homelands but this would have to be kept to the bare minimum. A policy had to be devised which provided for strict regulation of the number of 'legal' blacks living and working in the western Cape and for the 'repatriation' of shanty-town squatters many of whom were there 'illegally'. The government wanted to thwart the development of a permanent African working class in Cape Town. Once again the master-builders got to work.

The result was the Eiselen Plan introduced in 1955 by W.H. Eiselen, the then Secretary of Native Affairs. The plan declared the western Cape to be a 'white and coloured preferential area'. The plan involved the so-called Eiselen line, an imaginary border running roughly north to south through the Cape Province, from the western side of which all blacks were to be removed. The western Cape was to remain the 'natural home' of the coloured people, who would be given job preference and employment protection. Work began on clearing out the largest squatter camps. Coloureds and blacks were separated, the coloureds being removed to their own areas on the Cape Flats, the blacks elsewhere. The blacks were subjected to rigorous screening tests to discover who were legally entitled to remain in the Cape and to work there. Of 2,500 families tested, only 750 qualified. At least 1,200 families were ordered to separate, husbands to go to the single sex hostels, wives and children to the homelands hundreds of miles away. By 1960 most squatter camps had been demolished and the 'legals' were resettled in the town-ships.

Under the Eiselen plan, thousands of 'illegals' were weeded out. Between 1959 and 1961, 19,000 men and 7,300 women were 'endorsed out' of the western Cape. In the following seven years the full force of the plan was felt: the 'illegals' were continuously hounded in the townships; the African population was declared to be 'frozen' in order to reduce it by 5 per cent a year; black housing development was halted; labour offices began refusing work permits to employers of black workers if coloured labour was available. Pass law convictions in Cape Town rose from 8,434 in 1962 to 15,367 in 1967. But the boom of the early 1970s meant that the flood of illegal black labour was not going to be deterred by apartheid laws. By 1974 there were an estimated 90,000 'illegals' and squatting was again mushrooming. When the boom ended the 'illegals' stayed; but because not a single house for blacks had been built between 1972 and 1980 the squatter problem intensified. Shanty town camps sprang up at Maitland, Hout Bay, Table View, Modderdam and Unibell. The government moved in to demolish them systematically. Then came Crossroads, springing up over the Easter weekend of 1975 and slowly extending to its present size (officially put at 70,000 but generally believed to be much higher). The years during which the community withstood the hardships imposed by their living conditions and resisted all government attempts to move them have become stamped in the history of the struggle for black rights in South Africa.

As Crossroads grew, it became a severe embarrassment to the government as it appeared to represent a significant dent in the policy of influx control. The right wing of the National Party was up in arms; at the Cape congress of the party in 1978 the government declared that Crossroads would have to go. Demolition raids began. One resident was killed and many arrested. Still the bulldozers came. The camp dwellers were living in rudimentary shacks of cardboard boxes and plastic sheeting, their only protection against the bitter winds which sweep across the Cape Flats in winter and against the scorching summer sun. They became expert at burying the component parts of their shacks in the sand each morning before the demolition squads arrived, only to dig them out and re-erect them at night. A Save Crossroads Campaign was launched and, despite all the efforts of the authorities, the size of the community grew.

Then came what at first looked like a government reprieve. Piet Koornhof, the Minister of Co-operation and Development ('Piet Promises' as he became known after Crossroads residents began doubting his sincerity) said people living in Crossroads on 31 December 1978 could remain in the camp subject to certain conditions. The defiant resistance of the squatters, as well as the international publicity given to their plight, had apparently triumphed over the bureaucrats' determination to flatten the area. The squatters became optimistic about their future especially as the government agreed to build a new model township nearby, New Crossroads, to house some of the overspill squatters. The government invited the squatters' leaders to draw up a list of residents who were entitled to remain, triggering internal faction-fighting. The feud came to a head in April 1983 when seven people were killed and numerous shacks were razed to the ground. The split weakened the squatters' opposition to the government.

From the government's point of view this blot on the landscape close to Cape Town airport had to be removed. The thousands of shacks, housing a population which must have grown to around 100,000, presented an extraordinary spectacle stretching away into the distance. To study the problem for himself, P.W. Botha flew by helicopter over the Cape Flats on 4 March 1983, a crucial day in the history of the Crossroads community.

Botha's flight caused him considerable consternation as he saw how the squatter camps and black townships had spread. His solution to the problem was to have far-reaching consequences as became evident when the planners emerged with yet another blueprint.

It was called Khayelitsha ('new home'), a massive housing project of Orwellian proportions which eclipsed in its scale even the grandest designs of grand apartheid to date. It was the government's ultimate solution to the problem of how to weed out the blacks whose labour was not required and to consign those who were required to one plot of land, out of sight and out of mind. For Khayelitsha was to be a massive new township carved out of the windswept sand dunes on the coast at False Bay about 25 miles from the centre of Cape Town where many of the proposed township residents would work. After fifteen to twenty years its population was expected to rise to 240,000 people; by the end of the century it was calculated that half a million blacks would be living there. In short, it was to be the place where all the blacks of the Cape would have to live. The established black townships of Langa, Nyanga and Guguletu, closer to the city centre, would be destroyed and their settled communities would be forced to move to Khayelitsha. They would be going to a strange environment with few amenities and the cost of commuting, they believed, would increase, although the government denied this.

Khayelitsha was part of a broader strategy to isolate 'legal' blacks in one fairly remote location, making it simpler to control and administer them; to ferret out the 'illegals' and eradicate all the squatter camps in the area once and for all; and finally to insulate the Cape against the flood of blacks pouring in from the homelands. One civil rights worker described the scheme as a dumping operation involving the creation of a 'black homeland within South Africa to enable total social control over the black population of Cape Town'. The omens were not good for the government. Previous attempts to stem the black tide had been a failure. Blacks dispatched back to the homelands in mini-buses had simply turned round and come straight back again. Moreover, the determination of the Crossroads squatters to resist the move to Khayelitsha was growing. No longer was the Crossroads struggle just about poor housing, or the right to work where there were jobs, or the demand for families to live together. By now it had become a fight against apartheid laws which allowed the government to shift people around en masse like pieces on a draughts board. The government, though, was not to be deterred. A junior minister vowed that Crossroads would be 'disestablished' as soon as possible and the inhabitants dispersed throughout the new township of Khayelitsha 'to squash their spirit of defiance'. Crossroads had become a 'symbol of anarchy and chaos', he said, whereas Khayelitsha would be 'a beautiful city' comparable to the affluent white suburbs of Cape Town. The residents would even have their own seaside resort right on their doorstep.

Crossroads squatter camp. 30 January 1985. Foreign correspondents set off on a government-arranged tour of Crossroads and an introduction to Khayelitsha. The tour is being conducted by Timo Bezuidenhout, Chief Commissioner of the Department of Co-operation and Development in the western Cape.

At the perimeter of Crossroads policemen smash down squatters' shacks using iron bars to rip away corrugated iron fencing or boxwood roofs. The police officer in charge can hardly believe his eyes as he is confronted by a horde of journalists charging towards him. South Africa's Ministry of Bad Timing has struck again! The trip continues to Khayelitsha where architects and planners explain how the site will develop and how new road and rail links to Cape Town will be established.

Bezuidenhout is committed to Khayelitsha because he sees it as a place where people can live in simple but civilized surroundings instead of in filth. Bezuidenhout cares about these people. He meets their leaders, invites them to his office, talks to the ordinary people. 'How can you carry on living in these conditions?' he asks them. Bezuidenhout is a breath of fresh air among the ideological bookkeepers of apartheid and he almost certainly played a major role in convincing the government to take a fresh look at the squatter problem in the western Cape following the Crossroads violence.

The shift in policy had already been evident at the congress of the Cape National Party in September 1984 which saw some of the old shibboleths of apartheid come tumbling down. In a remarkably frank speech, P.W. Botha appeared to accept that the flood-tide of black workers towards the western Cape could not be turned back and that adequate housing would have to be provided for them. He conceded that if previous governments had accepted more of the economic responsibilities entailed in creating the black homelands 'we would have fewer problems today.' The congress scrapped the coloured labour preferential policy and Botha announced it was time to grant ninety-nine-year leasehold rights to those blacks who would be living in Khayelitsha and elsewhere. It amounted to the Afrikaners forsaking their last psychological safety net, one which had been with them throughout their history, namely that at the end of the day, when the black hordes were sweeping across the sub-continent threatening to drive the whites into the sea, the white and coloured homeland in the western Cape would be where they would make their final stand, the place to which they would retreat and where they would find Valhalla.

The government had done an about-turn on Crossroads, accepting increasingly that urbanization could not be held back. The problem was how to regulate it: which blacks would be allowed to stay – the 'illegals' as well as the 'legals'? The past had shown that even the most rigorous apartheid laws had failed to prevent the influx; indeed, one estimate suggested that since the Eiselen Plan the black population in the Cape, far from being reduced, had more than trebled. The Crossroads violence inspired a speedy government rethink. Just a few days after the unrest it was announced that those living in the established black communities of Langa, Nyanga and Guguletu would not be required to move to Khayelitsha. Bezuidenhout was a key figure in urging the saving of the three areas. The three communities were given leasehold rights and the freeze on housing development in the townships was lifted. Five days later came the reprieve for Crossroads itself. Black affairs Minister Gerrit Viljoen told the white House of Assembly that the government would allow the Crossroads site to be redeveloped, presumably into a conventional black township. It was the first indication from the government that Crossroads would be allowed to remain, and the second crack within a week in the policy of shunting all the western Cape blacks into Khayelitsha. Viljoen warned however that not all the Crossroads squatters could be accommodated at the site and many would still have to go to Khayelitsha to enable Crossroads to be developed. As Bezuidenhout explained it, until a sufficient number of people had left Crossroads, there just would not be space to start on the upgrading work.

But then an extraordinary thing occurred: with the element of compulsion lifted, several groups of Crossroads squatters suddenly announced that they were quite happy to move to Khayelitsha. The government had offered the cherry of allowing the 'illegals' to live 'legally' in Khayelitsha provided they looked for work during the ensuing eighteen months, after which their position would be reviewed. Coupled with a nod and a wink that they would not be deported back to the homelands even if they had not found work in the allotted period, it was enough for thousands of squatters to accept the deal and to leave their squalid conditions in Crossroads for Khayelitsha.

The Crossroads squatters had undoubtedly won. For ten years they had fought successive governments over their right to work where they chose, to live with their families and not to face the threat of removal to the bantustans if they became unemployed. The concessions announced by the government recognized that economics prevailed over political dogma, that tight influx control laws would never deter the individual who was set on reaching the big city to find work to earn even a small pittance to feed his or her family. For many people the policy changes were a reassuring sign that there were individuals within government who held broader views, who were not slaves to what had gone before.

As with other apartheid reforms, it begged the question: could policy failures not have been recognized earlier, sparing the killings, the demolition raids, the squalor and the misery during all those wasted years?

CHAPTER 9

'A People's War'
Uitenhage and the troubled eastern Cape

Sharpeville township. 21 March 1985. The black township dwellers started erecting barricades and burning tyres early this morning, the 25th anniversary of the Sharpeville massacre. By 10.00 am the police have already made several forays into the township to try to disperse mobs of black youths. The main access road is blocked by stones and broken glass.

We reach the scene of the 1960 shootings. A survivor who twenty-five years previously, as a youngster of thirteen, was among the crowd when the police opened fire, points to a nearby shop. He explains that it was through the store that he escaped when the shots rang out. The police station still looks much the same, he says. 'It was just here [he points to a patch of open ground in front of the main gate] that most of them died. You see the majority were all shot in the back. The police panicked, they were inexperienced.'

Leaving Sharpeville, the crowds are erecting new barricades. The car radio carries the lunchtime news. 'Fourteen people have been shot dead by police at Langa township near Uitenhage' says the announcer. 'Details are still coming in.' It hardly seems possible that on this day of all days, arguably the most sensitive anniversary on the South African political calendar, the police would open fire on blacks. But the black townships around Port Elizabeth and Uitenhage, in the industrial centre of the eastern Cape, have been simmering for weeks and were inevitably going to boil over.

But why the eastern Cape? Founded in 1799, Port Elizabeth is the third-largest port in southern Africa and was a perfect location for the giant motor companies which began to arrive in the area from the 1920s onwards. Ford and General Motors established plants in Port Elizabeth and a Volkswagen factory is at nearby Uitenhage. The port facilities handle car components imported from abroad. The black workforce for the car assembly lines comes from the many satellite black townships like New Brighton, Kwanobuhle and Langa. The townships are large, sprawling and close together and, according to some studies, have some of the worst conditions anywhere in the country; a quarter of a million people live in 30,000 mostly shanty homes.

Poor living conditions helped create solidarity as did the fact that a majority of the urban black population were Xhosa-speakers from Ciskei and Transkei. It is unusual in the major urban centres of South Africa for the black work force to be predominantly from a single tribe. Thus the proximity of the townships and their tribal uniformity meant that residents could be easily mobilized for political action. The eastern Cape has been the nursery school for many of South Africa's black leaders and senior political figures in other countries of Africa. Robert Mugabe of Zimbabwe is a graduate of Fort Hare University as are some of the major political figures in Uganda, Kenya and Nigeria. The area was also the political home of Mandela, Robert Sobukwe, who led the Pan-Africanist Congress, Tambo and Biko. The township of New Brighton has several long-established and influential high schools which each year produce well-educated, politically alert young people. The fact that many of them join the long queues of jobless after finishing school helps fuel their political consciousness. The main black political movements have had a firm base in the eastern Cape. Both the Black Consciousness movement of Steve Biko and the African National Congress have substantial support despite the bannings of these organizations.

Trade unionism in the eastern Cape dates back to the 1920s. The United Automobile Workers Union was established in 1974 and recognized by Ford and Volkswagen. In 1979 it merged with a trade union for coloureds to form the National Automobile and Allied Workers Union. Unionization, and the concentration of huge black work forces within just a handful of major companies contributed to worker solidarity. Many of the leading black organizers held vital jobs on the car assembly lines and could bargain from a position of strength. Local managements, anxious about the reaction of parent companies in Europe and America to news of strikes and unrest in

South Africa, often caved in to worker demands. In addition workers who had improved their wages during boom years adjusted to a higher standard of living. Expectations were raised and employers had to fulfil them. So both socially and economically, the blacks of the eastern Cape felt themselves to be part of a united struggle. As South Africa's recession set in, the struggle intensified. A number of factors had combined to produce South Africa's most serious economic crisis in decades. A prolonged drought had devastated parts of the country and by early 1985 inflation was around 14 per cent, three times greater than that of South Africa's major trading partners; the price of gold had collapsed and government spending was running well over budget, partly because of the vast sums being used to prop up the black homelands plus the costs incurred in creating two new parliaments.

Higher food and general living costs, lower wage increases, and several reductions in overtime payments (a 40 per cent shortfall in extra pay for the average black worker) had combined to produce a dramatic slump in the blacks' standard of living. Unemployment was rising. Simply to hold the current rate of unemployment in South Africa, the government has to create 200,000 new jobs each year. In the eastern Cape the three motor giants had a combined workforce of 17,048 in December 1982 and by March 1985 the figure had slumped to 11,334. The eastern Cape was beginning to pay the price for dependence on the car industry.

All these factors were coming together to undermine what had been a major plank in the government's approach to the country's black population. The government hoped black revolution could be bought off if a prosperous black middle class could be created which poorer blacks would aspire to. With the economy sinking the country could not lift the living standards of the blacks.

The townships around Port Elizabeth and Uitenhage had had continuous unrest throughout much of 1984 and early 1985. A work stayaway called by the UDF-affiliated Port Elizabeth Black Civic Organization (PEBCO), backed by the trade unions, was called for 21 March. In the days leading up to the boycott the situation in the townships was increasingly volatile. The weekend of the 16th and 17th saw rioting in many of the eastern Cape townships with the police reporting the situation to be extremely tense and announcing they were increasing their strength on the ground. By the morning of the 21st – Sharpeville day – the police were nervously on full alert while rioters were on a political 'high'.

The township of Langa in the eastern Cape (not to be confused with Langa near Cape Town) is unusually close to white residential areas. Townships are usually a fair distance from white suburbs. Soweto, for example, is several miles outside Johannesburg itself. But white residents were able to stand on a hilltop and look down on Langa below and watch the violence from a grandstand position.

When a large crowd of black residents formed early on the morning of the 21st and marched towards the white suburb, police units called out to intercept the marchers were uneasy. What took place in the minutes which followed deprived South Africa of nearly all the international goodwill generated by Botha's reforms. Police initially said a crowd of 3,000 to 4,000 blacks had left Langa township to march on the nearby white town of Uitenhage. About a mile out of the township, said the statement, the police had opened fire, killing fourteen. During the afternoon the number who died rose to seventeen and eventually to twenty.

That afternoon Law and Order Minister Louis le Grange told parliament that the police had been 'forced to open fire in self-defence on a crowd armed with stones, sticks, petrol bombs and bricks'. But le Grange's account was soon to be challenged. Survivors said the crowd was peaceful and on its way to attend a funeral. A crucial question to arise was why the police had fired live ammunition instead of tear gas, rubber bullets, or birdshot to disperse the crowd. An alarming picture of the police force began to emerge.

The violence which erupted in South Africa during early 1984 and which continued for months stretched the country's police force to the limit. The 1976 rioting was confined to the main townships like Soweto, but the latest disturbances spread into the rural areas.

After apartheid itself, the police force is possibly the most controversial aspect of the way South Africa is run. The security police, for example, armed with a wealth of detention laws allowing for long periods of confinement and interrogation, and protected by legislation which limits scrutiny of police actions by the media, have frequently been in major rows after leading activists have died in custody. Steve Biko's death in 1977 was a notorious example. Biko was held in jail in Port Elizabeth and was visited by two white surgeons who failed to have Biko undergo proper medical examination despite obvious head injuries. (Eight years later, after numerous calls for disciplinary action, the two doctors were found guilty by a medical board of disgraceful or improper conduct and one of them, Dr Benjamin Tucker, was subsequently struck off the medical register.) Biko was then taken naked in the back of a police landrover on a journey of several hundred miles to Pretoria where he was dead on arrival. The subsequent inquest concluded that no officer was criminally responsible for Biko's death.

A second case arousing international condemnation was that of Dr Neil Aggett, a white medical doctor and organizer of the Food and Canning Workers' Union, who died in detention at John Vorster Square police headquarters in Johannesburg (the security branch offices where, in the past, several detainees have died after 'committing suicide' by jumping from upper-floor windows). At the inquest on Dr Aggett an affidavit was presented alleging that he:

- was allowed to sleep for only a few hours during seven days of intensive interrogation.
- was made to stand naked for long periods with his right wrist and ankle handcuffed together.
- had a canvas bag placed over his head and was then pushed and kicked when his answers were unsatisfactory.
- was the victim of attempts to suffocate him.
- had his head banged against a desk repeatedly and was punched.
- was given electric shock treatment.

A magistrate ruled that Aggett's death was not caused by any act or omission on the part of the police and that he had died of suicide by hanging. The inquest verdict brought an outcry from within South Africa and abroad.

But if the security police caused concern, there was increasing alarm at the way the uniformed branch and riot squads were handling the violence in the townships. The intense unrest gave some young policemen their first taste of township violence. The Southern African Catholic Bishops' Conference accused the police of 'reckless or wanton violence involving the indiscriminate use of firearms, assaults and beatings, damage to property, provocative, callous or insensitive behaviour, indiscriminate or reckless use of tear gas and questionable police conduct at funerals of unrest victims'. Several examples of alleged police misconduct were documented in the bishops' report including what was described as the 'callous killing of a black youth' who was allegedly shot through the forehead at point-blank range while being held in a police vehicle. Two white policemen allegedly raped two black teenage girls in an armoured personnel carrier in Sharpeville. The bishops accused the police of the indiscriminate use of rubber bullets (quoting a doctor who said he knew of a child whose skull had been fractured by a rubber bullet and who had subsequently died of meningitis), of assaulting mine-workers during unrest in the pits (one miner testified that he had been hit by a pick handle) and of looting and damaging shops in Sebokeng. Conference president Archbishop Denis Hurley declared, 'There is now a state of war between the police and the people.'

Many of the young recruits to the police force come from the more conservative Afrikaner stock, many of whom have a poor command of English and often are not well-educated. Of late the number of English-speaking recruits has increased, since the government made it possible for youngsters to serve three years with the police force instead of doing their two years' national service, the latter involving long, lonely and often dangerous periods of duty fighting insurgents on the Namibian border with Angola. Many of the English-speaking policemen are sent to the bigger cities leaving the Afrikaners to control the situation in the rural areas like the eastern Cape.

Young Afrikaners' attitude to police work reflects their fore-fathers' feelings about blacks. Essentially it is a fight for survival by the whites against the 'swartgevaar' – the 'black threat'. The distinguished South African author Alan Paton put it like this:

> During the last century there was a long series of frontier wars between Afrikaner trekkers or frontiersmen going north and African tribesmen coming south. The memory of these wars lies deep in the Afrikaner mind and some of our white policemen are still fighting them.

The number of black recruits into the police has increased dramatically in recent years and they now constitute half the force. In the middle of 1984, the force consisted of 45,961 men and women, 22,964 of whom were black. The officer ranks are still dominated by whites, although in 1984 there were sixty black officers of whom two were colonels. Many of the country's police stations, especially in black areas, are manned and commanded entirely by blacks. But what is significant about these figures is the limited size of the South African police force compared to that of other countries. With 1.4

policemen for every 1,000 members of the population it is one of the smallest in the world, which explains why police are rarely seen on the streets of the major cities. If, as many of South Africa's critics claim, the country is a police state, then it is ironically a police state without enough policemen. In 1976 during the Soweto riots it was not unusual for fifty-man platoons to come face-to-face with crowds of up to 3,000. Taking into account officers who are on leave or off-shift, it has been calculated that the number of uniformed policemen on duty at any one time can be as low as 2,000, in a country which has a population of over thirty million. Overstretched as they are, it is not surprising that plans have been announced to double the numbers of the police over the next decade.

The South African police force faces problems rarely experienced by its European or American counterparts. In South Africa the police are not operating in built-up, closely-confined suburbs of cities like Belfast where unruly groups can more easily be contained through police charges or firing rubber bullets. In the open spaces of South Africa's black townships police units can easily be outflanked, rioters can run away in all directions, tear gas is blown away quickly by the wind rather than lingering between buildings and stifling those trapped in a corner of a street. Moreover, rioters in South Africa have shown on many occasions that they are quite prepared to kill any policeman they lay their hands on, a rare occurrence as far as European police forces are concerned.

The police are seen by most blacks as the instrument of the government's policy of suppression. Part of the problem is political control of the police. The Law and Order Ministry often seems unconcerned about international opinion of police action. Le Grange is a controversial figure who has presided over several rather inopportune actions by his department.

So, even before the Langa shootings, there was concern about the actions of the South African police, both security and uniformed branches, and about political control.

Specific concern about the police in the eastern Cape, particularly in Uitenhage, had also increased prior to the Langa shootings. On the weekend of 14–17 March the Black Sash civil rights organization held its national conference in Port Elizabeth and voiced the view – prophetically as it turned out – that recent events in the eastern Cape 'indicate that the country is on a disastrous treadmill of escalating, mindless violence'. Indeed, during the conference, several of the delegates were called away to Uitenhage police station to investigate the reported disappearance of six black youths. In a subsequent sworn affidavit one of the group, Mrs Molly Blackburn, said that she had been 'deeply shocked to see a young man lying on the floor next to a table with his hands handcuffed to the table leg. Bending over him was a black man in civilian clothes with a long orange plastic whip. I saw him assault this young man as I walked in. I called out "Dear God, what do you think you are doing?" I moved over to the young man and he was bleeding from lacerations on the left side of his face and had traces of blood on his mouth.' Mrs Blackburn also testified to what she claimed was the aggressive behaviour of a Lieutenant John Fouche, the officer who was to give the 'open-fire' order on the Langa crowd four days later.

Langa township. 25 March 1985. Four days after the police shootings, church leader Allan Boesak investigates the incident. He goes to the Catholic church in Uitenhage where an emergency relief centre has been set up by the Black Sash to assist the injured and to help parents looking for children arrested in township disturbances but who cannot be traced. Boesak hears from a survivor of the police shootings who, according to Boesak, tells him that afterwards the police had kicked the bodies to see who was alive or dead; those still alive were 'summarily executed' – 'cold-blooded murder', as Boesak describes it.

Boesak drives to Langa. He is stopped by a police road block. Boesak demands to know why he cannot go in. The police order everyone back 50 yards. Boesak explains he is a minister and has a right to enter the township. Photographers and cameramen film the scene. Officers manning the road block brandish their weapons threateningly and one of them begins counting from one to ten, the implication being that if Boesak and everyone else has not moved back after ten seconds we will all be shot. Another superb piece of public relations from the South African police! We retreat gingerly.

Cape Town. 26 March 1985. Boesak, Beyers Naude and other church leaders, including the Anglican priest in Kwanobuhle, gather at a downtown church to remember the dead of Langa. The church resounds to the singing of 'We shall overcome', reflecting Boesak's view that the struggle for justice in South Africa is akin to that of the civil rights movement in the United States. After the service the congregation lines up and begins a march towards parliament. After barely a quarter of a mile they are intercepted by the police and told they are staging an illegal protest. The marchers – some 500 strong – sit down on the pavement. Boesak, wearing his clerical robes, is first to be arrested. An officer takes him by the arm and leads him away. The rest are bundled into vehicles and kept overnight in the police station where they sing freedom songs until they are released next morning on bail.

Langa township. 27 March 1985. What is arguably the most important inquiry since the investigation into the 1976 Soweto rioting gets under way. Justice Donald Kannemeyer – appointed by the state president as a one-man commission of inquiry – visits the scene of the police shootings accompanied by a heavy police guard, although the township dwellers are not hostile. Lieutenant Fouche explains to the judge that two police armoured vehicles (casspirs) were parked on either side of the road and that the crowd had approached to within seven paces of the police. But Errol Moorcroft MP, a member of a PFP delegation which visited the scene the day after the shootings, paces out twenty-three steps to a spot where, he says, the bloodstains are still visible. Already, there is conflicting evidence on exactly how close the crowd were to the police when they opened fire.

As the commission hearings proceed, remarkable evidence is heard about the police role in the affair, much of it conflicting and revealing serious shortcomings in the Uitenhage police force. In his report Judge Kannemeyer lays the blame for the shootings firmly at the door of the police but takes pains to ensure, after careful consideration, that Lieutenant Fouche is not made the scapegoat. He faced 'an awesome decision', says the report, in deciding whether to let the march continue, possibly endangering white lives, or to halt it which would inevitably mean opening fire. The judge also rejects the evidence that the police fired on the injured lying at the scene. The report criticizes commanding officers who had allowed police to go out on patrol without conventional riot control weapons, only live ammunition. The conduct of several individual officers is attacked including a Uitenhage security branch policeman who had applied for the banning of the funeral on 21 March, causing confusion among the township residents. Had the banning order not been invoked, says Kannemeyer, 'there can be little doubt that the procession would have passed . . . without incident.'

The publication of the Kannemeyer report is accompanied by a memorandum issued by Louis le Grange. The document outlines steps which have already been taken to improve police procedures and announces that a board of inquiry has been appointed 'to consider matters relating to certain findings by the Kannemeyer Commission in respect of the South African police'. Despite Kannemeyer's considerable indictment of the police, there are no resignations from the force and the minister remains in office.

Outside the courtroom, the town of Uitenhage had undergone something of a transformation during the weeks of the inquiry. The white population had grown uneasy about the daily violence and the police and army vehicles touring the town further unsettled them. But it was not only within the white areas of the eastern Cape that the temperature was rising. Inside the black townships the wave of violence which had started in 1984 in Sharpeville and Sebokeng now exploded into a savage wave of killings, the target being black policemen as well as the councillors on the black local authorities who had little support from the blacks themselves.

Deprived of any effective outlet for their grievances and enraged by the Langa killings, the young blacks of the eastern Cape townships went on the rampage attacking anyone and anything associated, however remotely, with the white authorities. On 19 April 1985, a government spokesman reported that between September 1984 and February 1985:

5 black councillors and 4 black policemen were killed.
109 black councillors were attacked.
56 black police officers were injured.
143 black school buildings, 6 churches, and 9 clinics were destroyed.
66 black councillors' homes were burned.
516 private vehicles and 1080 buses for blacks were badly burned or damaged.
147 black councillors were 'forced to resign' and in some areas entire black councils had resigned.

The last remaining black councillor in Kwanobuhle who had refused to resign, Mr T.B. Kinikini, was bludgeoned to death along with one of his sons and two nephews, their bodies then doused in petrol and set on fire. This fate increasingly befell government officials. Later the black mobs would dance on the charred remains of their victims. Three Indians were dragged from their car near Port Elizabeth and attacked while the vehicle was set on fire. A petrol bomb was thrown into the home of the secretary of a black council and her four-year-old son burned to death. By the end of March 1985 the police were quite clearly unable to control the situation. Early on the morning of Sunday 31 March, as the dawn mists were clearing, the army moved into the riot-torn townships and were to remain there. But they too were unable to prevent the murderous vendetta against blacks who had decided to participate in local black bodies or serve in the police force. By the middle of 1985 violence was rife in nearly all the major black centres except, perhaps surprisingly, Soweto. There were several reasons for this: the comparatively wealthy black middle class in Soweto who did not wish to rock the boat, a politically sophisticated élite who believed that protests should be launched selectively and only when the time was right and the fact that after 1976 the government had ploughed millions of rand into improving the township. How long Soweto's relative immunity from the more general violence will last is uncertain. 1986 marks the tenth anniversary of the Soweto uprising and there will inevitably be several potential flashpoints as blacks commemorate those who died.

But how did the government react to the unrest? Government ministers publicly claimed that the violence in the black townships was the result either of straightforward criminality (in part they were right) or of a well-orchestrated campaign by the ANC and the South African Communist Party (also correct, up to a point). Convinced of this, the government rounded up all the alleged ringleaders of the conspiracy and put them on trial for high treason. It was an action in keeping with the way the South African government had historically handled outbreaks of violence or widespread protest campaigns. In addition to bringing court cases against activists, for example the 1956 treason trial, the government had enacted an all-embracing web of security legislation. The *Suppression of Communism Act (1950)*, the *Criminal Law Amendment Act (1953)* and the *Unlawful Organizations Act (1960)* led to the banning of the South African Communist Party (and also provided for extreme penalties for anyone found guilty of any action which could be remotely interpreted as communist activities) and of the African National Congress and the Pan-Africanist Congress. In addition the government had at its disposal a wealth of legislation which allowed for long periods of detention without trial for political activists. The *General Law Amendment Act (1964)* introduced the infamous '90-day clause' under which the police were granted the power to arrest without a warrant anyone suspected of sabotage and to detain him for 90 days for interrogation without having to bring him before a court. The period of detention was extended to 180 days under the *Criminal Procedure Amendment Act (1965)*. Both laws were superseded by the *Terrorism Act (1967)* which stipulated that a suspected terrorist could be detained indefinitely without trial and that no information about the detainee need be made public. South Africa's current security legislation is embodied in the *Internal Security Act (1982)* which not only provides for detention without trial but is also used for the arrest of suspected political agitators and to prohibit anti-government activities which would normally be regarded as part of the democratic process by most western societies.

But how did the government intend to neutralize those who, it believed, were inspiring the protests but who did not partake in violence? The answer came soon enough. The government's tactic was to link the UDF leaders with the outlawed ANC and SACP. The signs had been there early on. In October 1984, shortly after the outbreak of violence in the Vaal Triangle, le Grange declared to the National Party's Transvaal congress in Alberton: 'When the UDF's activities in South Africa are judged, there can be no conclusion other than that the UDF has the same revolutionary aims as the banned ANC and South African Communist Party and is actively preparing a revolutionary climate.' Le Grange claimed that 90 per cent of the UDF's office-bearers had previously been linked to the banned organizations. The UDF issued a strong statement in reply to le Grange, accusing him of making links between the UDF and the ANC which were 'totally without foundation' and could not 'be substantiated even on the basis of his own flimsy evidence'.

Le Grange had prepared the ground and soon moved against sixteen of the UDF leaders (including five of the Durban Six) by charging them with high treason. Amid an international outcry the sixteen seemed destined to remain in detention until their trial, the date of which seemed some way off and the length of which was indeterminable. The suspicion grew that the government was simply out to silence the UDF leadership so as to give its new constitution time to take shape, unassailed by internal political opposition. The government insisted that the decision to prosecute the sixteen had been taken by the attorney-general and that the government did not have a hand in it. Eventually the judge president of the Supreme Court in Natal ordered that the accused should be released on bail, pending their trial, although their bail conditions effectively stifled them as far as any political activities were concerned.

The indictment, when it appeared, turned out to be 600 pages long. The charges contended that the sixteen had supported a 'revolutionary alliance' comprising the SACP, the ANC and the South African Congress of Trade Unions. The UDF was an instrument of this alliance, the indictment alleged. Most of the charges concerned speeches or writings of the accused. The document contained no hard evidence of committing or conspiring to commit violent actions as such. The indictment, however, referred to a 'sinister web' of overlapping organizations which, through non-collaboration, boycotts, labour unrest, and by demanding the release of imprisoned leaders and the return of those exiled, had conspired with the 'revolutionary alliance' to bring about the downfall of the state. The charges left many observers uneasy. The Afrikaans newspaper *Die Vaderland* expressed concern that in the past the authorities had found themselves in a position where charges could not be pressed home; the paper hoped the government would not end up this time 'with egg all over its face'. The warnings were not heeded and in December 1985 the state dropped charges against twelve of the accused, who were then acquitted. The prosecution case had depended on the dubious evidence of 'expert witnesses' on revolutionary violence.

In any case the round-up of the anti-apartheid leaders failed to halt the violence. Young, mostly unknown, radicals were beginning to take control of the streets in several of the townships. The government waited a few weeks and then introduced even more draconian measures.

CHAPTER 10

Under Siege
The state of emergency

KwaThema township, east of Johannesburg. 9 July 1985.
Thousands of black township residents from the East Rand are
gathered in a sports stadium for a funeral service for previous unrest
victims. As the mourners move off in procession towards the cemet-
ery they leave behind in the centre of the sports ground the prone
figure of a young black man, beaten senseless by some of the crowd.
Accused of being a police collaborator, some of his fellow blacks had
turned upon him during the service with fists and stones. The
Anglican Bishop Suffragan of Johannesburg, Bishop Simeon
Nkoane, who lives in Kwa Therma, stands guard over the young
man along with a white priest to protect him from further assault.
Eventually an ambulance arrives to take the victim to hospital.

The KwaThema incident was one of three horrific attacks on alleged
black informers by fellow-blacks which took place during the early
part of July 1985 and which alarmed both the government and
moderate anti-apartheid leaders. They appeared to indicate that the
violence was assuming more frightening proportions. In Duduza
township, also on the East Rand, a mob dragged a young black from
his car, beat him and were about to throw him onto his car which had
been prepared as a funeral pyre when Bishop Tutu, who was
attending a nearby funeral, intervened and saved the young man's
life. A few days later at another funeral in Duduza a young girl, again
suspected of informing to the police, was stoned, stabbed and
beaten, then covered in sticks and grass which were set on fire.
    It was after this attack that Bishop Tutu announced that he would
consider leaving South Africa unless such incidents stopped, declaring that the television pictures of the young girl's death, beamed

around the world, had undermined the black cause and suggested to many that the blacks of South Africa were not, as many whites claimed, ready to govern themselves. But the attacks did not come as a surprise. They were the result of a determined effort by activists to make the townships 'no-go' areas for the authorities, especially the police.

The effort had begun soon after the African National Congress lost its military bases in neighbouring Mozambique after South Africa signed its peace treaty with the government in Maputo in March 1984. While not curtailing plans to launch guerrilla attacks inside South Africa, the ANC leadership in Lusaka decided to concentrate as well on bringing the black townships to a high state of politicization. The call went out from Lusaka to the black youths of South Africa to 'make the townships ungovernable'.

The vehicle for this was the Congress of South African Students which had earlier led the schools boycotts and which had been influential in organizing the Transvaal work stayaway. The security authorities were convinced that a small group of COSAS radicals were organizing the unrest, often using intimidation, particularly in the troubled townships like KwaThema and Duduza. A sixty-man special police squad was sent into the East Rand townships to hunt down the suspected ringleaders. Later COSAS itself was banned.

The government was disturbed by evidence that the radicals were trying to carry through a classic two-stage revolutionary programme in some of the townships. The first phase was to make the townships ungovernable as the ANC had urged. Local government in many areas had collapsed following attacks on black councillors and the resignation, out of fear, of others. Black policemen, also the victims of violence, had been evacuated from their homes and, along with their families, were living like refugees in tented camps behind barbed wire on the outskirts of townships. Law and order had virtually broken down with even the simplest burglary unable to be investigated unless an officer entered the township accompanied by armoured personnel carriers carrying police and troops.

Indeed it appeared to the authorities that the second phase of the activists' programme was becoming evident. Law and order, judicial functions and some essential services were increasingly being under-taken by COSAS activists in defiance of the recognized authorities. A worrying development occurred in the middle of July when for the first time there was an upsurge of serious unrest in Soweto, which until then had escaped the worst of the violence. A crowd of young high school pupils wearing their school uniforms tried to hold a meeting at the Regina Mundi church to call for a schools boycott in support of fellow-pupils detained by the police. The riot squads moved in with tear gas to disperse them, sparking off two days of serious rioting. Buses were hijacked and all services halted, cars were set alight, and a party of American and German tourists on a bus tour of Soweto were stoned and had to be escorted out of the township by police.

In Port Elizabeth a boycott of white-owned shops was called for. A black woman who defied the call was axed to death.

Concern mounted at grass-roots level in the National Party that the government was losing control and surrendering the townships to the rule of black radicals. The cabinet met, conscious of the mounting concern among many whites but aware too of the likely hostile international reaction to any new sweeping clampdown. The need to reassure whites was, however, paramount. On the evening of Saturday 20 July P.W. Botha went on nationwide radio and television to announce that a state of emergency would come into force at midnight. It was the first time in a quarter of a century that a South African government had assumed such powers, the previous occasion having followed the Sharpeville massacre in 1960.

The state of emergency was enforced in thirty-six magisterial districts, an area which covered most of the country's major trouble spots. It afforded the security authorities extensive powers of search and arrest and shielded the police from scrutiny of their actions. Hundreds of alleged activists were picked up during the first few days of the emergency and were held incommunicado. Eventually some were released but the arrests continued in the weeks and months which followed. The government toyed with the idea of invoking news censorship but settled instead for calling upon editors to scale down their coverage of the unrest. The authorities were convinced that rioting was being incited by television crews, that some inexperienced reporters were printing rumours and allegations about police action without checking the information, and that the saturation overseas news coverage of the unrest was giving a false picture of the extent of the unrest. Though there was justification for some of these beliefs, the government's approach smacked of blaming the messenger for the bad news. (In November 1985 the government announced sweeping restrictions on news coverage of the violence so that townships were effectively barred to journalists

during times of unrest unless they were escorted by the police –
anathema to most correspondents. The measures were aimed particularly at foreign television teams who were accused of acting as a
'catalyst to violence'. The clampdown also had a wider political
aim: to kill off South Africa as a world news story in the hope of
taking the international heat off the Pretoria government.)

In any case the emergency powers were clearly failing to stem the
violence. In the weeks which followed Botha's announcement the
number killed each day in violence remained high and the month of
August saw another escalation in the unrest with areas which
previously had been fairly peaceful suddenly becoming embroiled.

The upsurge of violence spread to black townships around Durban, sparked off by the murder of a leading anti-apartheid lawyer,
Nonyamezelo Mxenge, who was gunned down as she got out of a car
outside her home in Umlazi township. Mrs Mxenge whose husband,
also a leading civil rights campaigner, had been murdered in sinister
circumstances four years previously, was one of the principal figures
in the legal team defending the UDF sixteen in the Pietermaritzburg
treason trial. As she had played an important role in gathering
evidence for the defence, her death was seen by her fellow-attorneys
as a devastating blow especially as the trial was soon due to
commence. Her murder served to fuel the suspicions in some opposition circles that right-wing death squads linked to the government
were at work charged with eliminating activists, although no evidence ever came to light to substantiate the suspicions. The earlier
murder of four leading UDF activists from the town of Cradock in
the eastern Cape, which had also occurred in mysterious circumstances, lent further credence to the death squad rumours in the eyes of
many government opponents.

The funeral of Mrs Mxenge saw passions running high. The events
which followed have never been satisfactorily explained. The UDF
conducted memorial services and vigils, political acts which brought
them into confrontation with the rival Zulu-dominated Inkatha
movement. There were suggestions, never clarified, that Inkatha
members joined by the police attacked the UDF. The violence spread
from Umlazi to the township of Inanda and amid the general
mayhem the local Indian population, many of whom owned property or businesses in black townships, became the targets of a general
wave of violence. Homes and shops were plundered and then burned
to the ground, as were government buildings. After four days the
number killed had risen to over fifty, and some two thousand Indians

had fled their homes. Another casualty was the Gandhi Settlement, a school and library complex dedicated to the memory of the Mahatma's early years living in Durban.

Within a few days the violence had spread to Cape Town. The Reverend Allan Boesak announced a mass march on the city's Pollsmoor Prison to demand the release of Nelson Mandela. It promised to be one of the most emphatic demonstrations of anti-government feeling South Africa had witnessed, a protest in keeping with Boesak's design to turn the anti-apartheid campaign into a nationwide action in the style of the American civil rights movement of the 1960s. On the eve of the march Boesak was arrested and held for several weeks, eventually being freed on bail charged with subversion. The security authorities sealed off Athlone sports stadium, the venue for the start of the march, effectively preventing it from going ahead.

For two days afterwards street battles raged in several of the city's townships with the violence spilling over on one occasion into the white suburbs. Two cabinet ministers, le Grange and Defence Minister Magnus Malan, flew down to the Cape to demonstrate government concern at developments, a reaction to a strong statement from the right-wing leader Andries Treurnicht who accused the government of keeping the security forces 'on a leash and allowing them to use only birdshot and rubber bullets'. Around thirty people died in the violence and almost three hundred were injured.

The government's response, in keeping with the view that a militant minority was organizing the rioting, was to announce the closure of nearly half the coloured schools and colleges in the western Cape. The establishments were described by the minister responsible as centres of 'intimidation and disruption'.

With the state of emergency obviously failing to stabilize the situation and with international hostility towards South Africa growing, pressure mounted on the government to come up with new measures aimed at ending the crisis and at offering the blacks a fairer share in power. Already France had withdrawn its ambassador from Pretoria and announced a freeze on new investment in South Africa. The United States, which had recalled its envoy some weeks previously, refused to accredit the newly-appointed South African ambassador in Washington, while Norway decided to withdraw its senior diplomat. The member countries of the European Economic Community announced they were recalling their ambassadors for consultations and they later agreed on a package of political sanctions against Pretoria despite earlier British opposition to such moves.

By far the most crucial diplomatic move took place in Vienna in early August at a meeting attended by South African Foreign Minister Pik Botha and senior US administration officials including the National Security Adviser Robert McFarlane. In response to American calls for more far-reaching reform, Pik Botha assured the Americans that important changes were in the pipeline. He pointed to a speech which President Botha was due to make on 15 August in Durban as a major signpost. The US delegation came away convinced that the Durban speech was of crucial importance while in South Africa itself the news media were briefed in advance that Botha was going to announce major changes to apartheid.

On the eve of the speech a South African newspaper came out with the headline saying 'All eyes on Botha', but the mounting local and international expectations appeared to unnerve the cabinet and Botha. The familiar fear of being seen to bow to foreign pressure reasserted itself. By all accounts the speech was rewritten several times, gradually watered down so that it eventually turned out to be a damp squib. Pik Botha had oversold the significance of the speech beyond the ability of his president to deliver the goods. Faced with a golden opportunity to convince the world of his genuine reformist intentions, Botha had simply retreated into the laager declaring defiantly that:

> I am not prepared to lead white South Africans and other
> minority groups on a road to abdication and suicide. Destroy
> white South Africa and our influence and this country will drift
> into factional strife, chaos and poverty.

The speech was followed by a wave of disappointment and exasperation. The country's English-language financial newspaper *Business Day* called for Botha's resignation, describing him as a 'hick politician'. Subsequent announcements about major changes to the pass laws and to the rights of homeland blacks to enjoy South African citizenship were partly overshadowed by the growing mood of impatience with Pretoria both within the country and, more importantly, abroad.

The mood of frustration manifested itself most of all among foreign bankers and in the financial community generally. Confidence in the white government to set a course towards genuine reform evaporated. The South African rand plummetted from 52 US cents when the state of emergency was declared to under 33 cents at one point on 27 August. As the run on the currency gathered pace, the government announced a week-long closure of the money markets and the stock exchange. Against a background of mounting political and financial crisis the governor of South Africa's central bank Dr Gerhard de Kock embarked on an international rescue mission aimed at rolling over the country's $24 billion short-term debt, knocking on the doors of the Bank of England in London and of the Federal Reserve and Citibank in the United States, among others. De Kock's mission failed to win a breathing space for South Africa's debts to be rescheduled. No western country wanted to be seen extending credit to a government whose security forces were seen nightly on television confronting those whom the world perceived as freedom-seeking blacks.

On the eve of the money markets' reopening Finance Minister du Plessis announced a unilateral four-month suspension of South Africa's foreign debt repayments to protect the rand from further depreciation. It was a devastating blow for the political and business community. In the past South Africa had always prided itself on honouring its loan repayments on time. Now though, some were bound to bracket the country alongside third-world nations who are frequent and substantial defaulters, a measure of the extent to which Pretoria's political credit was drying up in western capitals. The drastic measures even overshadowed the traumatic effect of a decision by President Reagan to invoke limited economic sanctions against South Africa. The sanctions themselves were not particularly punitive, regarded by many as token gestures by the Reagan administration. The international financial cold-shouldering of Pretoria had come as a far greater shock and appeared to many to presage a period in which the South African government would come under mounting pressure from the western business community to change direction.

So what are the conclusions to be drawn from the most sustained period of black unrest in South Africa's history? For the blacks, the widespread violence did not begin as a specific protest against the new constitution although P.W. Botha's reformed parliament did remind blacks of their political deprivation; rather it was an expression of anger over local grievances which activists channelled into a wider national campaign. The vicious attacks on local black councillors and policemen marked a repudiation of all forms of representation which the government might impose on the blacks.

The young people taking part in the protests stayed and fought in the townships, unlike the 'children of Soweto' who fled the country in 1976 to join the ranks of the ANC. The government believed that the violence was due in the main to political agitators from the ANC infiltrating the townships and radicalizing the black youth. To a certain extent that was true. Deprived of its bases in Mozambique, the ANC had been able to establish its presence inside the townships although it appeared that local cells were operating independently of Lusaka's control. But then the ANC's influence among most politically conscious blacks had never really waned despite its banning. The support was already there and the black township activists were ready to respond to the ANC's political programme. For a start, there was a feeling among many blacks that 'history is on our side'. The ANC was also propagating the concept of a 'people's war' aimed at 'liberating' the townships. Whether ANC agitators were sent in to organize such rebellions inside the townships is uncertain; undoubtedly the ANC was encouraging them from afar.

As for the whites, the violence left them with a feeling of deepening uncertainty about their future. There was a run on guns and ammunition at weapons shops in white areas close to trouble spots; some whites were selling up their homes at a substantial loss and leaving for overseas; others researched their ancestry to assess the chances of being eligible for non-South African passports.

But there was no panic exodus. Indeed there was an intangible feeling among some whites that the unrest had at least cleared the political decks; that the issues had been more clearly identified than before; that problems of charting South Africa's future course were now well and truly out in the open and being discussed at every level of society.

The international consequences of the violence were twofold. South Africa's western allies and financial backers began to calculate that the price of continuing to sustain the Pretoria government was becoming too high. The argument advanced by countries like Britain, that more change could be achieved by maintaining political and economic ties with South Africa, appeared to look a little thin in the eyes of many.

Finally, the unrest and the government's reaction to it almost entirely overshadowed the earlier successes which Botha had notched up in the foreign policy field. But by mid-1985 these successes were themselves beginning to look less than resounding.

CHAPTER 11

Friends and Neighbours
Pretoria's breakthrough into black Africa

The single-track railway bridge drenched in the spray of the Victoria
Falls on the Zimbabwe-Zambia border is a lifeline for black Africa.
Every thirty minutes or so a Zimbabwean steam train carrying coal
and food arrives to be met by a Zambian engine which will take over.
From the opposite direction a Zambian train carrying copper
heads south for Bulawayo and for a port on South Africa's long
coastline. Victoria Falls is a key rail link between black Africa and
the 'racist régime in Pretoria' despite political differences. No appreciation of southern African politics can be complete without understanding the region's rail network.

Civil wars in several black states have made the South African link
even more vital for these countries. The Benguela railway linking
Lusaka with the Angolan Atlantic port of Lobito is closed because of
the civil war between the Marxist government in Luanda and South
African-backed guerrillas; the Chinese-built Tanzam railway con-
necting Lusaka with the Indian Ocean port of Dar-es-Salaam in
Tanzania has lengthy bottlenecks owing to maladministration at the
port; the short rail link between the Zimbabwean capital, Harare,
and the Mozambican port of Beira has been attacked during the civil
war between the Maputo government and rebel forces. In late 1983
an estimated 65–70 per cent of Zimbabwe's and 50–60 per cent of
Malawi's foreign trade was being routed through South Africa.
Zambian dependence amounted to 40 per cent of exports and 70 per
cent of imports. Lesotho, Botswana and Zaire are similarly dependent. The main exports are copper (2.5 million tonnes annually),
cobalt, chrome ore and ferro-chrome.

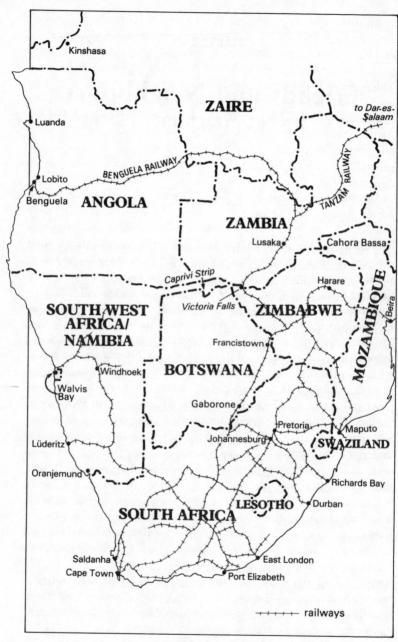

Southern Africa

All these exports find their way to the world market via South Africa's sophisticated ports at Durban, Port Elizabeth, East London and Cape Town, as well as two new harbours at Richards Bay close to the Mozambique border and Saldanha Bay north of Cape Town. This extensive rail and harbour network means that, should it so wish, South Africa could impose an effective stranglehold on the economies of several black African states. It is interesting that the African National Congress, while regularly attacking other economic targets in South Africa, has rarely sabotaged the strategic railway lines which link its host nations with the harbours of South Africa.

Another major source of black African dependence on South Africa is the earnings sent back by black miners from all over southern Africa who work in South Africa's gold and coal mines. Mozambique, for example, provides almost 50,000 miners and 60 per cent of their earnings are remitted directly to Mozambique. A similar arrangement applies to the 90,000 black miners from Lesotho whose remitted wages virtually keep that country afloat, and to the 12,000 from Malawi. Electricity produced by a hydro-electric project at Cahora Bassa in Mozambique is fed to the Mozambican capital Maputo not via the country's own electricity pylons but through the South African grid, which means South Africa could effectively plunge Maputo into darkness. The railways in Mozambique and the harbour facilities at Maputo are administered and maintained by South African officials. To sum up, without the South African link the economies of Lesotho, Botswana and Swaziland (which are part of the Southern African Customs Union under which custom dues are pooled) would probably collapse, while those of Zambia, Zimbabwe and Mozambique would find themselves in perilous circumstances.

Even African countries with the most hostile views about apartheid accept South African products. In the black homeland of KwaZulu, for example, a small business manufactures shirts with a 'Made in KwaZulu' label. These are exported to Kenya where the labels are unstitched and replaced with others saying 'Made in Kenya'. Similarly there is a sweet factory in Swaziland which is entirely South African-owned but which exports preserves to Nigeria with a 'Made in Swaziland' label. In 1985 the South African Trade Authority announced that South Africa traded directly or indirectly under a camouflage label with forty-five of the fifty members of the

Organization of African Unity and that during the first three months
of that year such trade had increased by 65 per cent, standing at
R309.2 million.

Moves to counter this black African reliance on the hated enemy
emerged among the five so-called front-line states (Zambia, Botswana, Tanzania, Angola and Mozambique) during the mid-1970s at
the time of the collapse of the Portuguese empire. These states were
initially concerned with resolving the Rhodesian and South West
African problems, but increasingly attention focused on forming a
regional organization which would render black Africa less dependent on Pretoria. The move was also inspired by resistance to the
idea, first floated by Pik Botha in a speech in Zurich in 1979, of a
'constellation of states' in southern Africa – moderate, non-Marxist
and working in harmony with South Africa. The result of the
deliberations was that in April 1980 the five countries, joined by
Malawi, Lesotho, Swaziland and the newly-independent Zimbabwe,
formally established the Southern African Development Coordination Conference (SADCC). Despite impressive strides in some
areas, SADCC's experiences have shown that the concept of black
Africa severing its links with South Africa is unrealistic. The Soviet
sponsors of several of the black African states, while forthcoming
with weapons (or at least sufficient weapons to keep the pro-
Moscow faction within the country in power) has shown little
readiness to foot the bill when it comes to feeding empty stomachs.
South Africa, in return for the assistance it was offering, started
demanding its pound of flesh. Pretoria increasingly assumed the role
of regional policeman. South Africa's opponents called this 'destabilization'. Pretoria itself called it looking after South Africa's interests. These interests are concerned mainly with neutralizing the
military capacity of the banned African National Congress with its
headquarters in Lusaka, bases in several countries neighbouring
South Africa from which to launch attacks and training camps
further afield in Africa.

The African National Congress is one of the most heavily-
infiltrated liberation movements in the world. The South African
security services are never far behind the moves of the ANC, its
strategy decisions and shifts within its leadership. The organization
is made up of two main camps. First there is the black nationalist
wing: exiles from the old congress movement, among them those

who retain the ideal of a non-racial South Africa and whose Christian humanitarian principles prevent them launching terrorist attacks against 'soft' targets inside South Africa. A car bombing in May 1983 in Pretoria that killed nineteen people (eleven whites and eight blacks) and injured over 200 was an exception. The bomb exploded prematurely, its radio control device apparently activated by the VHF radio signal of a passing ambulance. The explosion killed the two ANC bombers. The ANC leadership has gone mainly for economic or military targets like South Africa's first nuclear power plant which was sabotaged during its construction in December 1982 setting back by a year the moment when it came on stream. Wherever possible, the ANC has tried to avoid loss of life among civilians. The other wing is that of the South African Communist Party, among the most slavish followers of Moscow in the world and one which continually threatens to steer the ANC towards intensifying the terror campaign.

Although moderates still run the ANC this has not lessened Pretoria's determination to destroy its military capability. In the seven years up to the end of 1982, the security services logged a total of 217 attacks in which forty-eight people were killed. Damage was estimated at R600 million. Between 1977 and 1983 a total of 127 ANC men were arrested and forty-five killed. The South Africans have also built up a fairly detailed picture of the ANC structure as a result of infiltration and their interrogation of captured ANC suspects. Security officials said that the path trodden by a typical ANC member usually began with his recruitment either inside South Africa or in one of its neighbouring states. Transported to Maputo and accommodated in a safe house, he was then flown to the Tanzanian capital of Dar-es-Salaam and taught ANC history and security procedures. From there he was taken to the Angolan capital, Luanda where each recruit acquired his nom de guerre, after which only the ANC security department is supposed to know the recruit's true identity. The South African security apparatus identified five ANC training camps in Angola – Quibaxe, Pango, Malanje, Vienna, and Caxito. The new recruits were taught to march and drill, given firearms training, taught politics by SACP commissars, and instructed in the techniques of sabotage and explosives handling, map reading, field work and communications in a programme of up to two years. The most promising recruits were sent to the Soviet Union for further specialized training. Courses in guerrilla tactics, platoon commanding and infantry and artillery warfare are offered at the Privolnye military camp near Simferopel in the Ukraine, also in Odessa and 'Centre 26' near Moscow. Other specialist training centres are located at Teterow near Rostock in East Germany. South African intelligence estimate the ANC's field manpower at between 1,500 and 2,000 men of whom about 300 are deployed in the forward area at any one time.

With several black states hosting the ANC, Pretoria began offering a stark choice: either you are with us or against us. Being with South Africa did not necessarily have to mean recognizing the country by establishing diplomatic relations as Malawi had done, or even displaying open warmth towards Pretoria. It simply involved playing the game according to Pretoria's rules. Zimbabwe, for example, which publicly condemned 'racist South Africa' stridently, privately left Pretoria satisfied that its commitment to the anti-South African cause would not extend to offering sanctuary to ANC members. This was after Prime Minister Robert Mugabe had had several reminders of Zimbabwe's vulnerability; the blowing-up of 2½ months' supply of Zimbabwean oil at Beira in Mozambique was a spectacular example. Mugabe's government also accused South Africa of masterminding the 'super-dissidents' supposedly backing Zimbabwe's opposition leader Joshua Nkomo in Matabeleland (although Nkomo himself denied this). Such allegations were also rejected by Pretoria but they were sufficient to convince South Africa's opponents that Pretoria was prepared to engage in economic sabotage to ensure that neither Zimbabwe nor any of the other countries on its borders stood a chance of emerging as the model of a successful black state which might negate South Africa's implied argument that the blacks could not rule themselves. Nevertheless Mugabe got the message about harbouring the ANC. Those countries which didn't began to feel the heat.

In Lesotho, the tiny mountain kingdom landlocked by South Africa, Pretoria targeted on 11,000 or so South African exiles in the country, among them members of the African National Congress. In December 1982 South African commandos raided alleged ANC 'nests' in the Lesotho capital Maseru, killing forty-two people, twelve of them civilians. The other thirty victims were mostly ANC members, though whether they were part of the organization's military wing was uncertain. The Lesotho government soon began moving some 200 ANC members out of the country. Not content with this, Pretoria tried to press Lesotho into signing a fully-fledged mutual security pact, under which the government of Chief Leabua Jonathan would agree not to harbour the ANC, an offer which was politely refused. This, together with Chief Jonathan's invitation to the communist governments of North Korea, China, and the Soviet Union to establish embassies in Maseru (which served to fuel Pretoria's paranoia about the communist-inspired 'total onslaught' against South Africa), prompted further pressure. Chief Jonathan accused Pretoria of backing the shadowy Lesotho Liberation Army of Ntsu Mokhehle, a long-standing foe of Chief Jonathan. Later he accused South Africa of helping another Lesotho opposition group, the United Democratic Alliance. Pretoria dismissed these allegations as Chief Jonathan's 'antics'. Reading between Lesotho's neurosis about South Africa's intentions and the ambitions of South African realpolitik, it seemed that at the very least Pretoria was maintaining contacts with opposition groups trying to overthrow Chief Jonathan, although using such groups as a bargaining counter rather than preparing them to seize power.

South Africa has learned that today's allies can turn out to be tomorrow's liabilities once their usefulness to Pretoria has expired.

This certainly proved to be the case in South Africa's dealings with the Mozambique National Resistance Movement (RENAMO) which South Africa backed in its fight to overturn the Marxist government of President Samora Machel in Mozambique. Machel was allowing his country to be used as the main launching-pad for ANC attacks into South Africa.

RENAMO emerged during the twilight of Portuguese colonial rule in Mozambique as a rival internal guerrilla army to the Marxist FRELIMO movement which eventually took power. However, its survival would have been doubtful had it not been effectively taken over by the Rhodesian Central Intelligence Organization in the late 1970s. In 1965 the Rhodesian Prime Minister Ian Smith had issued a unilateral declaration of independence (UDI) from Britain to preserve his country's white minority rule. The rebel Smith régime soon found itself embroiled in a bitter bush war against two guerrilla armies: the Zimbabwean African People's Union (ZAPU) led by

Joshua Nkomo with bases in Zambia, and the Zimbabwean African National Union (ZANU) of Robert Mugabe which was allowed to operate from inside neighbouring Mozambique after the country became independent in 1975. The FRELIMO (Front for the Liberation of Mozambique) government under President Machel was hostile to the Rhodesian régime and supported the anti-Smith guerrillas. For the Rhodesians the RENAMO rebels served as an intelligence system to keep a watchful eye on the activities of Mugabe's ZANU guerrillas who launched their attacks against Rhodesia from bases across the border. The Rhodesians set up training camps run by exiled Portuguese who had contacts with Portugal's sinister intelligence service. When the Smith régime collapsed in 1980, following a British-sponsored peace settlement, and Robert Mugabe took over at the head of a black majority government, the RENAMO movement seemed to be heading for oblivion until it was again taken over, this time by the South Africans. RENAMO was transferred to bases in the northern Transvaal where it continued its operations, no longer against Rhodesian guerrillas but against the central government in Maputo. RENAMO was remarkably successful in its new role, virtually taking control of a number of Mozambique's provinces and rendering several others ungovernable.

Road and rail links were sabotaged and the Cahora Bassa power lines were frequently attacked, as were the oil pipelines to Zimbabwe. By early 1984 President Machel was presiding over a shattered economy. His people were starving (to such an extent that mothers were leaving their babies by the roadside hoping that others would find them and be able to feed them), the shelves in the food stores in Maputo were empty and motorists were paying unemployed youths to guard their cars in the queues (lasting up to thirty-six hours) for petrol. Machel had to start preparing his country for the unthinkable: a Marxist state making peace with the hated 'racist enemy'.

On 3 February 1984 Radio Maputo broadcast a report based on an official document circulated to embassies in the capital outlining the damage inflicted by Pretoria as part of its 'global strategy of reducing commercial and economic relations with Mozambique'. The radio reported the following details of 'economic sabotage':

- The number of Mozambicans working in South African mines had fallen by almost two-thirds, with the loss of $568m in

remittances; 70,000 workers had become unemployed.
- The most costly factor had been the cancellation of the agreement whereby South Africa paid one half of miners' wages in gold at official prices. The total loss to Mozambique was estimated at over $2.6 billion.
- Direct aggression by South Africa and by armed bandits sponsored by the régime had caused $333m damage. In 1982–3 the bandits (i.e. RENAMO) had destroyed 900 rural shops, affecting 4.5m people; almost 500 primary schools; and 86 secondary schools.
- In 1982 alone, RENAMO had destroyed 130 villages resulting in over 100,000 peasants losing their property.
- The total cost of South African aggression and economic destabilization was estimated at almost $4 billion – three times more than Mozambique's total indebtedness to western countries.

How much of this was due to South African action or indirect action is, of course, impossible to quantify. Apart from the effects of the civil war, the country was also suffering from a prolonged drought, not to mention administrative incompetence. It was probably a combination of all three factors which had brought Mozambique to its knees. A stark reminder of the firepower which South Africa could muster to punish those who harboured the ANC came with an air attack on Maputo, following the Pretoria car bombing, and the sabotage of an ANC office in the city in late 1983. South Africa claimed that all the casualties from the air attack were ANC personnel, but this was contradicted by Mozambique which said that the dead had been civilians.

The spiralling violence in the region concerned the United States which calculated that if Pretoria's security anxieties over the ANC could be eased it would adopt a less hostile stance towards its neighbours, leading in turn to peace in the area. With the US playing an active role behind the scenes, joined later by Portugal as the former colonial power, contacts between South Africa and Mozambique began during the latter half of 1983 and were formalized during January 1984, with working parties set up to establish areas of mutual interest. Within a few weeks both countries had worked out the framework for a non-aggression pact.

Komatipoort, on the South Africa-Mozambique border. 16 March 1984. A stretch of land close to this border town has been declared a 'no-man's land' for the occasion, though it is technically part of South Africa. A huge tented camp has been set up by the South African Defence Force who had less than a fortnight to prepare for the occasion. Vast quantities of 'LM prawns' (LM stands for the former name of Maputo – Lourenço Marques) have been brought in from Mozambique as well as crates of South African white wine from the Cape. The South Africans have installed dozens of telephone and telex lines at the remote site for the hundreds of local and international news people covering the occasion. Komatipoort railway station has been spring-cleaned for the historic meeting between Prime Minister Botha and President Machel, and a special railway platform straddles the border. South Africa's state train (the 'white train') has been brought in for the summit meeting. It was used for a royal visit to South Africa in 1947 by King George VI, Queen Elizabeth and the Princesses Elizabeth and Margaret, and for a 1975 summit on the Rhodesian crisis between South African Prime Minister Vorster and Zambian President Kenneth Kaunda on the Victoria Falls bridge.

From the Mozambican side of the border Machel arrives in full military regalia, while Botha is wearing a dark suit and a hat which he removes to shake hands with Machel who first salutes, smiling broadly, and then shakes hands with Botha. The summit meeting lasts ninety minutes. Botha emphasizes the benefits to South Africa and Mozambique, though ideologically opposed, of joining together to rationalize food production, develop regional trade, establish housing and education programmes, health services, employment opportunities, and many other schemes. Turning to the Mozambican delegation, Botha declares: 'We are both African countries, inhabited by African peoples whose past and future are firmly entrenched in the southern part of the African continent. We are of Africa.'

The essence of the Nkomati treaty was that both countries would not allow their territories to be used as a base for hostile forces to launch attacks against the other. Mozambique had agreed to end the ANC military presence in its territory (leaving a small political bureau in Maputo) while South Africa had committed itself to pulling the rug out from beneath its former protégé, RENAMO.

For P.W. Botha the Nkomati accord and a similar agreement with Swaziland signed secretly two years earlier were blueprints for what he hoped would be a series of non-aggression agreements with other black states. The aim was to castrate the military capability of the ANC and to lock southern Africa into what one observer called 'Pax Pretoriana'. Five months after Nkomati – in what was his final address as South Africa's last prime minister – Botha said that the Mozambique and Swazi agreements had opened the door towards a 'new order of co-operation and development in southern Africa'.

But how successful would be South Africa's bid to establish a modus vivendi with black Africa? For thirty years Pretoria had been trying various openings. Advances under Prime Ministers Strijdom and Verwoerd were scuttled in 1960 when South African police shot dead sixty-nine blacks in the Sharpeville massacre to the horror of black Africa. The period of détente under John Vorster saw South Africa establishing contacts with Hastings Banda in Malawi (which led to full diplomatic relations), Houphouet-Boigny of the Ivory Coast and Kofi Busia of Ghana. But this period ended with the 1969 Lusaka Manifesto drawn up by black African states which stated that:

> The actions of the South African government are such that the rest of the world has a responsibility to take some action in defence of humanity. On the objective of liberation we can neither surrender nor compromise. [But] we should prefer to negotiate rather than destroy.

South Africa, however, rejected any suggestion of other countries becoming involved in its internal affairs. In June 1971 the Organization of African Unity consequently voted against dialogue with Pretoria and implicitly came out in favour of armed struggle. South Africa tried again to reach an understanding with black Africa following Portugal's withdrawal from the subcontinent, when the downfall of the colonial régimes in Mozambique and Angola removed an effective cordon sanitaire on South Africa's borders.

But South Africa's support for the embattled white minority régime in Rhodesia acted against bridge-building towards the black states. John Vorster soon realized the impediment and piece by piece began removing the props which had helped the Smith government to stave off the effects of international economic sanctions and which had assisted the régime in waging the bush war against the guerrilla armies. In 1975 South African police units were withdrawn from Rhodesia and Vorster exercised all the leverage he could muster (bearing in mind there was little love lost between the two men) to urge Smith to reach a settlement with the nationalist leaders. Vorster had by then concluded that the Smith government was doomed, a cause which was not worth risking his regional policy for. In any case an early settlement, he reckoned, might produce a less hostile government, possibly under the moderate black leader Bishop Muzorewa, rather than a rabidly anti-South African Marxist régime later. Vorster forced Smith to meet the black leaders, a meeting which, though not successful at the time, was a significant step towards the peace settlement which was to emerge four years later when Britain brought Rhodesia's white and black leaders together at Lancaster House in London and obtained their reluctant agreement to a deal under which Smith would surrender power to a black majority government, though with guarantees of security for the whites. Vorster's policy was on course but was sunk within eighteen months, both by South Africa's invasion of Angola in 1975–6 in support of anti-Marxist guerrillas and by the unrest in South Africa's black townships in 1976–7 which left over 500 dead and alienated black Africa. The policy of dialogue with black states clearly had not worked. Under Botha, South Africa changed tack and applied the policy of machtpolitik.

But would Botha's approach prove any more fruitful than previous attempts to break through into black Africa? In one sense Botha had already broken new ground. Where previous attempts at dialogue had foundered on South Africa's internal policies, here was Mozambique signing a peace treaty with Pretoria, apartheid and all, and expelling from its territory the very organization which was in the vanguard of the anti-apartheid struggle. In expelling the ANC Mozambique had stuck to her side of the bargain, but could Pretoria honour hers?

At the moment South Africa and Mozambique signed the peace accord a RENAMO radio station in South Africa which broadcast anti-FRELIMO propaganda went off the air, shut down permanently by Pretoria. South Africa did not find it so easy to turn off RENAMO's military activities and allegations increased that Pretoria was still aiding the rebel movement. There were reports of night-time air drops into the northern Mozambican provinces to

RENAMO forces on the ground and rumours of mysterious flights across the Kruger National Park, the game reserve which lies along much of South Africa's border with Mozambique. How was RENAMO able to keep going? Where were its finances coming from? Who was supporting it – the South Africans still, or were other interests at work?

The non-military agreements of Nkomati were beginning to take shape. Within six weeks the two states had agreed on tapping power from Cahora Bassa. Planned by Portugal before its retreat from Mozambique, financed largely by South Africa, and constructed by a European engineering consortium, the hydro-electric project had been severely affected by the civil war, principally because of RENAMO attacks on the power lines. Working parties studied other joint projects like improving tourist facilities along Mozambique's superb Indian Ocean coastline, where South African tourists had flocked before independence, and joint agricultural schemes. But the success all hinged on improved security. RENAMO's activities had if anything increased since the Nkomati signing. Hard-line Marxists within FRELIMO, who had had reservations about the agreement in the first place, were increasingly expressing their concern. Among Mozambique's allies there were strong reservations, not voiced publicly, about the wisdom of Machel making peace with the enemy. In May 1984 Machel travelled to Arusha in northern Tanzania for a one-day summit of the leaders of the six front-line states. Opening the summit President Nyerere of Tanzania, who had accepted the necessity of the Nkomati accord with great reluctance, declared that through a combination of threats and promises, South Africa was trying to steer SADCC member nations towards a long-term dependence on Pretoria, offering 'the mirage of quick economic prosperity in co-operation with apartheid South Africa.' The final communiqué made scant mention of the peace accord. It simply stated that the front-line leaders 'expressed the hope that the South African government will live up to its commitment to cease its acts aimed at the destabilization of Mozambique through the use of armed bandits.' They expressed appreciation of Mozambique's commitment to continued moral, political and diplomatic support for the ANC. Lukewarm praise indeed. Machel was looking an increasingly lonely man.

Within a month Pik Botha was called to Maputo for an urgent meeting. Botha reassured Machel of Pretoria's good faith but South Africa still failed to curtail RENAMO. The security situation deteriorated and Maputo increasingly took on the appearance of a city under seige. How could RENAMO keep going?

The respected International Institute for Strategic Studies in London attributed the RENAMO resurgence to a South African decision to provide RENAMO with a massive supply-drop around the time the Nkomati accord was signed. The institute added that Pretoria also seemed to have allowed more than 1,500 trained RENAMO personnel to enter Mozambique with their weapons before it closed the movement's camps in the Transvaal. Was the South African military, or sections of it, acting alone? Or did the government know what was going on? After all P.W. Botha had strong links with the military, having been Minister of Defence in the 1970s. Were there right-wing elements within the army who were responsible for continuing to supply RENAMO? Or were army commanders in the eastern Transvaal neighbouring Mozambique turning a blind eye to secret supplies sent in by RENAMO supporters among the 600,000-strong Portuguese exiles in South Africa? The picture became clearer as South African agents and diplomats around the world traced the source of the RENAMO supply line.

RENAMO, or rather its suppliers, had simply reactivated the former sanctions-busting trail which was used by mercenaries and middle-men to enable Rhodesia to survive during UDI when the illegal Smith régime was subjected to an international economic embargo. Ex-Rhodesian officers, some in London, had established a supply line down the east coast of Africa. One of the countries involved was the Gulf state of Oman. Centuries ago Mozambique was part of the Omani empire; indeed RENAMO exploited the concept of an east African Islamic consciousness to win support. Another link in the chain was the Comoro Islands, whose government was established as the result of a mercenary coup several years ago. It seemed that remote parts of Tanzania and Malawi were being used for arms drops, though without the knowledge of the respective governments.

South Africa unveiled a plot by Portuguese businessmen and financiers to overthrow Machel and reinstate a pro-western capitalist government which would allow Portuguese entrepreneurs to exploit Mozambique's substantial resources. Pik Botha referred to it as 'an international web of bankers, financiers, and businessmen with large political and economic interests in Africa, Latin America and Europe, who were hostile to President Machel and who were determined to turn Mozambique into their own private economic preserve'. Senior figures in Portugal's socialist government were among those who also lent strong support to RENAMO. In addition, right-wing political interests in West Germany were believed to have links with RENAMO.

By October 1984, with Nkomati six months old, the intensifying RENAMO effort was becoming acutely embarrassing for South Africa. Pik Botha brought FRELIMO and RENAMO together for talks in Pretoria on 30 October 1984. Botha said that under an agreement reached at the meeting RENAMO would recognize Machel as the Mozambican leader and both sides would cease all armed conflict and hostility. But shortly after the ceasefire announcement RENAMO declared the war would go on and nothing agreed in Pretoria would stop its bid to topple Machel.

In January 1985 two Britons travelling from Johannesburg to Maputo by road crossed the border at the frontier post of Ressano Garcia and were stopped by RENAMO, ordered out of their car and then taken into the bush. When Mozambican soldiers arrived at the scene they found the two Britons bayonetted to death. The incident, occurring so close to the border with South Africa, again caused the government in Maputo to raise the issue of whether RENAMO was not operating from the sanctuary of South African territory, possibly with South African military assistance. The killing of the two Britons prompted a full-scale search for RENAMO supporters in the South African Defence Force. A handful of dismissals occurred, seen by many as token. Still the suspicions lingered in certain quarters that sections of the military were giving a nod and a wink to RENAMO activities in the border area.

It was a story of increasing gloom. Pik Botha said at the end of January 1985 that the destruction caused by the civil war was plunging Mozambique further and further into economic chaos. At the time of writing the civil war continues to destroy the country with little sign of peace. South Africa has almost given up its attempts to bring the two sides together. Instead it has come down firmly on the side of President Machel hoping to ensure his survival and with it the survival of the peace treaty.

And yet the situation was not altogether to South Africa's disadvantage. Pretoria had achieved its main objective of neutralizing the ANC in Mozambique. Machel knew that if he dared re-admit the ANC into his country the South Africans would strike again, and hard.

But had South Africa, in the process, bitten off more than it could chew? South Africa had unleashed the RENAMO beast but who was going to tame it? The South African public (the whites that is) would not tolerate large numbers of South African soldiers going into a foreign country to prop up a black Marxist régime.

In desperation Machel turned to his front-line partners for help. At a summit in June 1985 in Harare, Prime Minister Mugabe of Zimbabwe and President Julius Nyerere of Tanzania pledged that they would deploy their own troops inside Mozambique to assist FRELIMO to hunt down RENAMO. Zimbabwean troops were already guarding the oil pipeline from the Mozambican port of Beira, as well as the road through the Mozambican province of Tete which links north-eastern Zimbabwe and Malawi. But following the summit decision several thousand Zimbabwean troops were poured into Mozambique and soon scored a major victory, seizing a RENAMO base in the Gorongosa National Park in Mozambique's Sofala province. During the raid a diary belonging to the secretary of the RENAMO leader, Alfonso Dhlakama, was captured and it revealed that despite its denials South Africa was still in touch with the right-wing rebels. The diary referred to South African arms drops and visits to the movement's headquarters by the then Deputy Foreign Minister in Pretoria, Louis Nel. His chief, Pik Botha, acknowledged the authenticity of the diary and conceded that the contacts had taken place, an admission that sections of the military seemed intent on jeopardizing the Nkomati accord.

South Africa also appeared to have underestimated the cost of those parts of the peace agreement which it *was* honouring. South African officials were appalled at the scale of destruction in the areas worst affected by the civil war. A sprinkling of aid donations from other governments would not be the answer. What was required was a massive rescue plan and who would come up with that? The South Africans were in the depths of the worst economic crisis in decades, so their capacity to help was limited. As for the United States, right-wing senators would be happier to see Mozambique collapse than grant aid to the Marxist régime. The best that could be hoped for, in the view of one observer, was a 'gradually-improving shambles'.

So, South Africa is in a dilemma. What would be the point of helping RENAMO to try and seize power? The movement is run by middle-men and mercenaries for the benefit of foreign economic interests. It has no political philosophy, no charismatic leadership, and its level of support among the people is questionable. Pretoria was stuck with Machel and had to try to encourage him away from his hard-line Marxism to a pro-western view, which is the only way Mozambique is going to attract the life-saving capital it needs.

All the time there was the danger that Machel might be toppled by the hard-liners. Or that he himself might decide his political survival demanded jettisoning Nkomati and breaking off his mild flirtation with the west, turning back to the Soviet Union for assistance in ridding the country of RENAMO and reinstating his authority over the country. The Soviets might be hesitant to commit themselves on a large scale. But if there was a need for them to notch up a foreign policy success, or to counterbalance an American advance elsewhere in the world, Mozambique might be the place to do it, in which case South Africa could end up with an army of Soviet and eastern bloc advisers on its doorstep as well, possibly, as several thousand Cubans. South Africa would then find itself in a worse position than it was in before Nkomati.

Nor had the closing down of the ANC bases in Mozambique led to the neutralization of the organization's military threat against South Africa, as many in Pretoria had hoped. In the months following the Nkomati signing several violent attacks in the northern Transvaal suggested to South African security officials that the ANC was beginning to open up a new channel of infiltration into the country via Botswana. Pik Botha's officials maintained that this was pointed out to the Botswanan government of President Quett Masire but that no action had been taken by the authorities in Gaborone to close down the ANC centres. Clearly South Africa was hoping to encourage Botswana to sign a security pact along the lines of Nkomati although they would probably have been satisfied with an agreement that the two countries' security services should work more closely together.

During the early part of 1985 security sources in Pretoria said they were expecting an increase in ANC activity prior to a major conference of the organization which was due to take place in June. The conference was called to review ANC policy in the wake of Nkomati and a confrontation was expected between the old guard, who still recoiled from a commitment to out-and-out terrorism, and the hard-liners, especially the post-1976 fugitives who had been languishing in training camps and who wanted to see more violent action against the Pretoria government. Pretoria was convinced that hard-liners were anxious to put on a display of ANC firepower inside South Africa prior to the conference so as to demonstrate that, despite Nkomati, the ANC could still get its men inside the enemy camp and could still act effectively.

Several of the attacks during the early part of 1985 bore the stamp of trained ANC cadres. But there were others which seemed to reveal that activists inside South Africa were to a considerable extent acting alone, perhaps maintaining distant links with the ANC leadership but having been given the freedom to act without orders from on high. One example of this was the bomb attacks on the offices of the Anglo American and Anglo Vaal mining companies within hours of their having dismissed thousands of their workers. Such an attack could not have occurred so quickly had it been instigated in Lusaka or even in Gaborone. The final straw, as far as the South African authorities were concerned, came with hand-grenade attacks on the homes of two coloured politicians in the new three-chamber parliament, one of whom was lucky to escape with his life. This was the first time that politicians associated with the new constitution had been attacked in this way since the inception of the parliament. It was not the ANC's style to mount such attacks, but neither could it be ruled out. The ANC denied responsibility for the blasts. A telephone caller claiming to speak for the previously unknown 'Western Cape Suicide Squad' told a news agency office in Cape Town that his group had carried out the attacks. The Law and Order Minister Louis le Grange was convinced the ANC was behind the blasts and within a few days South African commandos launched an early-morning raid into Gaborone, attacking a number of private homes and offices which they said were ANC planning centres.

Visiting the target buildings later that morning, it was evident that the South Africans had known exactly whom they were looking for. The commandos had crossed the border in vans with civilian number-plates, entered the suburbs of Gaborone at about 1 am, pinpointed the targets from intelligence information in their possession and then gone into each of the homes and offices, shooting dead targeted individuals and blowing up one or two of the buildings. The most up-to-date intelligence on the targets would probably have been provided on the day before the raid. Their strike rate in the operation was probably about 70 per cent. Not surprisingly the raid was followed by an international outcry. The Botswanan government complained to the United Nations Security Council that the victims had been innocent South African refugees who had had nothing to do with planning acts of terrorism. Concern mounted in South Africa itself. Three leading newspaper editors and an academic expressed the view on a television discussion programme that the attack may have been necessary but that it was vital for the security authorities to produce the evidence that the targets were ANC activists. The following day at a news conference in Pretoria two of South Africa's most senior intelligence chiefs, Brigadier Herman Stadler and Major Craig Williamson, put on show some of the items which they said the commandos had brought back from Gaborone. The captured weapons included an AK Soviet-made rifle with a silencer which, according to Major Williamson, is issued to Soviet special forces. He said the silencer would prove a major capture for western defence experts. ANC propaganda documents were also shown as well as a computer on which further propaganda material was stored on the floppy discs. Major Williamson could speak with some authority about the inner workings of the ANC as he was once a South African spy within the organization. Recruited by the South African police, Williamson disappeared for six months in the early 1970s and then reappeared as a student activist at the University of the Witwatersrand in Johannesburg, playing a leading role in student politics, even being arrested on one occasion. In 1977 he 'fled' the country into Botswana and then turned up in Geneva from where he ran anti-South African programmes and joined the ANC. He blew his cover and returned home in 1980 after a former fellow-campus spy and by then an agent of BOSS (the Bureau of State Security) defected to London and who, it was feared, might spill the beans and place Williamson's life in danger.

Whether Gaborone had become an ANC nerve centre, as Pretoria claimed, or whether the victims were simply refugees, as Botswana maintained, the raid indicated that the hawks were back in control within the South African government. Threatened by economic sanctions, lambasted at the United Nations, a mood of 'what the hell' had crept into the higher ranks of government. Even officials from the Foreign Affairs Ministry, who often conflict with the more robust military men, were expressing the view that South Africa was not going to have its interests dictated from Washington, London or elsewhere. In a speech to parliament following the raid, President

Botha outlined five principles under which South Africa was prepared to live in peace with the front-line states. These were a ban on cross-border violence; the removal of foreign forces hostile to any country of the region; the peaceful resolution of disputes; regional co-operation; and toleration of different socio-economic and political systems. The speech marked the opening shot in Round Two of Botha's demonstration of machtpolitik towards South Africa's neighbours. Round One had resulted in the co-operation of Mozambique, Swaziland and Zimbabwe. Round Two will place Botswana, Lesotho, Angola, and even Zambia and Tanzania in the firing-line.

All in all then, South Africa's first formal peace treaty with a black African state had satisfied Pretoria's immediate ambitions but presented long-term problems. Peaceful coexistence between black and white Africa was still a dream. The Mozambique accord brought disillusionment. But so did South Africa's attempt to secure peace with another of her neighbours, Angola, a peace which it was hoped would finally lead to independence for Africa's last remaining colony – Namibia.

CHAPTER 12

A Mirage in the Desert
Namibia's elusive search for peace

On the night of 22 May 1985 Angola's Marxist government announced that a South African commando unit had been surprised while attempting to blow up an American-owned oil refinery in the northernmost province of Cabinda, a coastal enclave separated from the body of Angola by the Congo River and a narrow strip of Zairean territory. Two of the commandos had been killed, several had escaped and one was captured, said the Angolans.

In Pretoria a defence force spokesman promptly denied the Angolan statement. But the following day the story changed. Even though South Africa had announced in April that all its troops had withdrawn from Angolan territory following previous incursions, the armed forces chief General Constand Viljoen was forced to admit that South Africa still had units inside Angola. They were not saboteurs, he contended, but an undercover intelligence team gathering information on the Angolan bases of the African National Congress and of the South West African People's Organization (SWAPO), fighting South Africa's occupation of South West Africa/ Namibia, the contested territory separating South Africa and Angola. (South West Africa is the South African name for the territory while the United Nations refers to it as Namibia.)

Several questions arose from the incident. Why was the alleged intelligence unit in Cabinda when, as far as was known, there were no ANC or SWAPO bases inside the enclave? If the unit had been en route to northern Angola (where there *are* bases) from Zaire, why pass through Cabinda which is crawling with Russian advisers and Cuban troops supporting the government? Had South Africa's

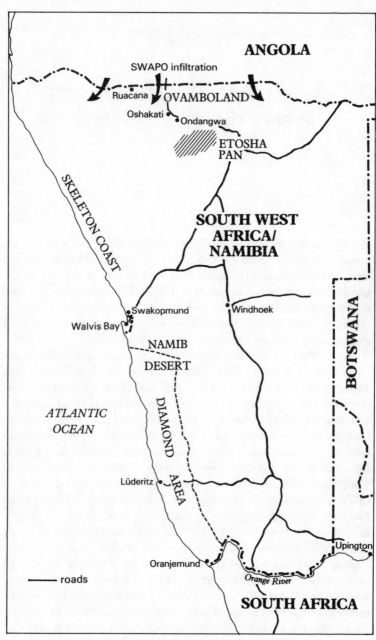

South West Africa/Namibia

Foreign Affairs Ministry been aware of the operation? Or was it a mission ordered by the generals without political clearance, another example of the well-known division between South Africa's military and political establishments?

If these kinds of questions were not embarrassing enough for Pretoria, the soldier who was captured by the Angolans, Captain Wynand du Toit, admitted before an Angolan-arranged news conference in the capital, Luanda, that the Angolan version of the episode was correct. He said his team had landed from a South African boat, that their task had been to blow up an oil refinery and to make it appear as though the South African-backed, anti-Marxist guerrilla army in Angola, UNITA (National Union for the Total Independence of Angola), led by the charismatic Jonas Savimbi, had been responsible. The South Africans maintained du Toit had been brainwashed, although that appeared unlikely given the short period between his capture and the news conference. South Africa said he was a member of a highly-trained unit along the lines of Britain's SAS (Special Air Service). But the fact he spilled the beans so quickly, whether or not he was under pressure, raised doubts about the quality of South Africa's crack commandos and of its intelligence-gathering. Initial reconnaissance for the mission had been carried out during the dry season when the grass was short, whereas the mission itself was mounted at the end of the rainy season when the bush was thick. The unit's trail through the undergrowth was spotted by a Soviet technician who pointed it out to the Angolans who then moved in for the ambush.

The incident aroused widespread international condemnation; South Africa was accused of being caught red-handed trying to destabilize a neighbouring black state; the incident again focused attention on Pretoria's continued occupation, in defiance of world opinion, of Africa's last colony, Namibia, whose destiny and that of Angola are inevitably intertwined.

Seized by the Germans during the nineteenth-century scramble for Africa by the colonial powers, Namibia is the final unresolved legacy of the German defeat in the First World War. The territory was placed under South African administration by a League of Nations mandate in 1920, although this was revoked by the United Nations in 1966. Since then, however, South Africa has refused to surrender the territory, fearing it would quickly have a hostile Marxist state on its borders. While international efforts to bring the territory to independence have been fruitless, a fierce bush war has been raging between SWAPO, fighting for Namibian liberation, and South Africa, determined to forestall a guerrilla takeover. Since it began in 1966 the war has cost over 500 South African lives while according to Pretoria, over 9,000 SWAPO insurgents have been killed or captured. It is one of the many tragedies of Africa's post-colonial history that a country so vast, so beautiful, and with such a diversity of peoples should have endured such a pitiless conflict.

It used to be submerged beneath the Atlantic Ocean. But now it is one of the most dramatic landscapes in the world: mile upon mile of desert suddenly rising up into great mountain ranges shaped like a row of dinner plates stacked in a washing-up rack. The Namib is one of the loneliest places on earth, a vast space of searing daytime temperatures and freezing nights, of crystal-clear skies yet raging sandstorms which obliterate everything in sight beyond a few yards.

Driving through the Namib desert, which comprises one-sixth of Namibia's land mass, from the territory's capital, Windhoek, to the Atlantic coast there emerges from the haze of heat and sand the outskirts of a town which, one soon discovers, seems oddly out of place with its surroundings. This is Swakopmund, the last outpost of the German colonial tradition in Africa.

The German influence is obvious in the suburbs with rows of palm trees along the pavements, regimentally spaced. The railway station appears to have been transplanted from Lower Saxony. Swakopmund looks like the film set for a movie about imperial Germany, were it not for the sun and the sand. The street names have an imperial echo as well. There is a Moltkestrasse and a Kaiser Wilhelm Strasse. The burghers of Swakopmund deny that they still celebrate the Kaiser's birthday. 'It just so happens that that is the day when the rains usually start, so we celebrate', says a local shopkeeper. But they do still sing 'Wir wollen den alten Kaiser Willi wieder haben' ('We want old Kaiser Willi back') along with other German volkslieder when they are in their *kleine Stuben* on a Friday night.

The town was founded in 1892 at the height of German colonization of South West Africa and soon became the main point of entry for German merchants and for the large number of troops who were sent to the colony to quash a revolt in 1904 by the Herero tribes-people who were reduced to 25,000 from 70,000, an extermination campaign which in ambition if not in size was on a par with the attempted annihilation of the Jews forty years later.

The outbreak of war in Europe in 1914 and the South African invasion of the German colony in support of the allies brought the troubles of a wider world to the doorstep of Swakopmund and the surrounding area. When the South Africans captured Swakopmund the townspeople resolutely refused to speak anything but German, a determination which hardened when the League of Nations granted South Africa the mandate for the territory. Despite its remoteness from Europe, Swakopmund continued to reflect faraway events, albeit in toytown fashion. In the 1930s a branch of the Nazi party was active and swastika flags were flown. During the Second World War the male population of the town was interned in South Africa, near Kimberley, and did not return until 1947. Today, as in West Germany, there is in this German enclave a fundamental abhorrence of nationalism. Seventy per cent of the white population of the town continue to speak German as their main language even though the younger generation have travelled further than their parents and are more exposed to English as an everyday language.

Less than half an hour's drive south from Swakopmund is the port enclave of Walvis Bay, another of the geographical anomalies resulting from colonial rule in Africa. The bay was seized by the British in 1878 in the name of Queen Victoria to counter Bismarck's colonial ambitions. When the Germans went ahead and took over South West Africa, the governor of the Cape Colony, in what was then British-ruled South Africa, annexed Walvis Bay. It is now part of South Africa proper even though it lies some 500 miles north of the nearest South African territory. Today it is a dreary, depressed place. The mayor of Walvis Bay, Christo de Jaager, bemoans the destruction of the port's fishing industry by Russian trawlers. Apartheid exists in the enclave (it being part of South Africa) while across the border from Walvis Bay it does not. South Africa's race laws have been phased out in Namibia as a prelude to independence for the territory, whenever that might happen. If it happens then Walvis Bay could figure prominently in the negotiations. South Africa is certain to retain the enclave as a lever against any future, hostile government in an independent Namibia. It is the main port handling freight for Namibia and the South Africans would be certain to bargain hard over it.

The British occupation of Walvis Bay did not however halt the German colonization of the territory. The Germans founded the capital, Windhoek, in 1890. Today the city is a curious mixture of black Africa, South Africa and Germany. The colour is provided by the Herero women wearing their expansive, multi-coloured dresses and queerly-shaped headgear like upturned Napoleonic hats. They mingle with white South African soldiers on leave from border duty. The German influence is there in the coffee houses where local politicians meet to discuss how to resolve the problems of the territory which, with only one million inhabitants, is one of the most sparsely-populated countries in the world. The ethnic groups include a mixed-race people known as Bastars (literally 'bastards'), a name of which they are proud, insisting that whereas the mixed-race coloureds of South Africa are the result of unions between whites and slaves, the Bastars are descended from relationships between whites and noble African women. The whites of Namibia are also divided ethnically, including German, English-speaking and Afrikaner communities. There is a branch of South Africa's National Party in Windhoek which is even more nationalist than its mother party.

Namibia is not a rich country. The territory has a very narrow economic base and is supported by an annual subvention from Pretoria which would be called into question in the event of Namibia becoming independent. The wealth which Namibia does enjoy, much like that of its minder, lies beneath the ground. South Africa's gold accounts for almost half its foreign earnings; Namibia's income is from diamonds along the territory's coastline and to a lesser extent from uranium. But many of the mineral deposits are not commercially exploitable and the reason they *have* been extracted is the long tax holiday which the mining companies have enjoyed in the past. A visit to one of the diamond excavation sites – Oranjemund – just north of the South African border reveals the ferocity of the landscape, the scale of the mining operation and the wealth that is found there. Oranjemund (literally, mouth of the Orange River) lies in one of the most inhospitable places on earth: bleak, unrelenting sand dunes and fierce winds off the sea causing sand storms up to 100 miles inland. Further north the landscape is even more remote and hostile. It was while constructing a railway line inland from the bay of Lüderitz that German excavators first discovered the glistening stone beneath the sand which would make the area the richest source of gem-quality diamonds in the world.

The discovery of diamonds in South West Africa, like the gold finds in Johannesburg, set off a klondike rush. German prospectors poured in; German financiers put up the capital. The Germans were eventually seen off both by the South African seizure of the territory and by the collapse of the German currency in the Depression. The mining companies subsequently merged to form Consolidated Diamond Mines, a subsidiary of the giant de Beers company, which is in turn linked to Anglo American. The CDM/de Beers/Anglo American tie-up comprises one of the most formidable business empires in the world.

De Beers mines within a huge concessionary area known as the Sperrgebiet (forbidden zone) which extends along the so-called Diamond Coast and which is sealed off to outsiders. The mining camps are self-contained, no vehicles are allowed to leave the fenced-off areas and workers are screened whenever they leave.

At Oranjemund a huge sea wall is being built which will push the sea back by up to 200 yards to enable diggers to get down to bedrock where diamonds are lodged. Once the bedrock is dug out it is then ground into even smaller pieces until the actual diamonds are sorted with tweezers under top-security conditions. Over 35,000 tonnes of bedrock are removed here each day at the end of which de Beers can boast another dinner-plateful of diamonds, a profit of $78,000 per day after tax. De Beers, through its own Central Selling Organization, controls 80 per cent of the world's diamond sales including most of the gems put onto the market by the Soviet Union.

The recent decline in the diamond market has meant that production has fallen from two million carats in 1977 to 930,183 carats during 1984. De Beers' tax contribution to the Namibian exchequer has consequently slipped from 50 per cent to 12 per cent. However, a commission of inquiry is investigating charges that de Beers deliberately stripped Namibia of its most valuable diamonds during the 1960s and 1970s and stockpiled them abroad as a hedge against the territory becoming independent under a Marxist government intent on nationalizing the diamond-mining industry. The prospect, however remote at present, of a communist government means de Beers, perhaps more than most, is observing political developments in the territory closely.

Watching developments equally attentively is the London-based Rio Tinto Zinc company which owns the Rossing uranium mine in northern Namibia, the largest open-cast uranium mine in the world. Developed during the early 1970s at the time of the worldwide drive towards nuclear power, Rossing's share of RTZ's profits reached about 26 per cent in 1982, although it has slipped back since then, partly due to the question mark hanging over the nuclear energy industry following the alert at Three Mile Island in the United States and partly because of the sensitive political position the company has acquired through operating in the territory. Rossing mines and sells uranium from South West Africa in defiance of a 1974 United Nations ruling that no minerals should be extracted from the territory without UN permission. Rossing has been the target of a campaign in Britain aimed at urging countries to cancel all contracts for the purchase of uranium from South West Africa. SWAPO has threatened to hold companies like Rossing liable for reparations, if independence comes, for 'stealing' the country's natural resources.

It was not until 1960 that a Namibian liberation movement became established. Two factors provided the impetus for SWAPO's emergence: a wave of nationalism sweeping the whole of Africa, and the Odendaal Plan of 1964 under which Pretoria sought to introduce apartheid-style homelands in South West Africa, with whites enjoying most of the land. SWAPO, founded in 1960, began its bush war in northern Namibia in 1966. The war has steadily increased in scale, with SWAPO fighters annually infiltrating Namibia from their Angolan bases during the rainy season for a spring offensive. SWAPO units benefit from the vast area that the South Africans need to watch and they rely on the support of the Ovambo tribespeople whose territory straddles the border between Namibia and Angola. SWAPO's campaign has tied up large numbers of South African and Namibian troops on the northern border, and border towns like Ruacana, Oshakati and Ondangwa are virtually armed camps. In the operational area the 'boys on the border' (South African troops) travel in air force planes and helicopters flying at tree-top level to avoid ground-to-air fire and in armed convoys on the roads. At night searchlights on the armoured vehicles sweep the road for potential ambushes.

The South Africans have a specialist undercover unit to track down the enemy guerrillas and eliminate them. The unit is known as 'Koevoet' (crowbar) whose officers include former Rhodesian Selous Scouts who operated previously on the side of Ian Smith's government against the guerrillas fighting Rhodesia's white rulers. The bulk of the force, though, are blacks from northern Namibia. They are experts in bush-tracking, so that most of their operations involve picking up the trail of SWAPO infiltrators and pursuing them until they can be eliminated. They boast of their 'kill rate'. Much of their intelligence, of course, comes from the local population against whom Koevoet has been accused of committing atrocities. In May 1982 a report was published by the Southern African Catholic Bishops' Conference following a visit to the territory by a six-man team led by Archbishop Hurley. The team reported that they had found a pervading fear of the security forces and that they had spoken to civilians who alleged beatings, torture and solitary confinement. South Africa complains that atrocities committed by SWAPO are given little attention: for example, bombs placed in public places like post offices or in garages which kill innocent civilians.

Whatever its record of conduct, Koevoet has proved effective in controlling the flow of SWAPO special forces into northern Namibia. Very often though, South Africa has struck across the border into Angola itself to attack SWAPO bases. Such operations have plunged the South African forces into the cauldron of Angolan politics, setting the military against not only SWAPO but also the Cubans, the East Germans and the Soviets, and thrusting Pretoria into superpower politics. Angola has become a chess board on which the various players in the southern African game make their moves.

Angola is potentially the granary of Africa. Once a food-exporter, the country is now believed to be importing around 90 per cent of its food requirements. Its agriculture has been devastated by the civil war with UNITA and by appalling mismanagement. Rich in diamonds and oil, the country is having to spend 70 per cent of its economic resources on defence. The country's leader, President Eduardo dos Santos, lives in a fortified bunker in the capital, Luanda. His government can claim to control only eleven towns in the entire country. Without its Soviet and Cuban shields, the government would be overrun by UNITA. It is impossible to venture more than a few miles outside the capital for fear of ambush. The organs of state barely function. The food shelves are empty. The once-graceful streets are filthy.

Part of the reason is the state in which the Portuguese left the country in 1975, but by far the worst devastation has been caused by the bitter civil war which broke out after the collapse of the shaky post-independence coalition comprising the Marxist MPLA (People's

Movement for the Liberation of Angola), the pro-western UNITA under Savimbi and the smaller, less effective FNLA (National Front for the Liberation of Angola). It was the FNLA which recruited a group of British and American mercenaries led by the notorious Costas Georgiou (alias Colonel Callan). Callan ordered the execution of fourteen of his men for 'insubordination' before being captured in 1976 and himself executed by an MPLA firing squad along with three fellow-mercenaries. Another thirteen (ten British and three Americans) were sentenced to long terms of imprisonment in Angolan jails but were released in small groups until the last of them was set free in 1984. At the outbreak of the civil war the MPLA called on the Soviets and Cubans for help. A few weeks later South Africa, privately encouraged by the United States, sent its columns into Angola, advancing so far north that they could see the lights of Luanda. The Americans, coming under domestic pressure, got cold feet and withdrew their tacit support from the South Africans who were left high and dry politically and finally staged a strategic withdrawal. Savimbi had meanwhile tactfully withdrawn to the fastness of his stronghold in the south-eastern wilderness of Angola. From there he was able to build up his forces till today they claim to control one-third of the country and are fighting once again for UNITA to have a share in government.

Since the South African intervention in the Angolan independence war its forces have launched major operations at various targets in Angola almost every year. Those which were publicly disclosed were:

- Operation Reindeer, May 1978. An attack on SWAPO bases in southern Angola. This was followed by reprisal shelling by SWAPO and the Zambian National Defence Force of the Caprivi strip (the pointing finger of Namibia which meets Zambia and Zimbabwe close to the Victoria Falls).
- Operation Sceptic, June 1980. A South African force thrust 90 miles into southern Angola and destroyed a major SWAPO base.
- Operation Klipkop, July 1980. A small attack on SWAPO headquarters at Chitado.
- Operations Carnation, Protea and Daisy, 1981. In Protea 4,000 South African troops swooped on a SWAPO force, killing 1,200.

- Operation Super, January 1982, and Operation Mebos, August 1982. Both targeted on SWAPO transit camps or forward bases.

One of the largest operations by South African forces in southern Angola began a couple of weeks before Christmas 1983 and shocked South African military planners into considering the consequences of future involvement inside Angola.

Throughout 1983 the civil war in Angola had intensified. UNITA made several advances, blowing up sections of railway lines, destroying locomotives and wagons, attacking hydro-electric projects, and gradually advancing into the diamond-mining region of north-eastern Angola. UNITA was edging closer to Luanda, attacking town after town, though not being able to hold them. An Angolan airliner was shot down shortly after take off from Lubango in the south-west of the country; among the casualties were Angolan and Cuban officers. UNITA intelligence officers claimed that the organization had 20,000 guerrillas and 20,000 'semi-regulars' deployed against the MPLA's army. Along the eastern side of Angola a 'Savimbi trail' exploited the network of bush roads to carry supplies north of the Benguela railway to the front lines. But UNITA suffered from a lack of airpower and its forces remained vulnerable to attacks by Soviet MIG-21s. Nevertheless the UNITA offensive posed a serious threat to the Luanda government. Concerned that its Marxist client was about to be toppled, the Soviet Union moved quickly. In September 1983 Moscow began pouring arms into Luanda. In the city's harbour ten Soviet freighters were unloading weapons around the clock, including Russian-made T62 tanks, helicopters, spare parts for fighter planes, surface-to-air missiles, transportable bridges and other weapons. In November the Soviet Union told South Africa that its continued occupation of southern Angola was unacceptable. Reports also suggested that the Soviets had warned South Africa that any attempt to overthrow the MPLA government and replace it with UNITA would not be tolerated by Moscow. The Soviet message to Pretoria followed a visit to Moscow by a high-level Angolan delegation which had outlined the seriously deteriorating situation in Luanda. At that stage, however, the South African government was not exceptionally perturbed by the Soviet threat or by the military build-up, believing that the Cubans and their Soviet advisers would mount only token resistance to attacks against SWAPO forces. But events proved them wrong.

Shortly before Christmas 1983 a report by the officially-controlled Angolan news agency claimed that South African Mirage and Buccaneer aircraft had launched an eight-hour bombing attack on the southern Angolan town of Caiundo. The report claimed that dozens of the inhabitants of the town were killed and a hospital and a school destroyed. A spokesman for the South African Defence Force dismissed the claim, saying there was no point in reacting to 'repetitive allegations'. But then on 23 December South African defence chief General Constand Viljoen announced that units were carrying out a 'limited operation' inside Angola aimed at wiping out pockets of SWAPO forces along the main infiltration routes into Namibia. In fact there is evidence that the operation had far wider ambitions than those of a 'limited' action and that among the possible objectives was the capture of the town of Lubango (an MPLA, SWAPO and Cuban headquarters 150 miles inside Angola) and even a full-frontal attack on the capital, Luanda, almost 600 miles across the border, though this idea was scotched by the doves within the military establishment. As things turned out, even the 'limited operation' proved tough going for the South Africans. The South West Africa Territory Force (the Namibian armed forces) announced that five of its soldiers had been killed in action and that one was missing, presumed dead. The bodies were coming home and so South Africa had to make public details of the military operation known as 'Askari'.

As news of the operation gradually seeped out over Christmas and the New Year, it became clear that Askari was bringing the South Africans into greater contact with the Angolan army, the Cubans and Warsaw Pact technicians than ever before. A major battle lasting four days took place at the town of Cuvelai 100 miles inside Angola. A combined force of Angolan and SWAPO units joined two battalions of Cubans pounding away at a South African position. The result, according to General Viljoen, was that 324 Angolans, SWAPO and Cubans had been killed and that seven South African soldiers had died. The South Africans fought their way determinedly out of the ambush but the engagement provided a foretaste of the enemy in southern Angola. By 10 January the number of South African dead had risen to twenty-one, the highest since the 1975 invasion. It had been a sobering experience for the South Africans whose unchallenged military control over southern Angola could no longer be taken for granted.

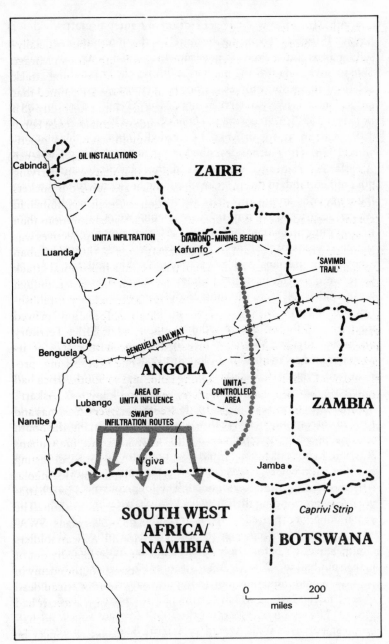

Angola 1983

South Africa needs a new generation of fighter aircraft which it is having difficulty acquiring because of the international ban on selling arms to the Pretoria government: its planes are now vulnerable to Soviet-made SAM missiles. Without control of the skies, the safety of the ground forces cannot be guaranteed especially as the Soviet Union is likely to ferry in more MIG-23s piloted by Cubans to bolster the MPLA. According to *Jane's Defence Weekly* (4 December 1984) Cuban troops in Angola exceeded 30,000 for the first time since 1976. The journal described the main aims of the Cubans in Angola as 'securing the position of the Marxist-oriented MPLA government and, in doing so, maintaining Soviet interests; developing Angola as an advance base for Soviet domination of southern Africa; securing work for otherwise unemployed Cubans and thereby providing an income for Cuba.' The Cuban presence in Africa as a whole stretched to eighteen countries, said *Jane's*, most of them acting as 'technicians' and 'advisers'. *Jane's* estimated that in Angola there were sixteen motorized infantry regiments, varying between 1,300 and 1,600 men, totalling 23,600 personnel; one anti-aircraft brigade of 500 men; one medium artillery regiment of about 975 men; about 500 air force personnel; about 1,000 military advisers and instructors and about 400 men involved in support services such as maintenance, medical, and logistical back-up.

In future the MPLA is likely to have more assistance from Soviet and East German technicians and advisers. In January 1984, as South Africa was scaling down its military operation in Angola, foreign correspondents were flown by helicopter into the area which was being vacated. Intelligence officers put on display captured Russian handbooks, maps and diagrams found in underground bunkers from where, it was concluded, the battles against the South Africans had been master-minded. The long convoys of armoured vehicles were winding their way back south, carrying with them the vast number of captured weapons, including three grenade launchers of a type which, according to South African officers, the Soviet Union had used before only in Afghanistan but which were now being supplied to SWAPO. At an air force base in northern Namibia we saw the mounted tailfin of an Impala fighter with a SAM missile lodged in the frame, which fortunately for the pilot had not exploded. The lesson of Askari for the South Africans was that future involvement in Angola would cost more lives and need greater firepower.

Perhaps with this in mind the South Africans signalled to the Angolans in December 1985 that they would withdraw totally from the south of the country provided the MPLA was prepared to rein in SWAPO. Negotiations resulted in a signed agreement in Lusaka in February 1984, under which South Africa and Angola agreed to create a Joint Monitoring Commission (JMC) to oversee the disengagement of forces and the withdrawal of South African troops. The Americans offered to liaise. Despite co-operation on the ground between the units from both countries, the withdrawal of South African troops took considerably longer than had been contemplated. Pretoria considered that there were elements within the Angolan army who, far from curtailing SWAPO's activities, were actively assisting them to regroup. A number of alleged violations of the disengagement agreement were reported to the JMC. Slowly, though, the South Africans pulled back until they reached the town of Ngiva, just 20 miles inside the Angolan border, where they remained, only a small token force but nevertheless infringing the restored sovereignty over the country which the MPLA hoped for after the Lusaka agreement. Also, there seemed little doubt that Pretoria wanted to keep at least one political card up its sleeve in the wider negotiations over Angola and Namibia. In the end, it was probably American pressure that compelled South Africa to complete the withdrawal. It was perhaps no coincidence that the final pull-out came in the same week that the American State Department expert on southern Africa Dr Chester Crocker was under fire before his critics on the House of Representatives Committee on Africa because of the Reagan administration's policy of maintaining friendly dialogue with Pretoria, and in the week that the Secretary of State George Schultz was to deliver a major address on southern Africa. The completion of the withdrawal has not, however, led to the elusive breakthrough in the search for peaceful independence for Namibia, a search which has now occupied the diplomatic community for two decades and which has defeated everyone who has become involved in it.

The long-running saga of Namibia has what, on paper, appears to the uninitiated as the perfect answer to the territory's problems. The document is United Nations Security Council Resolution 435. It is based on a letter to the president of the Security Council dated 10 April 1978 from the permanent representatives to the UN of Canada,

France, West Germany, Britain and the United States, the five nations who form the 'contact group' which since 1978 has tried to ease Namibia towards independence. The document includes a detailed independence timetable under which South Africa and SWAPO would stage a gradual withdrawal of their forces from Namibia, under United Nations supervision, paving the way for elections for a constituent assembly, a process which, it was visualized, would be completed within about four months. Eight years later the participants in the proposed plan are not even on their starting blocks.

South Africa co-operated on the drawing up of 435, which has since become the diplomatic benchmark regarding Namibia, but did not really have its heart in it. Pretoria suspected that the United Nations (from whose General Assembly South Africa was expelled in 1974 and which Pretoria regards as a theatre of hypocrisy) would not be sufficiently impartial to supervise independence elections. There was concern on the part of South Africa about the General Assembly's recognition of SWAPO as the 'sole authentic representative' of the Namibian people. Pretoria's view was this: how could any organization which ascribed to itself the right to determine who speaks for whom in any given country be trusted to see fair play in the run-up to Namibian independence?

Progress towards independence turned into another blind alley when in 1981 Washington suddenly raised the spectre of the Cuban presence in neighbouring Angola. State Department officials calculated that if the US could get the Cubans out of Angola, Pretoria would 'go for 435' and thereby provide the newly-installed Reagan administration with an early foreign policy success. The South Africans, though sceptical about Washington's chances of pulling it off, went along with the idea; in fact the American suggestion was like manna from heaven, providing a further delaying tactic. Thus was born the concept of 'linkage' and it still underpins American and South African policy towards Namibia, i.e. no independence for the territory until there is agreement on the Cubans withdrawing from Angola. The South Africans have capitalized on the American introduction of the Cuban factor by constructing a whole rationale for 'linkage'. Its thrust is that free and fair elections in Namibia cannot be possible if just across the border there are thousands of Soviet puppets threatening the Namibian people. Pretoria feels that just as many black Rhodesians voted for Mugabe simply to end the bush war, so Namibians would feel compelled to vote for SWAPO otherwise there would be no peace, as the Cuban presence across the border would remind them.

Pending a solution to the Cuban withdrawal issue, South Africa has tried to build up a credible alternative to SWAPO among what it sees as moderate parties in Namibia. The first attempt at this came in 1977 when a grouping of eleven political parties (one for each ethnic group) came together to form the Democratic Turnhalle Alliance (DTA), winning 80 per cent of the vote in the election which was held in December 1978. (Turnhalle means 'gymnasium' in German; it was the Windhoek gymnasium where they met.) However SWAPO and other important parties boycotted the election. The DTA performed less well in later elections and the Alliance was soon reduced to five ethnic parties. In January 1983 its leader and chairman of the council of ministers Dirk Mudge resigned and a South African-appointed administrator-general took over the running of the territory. Later that year a new, broader alliance of parties called the Multi-Party Conference (MPC) was established, though again SWAPO and at least one other important party remained outside. The MPC, SWAPO and the South Africans (in the shape of the administrator-general) were brought together in Lusaka in mid-May 1984 for what appeared to be an encouraging breakthrough in the diplomatic impasse. Pressure on SWAPO to attend the talks and to sit down with Namibian parties which, in SWAPO's eyes, had no legitimacy came from both the Angolans, who viewed SWAPO's continued hostile acts against South Africa as an invitation to further military action by Pretoria, and from President Kaunda of Zambia who, indirectly, was in touch with all sides and who feared more violence if the Namibian question was unsettled. For its part, the South African government wanted SWAPO to ditch its military campaign and join the political process inside Namibia. Pretoria had even gone so far as to release the founding father of the Namibian freedom movement, Herman Toivo ja Toivo, who was serving a twenty-year prison term on Robben Island. South Africa calculated that the return of Toivo into SWAPO ranks might introduce a more moderate element and encourage the organization towards talks. In fact, Toivo was so suspicious of South Africa's motives in releasing him that he virtually had to be dragged out through the prison gates. There is little evidence that he has influenced SWAPO thinking since his release, nor has he mounted a challenge to the leadership of Sam

Nujoma who is seen by South Africa as little more than a Soviet stooge.

The Lusaka conference was also part of another major plank of South Africa's policy on Namibia: to try to find an independence agreement which would find favour with a number of black African leaders (especially Kaunda) and which could side-step the deeply-mistrusted UN plan. The conference did, in fact, achieve a great deal; the very fact that SWAPO and the MPC were attending the same negotiations was in itself a step forward. But in the end it broke down following divisions within the MPC and after reports that a Soviet diplomat had put strong pressure on Nujoma not to concede any-thing, especially as far as 435 was concerned.

Following the failure of the talks, Pretoria turned once more to boosting the status of the MPC, with P.W. Botha announcing in early 1985 that Namibia was to have an 'interim administration' of its own. In effect, this was a return to the days of the DTA administra-tion and, despite the howls of anguish from the West about South Africa going for a 'UDI-style' solution, the devolvement of power hardly mattered in terms of the territory's future. Certainly it served as a warning from Pretoria that it was not prepared to wait for ever for SWAPO to switch from the military to the political option, and that the interim government was intended to strengthen the position of the MPC. But South Africa knows that a Pretoria-imposed solution to the Namibian question will not be accepted interna-tionally and will not end the bush war.

While Pretoria has been tinkering with the Namibian issue, the Americans, through the indefatigable Crocker, have been mediating between Pretoria and Luanda on the Cuban withdrawal. Something of a breakthrough occurred when Crocker won from the Angolan leader dos Santos a conditional agreement to send the Cubans home. Not the least of dos Santos' considerations in making this offer is the fact that the MPLA does not get the Cubans free – it has to pay Havana for them: one reason, perhaps, why President Castro is not over-keen to withdraw them. Talks in the Cape Verde Islands between the United States, South Africa and Angola resulted in Pretoria and Luanda each coming up with a timetable linking a Cuban withdrawal with the implementation of Resolution 435. The two timetables were far apart. South Africa wanted the Cubans out within weeks of the start of the implementation of the UN plan. The Angolan proposals foresaw a partial Cuban withdrawal over three years and even then 15,000 were to remain to guard Luanda and the country's oil installations.

The two sides are too far apart at present to pull off a compromise especially as Reagan's policy of friendly dialogue or 'constructive engagement' towards South Africa is under assault from opposite directions in Washington. From the left, the anti-apartheid lobby is claiming ever more loudly that the policy has brought little change to South Africa's internal policies, and that Pretoria still seems unprepared to scale down its involvement beyond its borders. From the right, Crocker is accused by men like the right-wing Republican Senator Jesse Helms of being 'soft on communism' and is advised that America's interests would be best served by giving stronger support to South Africa and its protégés in the region. Crocker's negotiating style is like an academic exercise in diplomacy which concentrates on nuances rather than the broader picture. For example, the attempt to bring South Africa and Angola together is fine but at what point do the diplomats start tackling the question of UNITA? Crocker's approach seems to assume that once Pretoria and Luanda have struck a deal, UNITA simply becomes an internal matter to be dealt with by the Angolans. But is a wider settlement possible unless UNITA is included in the negotiations at the start?

It would be foolish to underestimate the degree of respect which South Africa has for the UNITA leader, Jonas Savimbi, a respect which was shown by the invitation to him to attend the swearing-in of P.W. Botha as state president. South Africa may well have ditched its other protégé, RENAMO, but there is little sign at present that it would do the same with UNITA. The military in Pretoria accepts that Savimbi is unlikely to win the civil war outright by seizing and holding Luanda, but it feels that at the very least he is entitled to a share in a coalition government. China, Saudi Arabia, Morocco and Zaire also support UNITA.

From time to time Savimbi invites foreign correspondents to his camp at Jamba in south-eastern Angola. Many of these visits coincide with the freeing of foreign hostages captured by UNITA during its advances into the diamond-mining region where foreign technicians are employed. One such visit took place in May 1984 when Savimbi released sixteen British hostages. The flight to Jamba lasting five hours is on an ageing Dakota which often has to be given a push to get it started on the return leg. On landing at a remote bush air strip, a UNITA lieutenant welcomes you with orange juice and lunch. After 'immigration formalities' the party climbs into the back of a captured Soviet lorry for the thirteen-hour ride (recently cut to two hours after a second air strip was opened) over bumpy dirt roads to the Jamba HQ. Visitors are accommodated in immaculately clean thatched huts known as rondavels. South African wine is served as well as piping hot Irish stew.

Before the hostages are produced journalists are normally given a tour of the camp, including the hospital and the weapons factory where UNITA members, often assisted by their children, strip down captured Angolan weapons ready for use by UNITA forces. Savimbi also likes to put on a cultural evening for visiting correspondents. It is usually at the end of the festivities that Savimbi formally releases his hostages and they hold a news conference conducted by a young, western-educated UNITA brigadier who speaks fluent English. Most of the captives recount the long march through the Angolan bush following their capture to Jamba: the sore feet, the swamps, the endless trudge often in darkness, the danger of attack from Angolan helicopter gunships.

From what one observes at Jamba, UNITA appears to be an impressive force. It is not a here-today-gone-tomorrow renegade army. It has a solid base of support among the Angolan tribes including the Kimbundu (which once supported the MPLA), the Chokwe, the Songo and the Sele. On the other hand, there have been reports of tribal divisions within UNITA's ranks leading to several defections to the MPLA.

UNITA's strategy is to hit hard at the diamond-mining region so as to strangle the Angolan economy and to force the MPLA to the negotiating table. It also plans to step up its attacks on the Cabinda refineries. It is one of the ironies of Angolan politics that the country's Marxist government receives 90 per cent of its foreign earnings from oil produced by the American Chevron/Gulf company, whose installations are guarded by Soviet technicians and Cuban troops.

The South African commando operation into Cabinda raised doubts about the continuation of the talks between Pretoria and Angola and provided Dr Crocker with a headache he could well have done without. Indeed Angola announced in July 1985 that it was severing its contacts with Washington after Congress voted to resume funds to UNITA, a move which signalled a much tougher anti-Marxist stance by the US.

So eight years after the UN drew up the 435 peace plan for Namibia, during which time South Africa has tried to counter SWAPO by boosting the internal parties and the issue has been further complicated by the Cuban presence in Angola, what are the prospects for peaceful independence for the territory?

Most of South Africa's political leaders genuinely want to shed the country's responsibility for the territory, for a number of reasons. First, there is the cost. In 1983–4 South Africa contributed R241 million to the Namibian exchequer; in addition most of the territory's defence costs are met from the South African budget. Then there is the cost in terms of lives, seventy-seven members of the security forces dying during 1982 for example. Finally, there is a simple sense of weariness that South Africa is still burdened with the Namibian problem. Pretoria feels that it is all very well for the West to complain about South Africa stalling on a settlement, but how would the West itself like to 'take over the whole shooting-match and sort it out' as one official once put it to me. This mood of total frustration was summed up by P.W. Botha in a speech in early 1984 when he asked:

> Can it be expected from the Republic of South Africa to continue to bear this burden under circumstances where we don't claim sovereignty over the territory, where we are exposed to criticism from the internal parties of South West Africa, where we are severely condemned by the West and where the United Nations is threatening us with enforcement measures?

But South Africa is not about to throw in the towel, to surrender Namibia at any price. Barring unforeseeable circumstances Pretoria will never allow Namibia to be 'liberated' by SWAPO units marching into Windhoek as the guerrilla armies arrived in triumph in Salisbury during the winding-down of Ian Smith's illegal régime in Rhodesia. An unconditional pull-out from the territory is at present unthinkable. For a start, it would be resisted by the South African military who are not prepared to pull back the frontiers keeping out the perceived communist threat. It would be seized upon by the right wing in South Africa, who would capitalize on it. It would be read in the black townships of South Africa that Pretoria's white rulers had capitulated, that the will to govern had weakened and that only a final push was required to bring about black majority rule.

All in all, then, it is deadlock. Nobody is prepared to move. But then some of the parties involved may not be unhappy that the situation remains unresolved. The United States would like to get the Cubans out of Angola in order to register a moderately significant foreign policy success. But given that many Americans do not even know where Angola is, the United States administration is not going to risk a showdown with the Soviet Union over the issue and jeopardize co-operation on what are, for the US, far more important questions like arms control. The Soviet Union is probably quite happy with the way the conflict is ticking over at present. The MPLA may be in serious straits but regular topping-up with Soviet weapons should enable it to stave off UNITA, while Angola gives Moscow an important toehold in southern Africa. The Kremlin will not be contemplating an immediate assault, through its clients, on South Africa itself. It realizes that this would be suicidal, that Pretoria is a formidable regional power that is not about to be toppled. Moscow has learned from experience the dangers in backing proxy states and liberation movements in Africa. The late President Sadat expelled all his Soviet advisers in 1972 and then sought help from the West, Somalia switched allegiance in similar fashion in 1977, and in the Rhodesian bush war Moscow backed the wrong horse by supporting Nkomo and not the eventual victor Mugabe, who originally obtained his assistance from Communist China. So Africa is not an area of the world where the Soviet Union is likely to take risks. But it will be calculating that circumstances in ten, fifteen, or twenty years from now could change, could be more susceptible to Soviet expansion. The Soviets are prepared to play the waiting game.

As for South Africa, despite the shocks it received in Operation Askari, it still feels confident that it can handle itself militarily in the region. Consequently it believes it can hold out for the best possible deal over Namibia.

UNITA is well dug in throughout much of Angola and can turn to South Africa for help when a reverse is threatened. This is believed to have happened in September 1985 when Pretoria launched a one-week-long incursion into southern Angola, saying publicly it was to seek out SWAPO pockets, although there was little doubt the mission was in aid of hard-pressed UNITA guerrillas facing an intensified Angolan offensive taking place at that time. The MPLA has little choice but to continue the war against UNITA. Any attempt to negotiate with Savimbi, or to conclude a deal with the Americans to the detriment of the Soviet Union, would probably lead to the removal (or worse) of the Angolan leadership and their replacement with politicians more loyal to Moscow.

Surveying newspaper headlines about Namibia over the past decade it is staggering how many commentators have been seduced into believing that meaningful progress is taking place. 'UN claims new breakthrough in Namibian talks', 'Crocker punts new SWA deal', 'Looming watershed in Namibia's future', 'Namibia moves inch-by-inch towards independence' are just a few examples. Inch-by-inch progress it may well be. The trouble is that no sooner are a few steps of progress made than someone moves the finishing tape back further or transfers the race onto a different track altogether. Nevertheless, the failure to bring Namibia to independence has combined with South Africa's internal upheavals to give a new lease of life to the campaign, particularly in the United States, in support of economic sanctions against the Pretoria government.

CHAPTER 13

Turning the Screw
The American call for sanctions

Edward Kennedy, the liberal American senator whose brother Robert had triumphantly toured South Africa in the early 1960s, was shaken. A fighter for black rights in his own country, he had flown to Johannesburg to join the struggle for political freedom for the blacks living under apartheid. But what was this? Black demonstrators on the airport concourse shouting 'Kennedy go home'? The anti-apartheid bandwagon on which he had jumped assumed a united black struggle against the white minority government. Yet here were some of the subjugated black masses shouting at their 'champion' to forget it and return home. Was there more to the South African situation than the anti-apartheid voices back home had led him to believe?

Mounting American hostility towards South Africa which began in late 1984 had more to do with American politics than with events inside South Africa. The United States has always had a small and ineffectual anti-apartheid movement compared, say, to that in Britain. The London office of the African National Congress is the organization's most important bureau overseas. It serves as a centre for co-ordinating the propaganda campaign against the South African government both through the dissemination of literature and the organization of frequent demonstrations outside the South African embassy and elsewhere. South African security authorities believe that the London office is also the base from which white ANC members or sympathizers are sent into South Africa to reconnoitre possible targets for insurgency missions. Over the years there have been several bomb attacks on the ANC's office in London and these have been attributed by British security officials to South African government agents. The British capital is also the city in which large numbers of South African refugees are gathered. Several white exiles (journalists, political activists, etc.) among them devote their lives to expounding the views of the anti-apartheid lobby to a wider international audience, mainly in Europe, but with only limited success in the United States where the South African issue has rarely stirred the consciences of the liberal community. The anti-South African campaign in the US could boast few influential figures. The movement was not going to make much headway under its own steam; it needed a catalyst.

The catalyst appeared in the shape of Ronald Reagan's overwhelming second-term victory in the presidential election in 1984, which was a shattering blow for the defeated Democratic Party and also for the blacks who felt that Reagan's policies and his election platform had disregarded them. The blacks were also bitter that Walter Mondale had won the Democratic nomination over the black candidate, Jesse Jackson. For the blacks and for the demoralized Democratic Party as a whole South Africa became a unifying issue, rallying all sections of the party. It was a useful stick to beat the Reagan administration, whose policy of 'constructive engagement' towards South Africa was seen by Democrats as occasionally rapping Pretoria's knuckles while turning a blind eye to the country's apartheid policies and its destabilization of neighbouring states. South Africa did not help itself. Its police actions in quelling unrest in the townships, the detention of political and labour leaders, its attacks on neighbouring states and the delay in pulling out of Namibia fuelled the campaign.

The demonstrations began two weeks after Reagan's re-election on 6 November, most of them outside the South African embassy in Washington but soon spreading to other cities with South African consular offices. By late November there were protests almost daily in Washington. Several hundred people were arrested, many of them prominent figures. Early in 1985 the American soul singer Stevie Wonder dedicated his Oscar award for the score of the film *The Woman in Red* to Nelson Mandela. The South African Broadcasting Corporation promptly banned the Stevie Wonder record 'I Just Called To Say I Love You' from its airwaves, a controversial decision even by the SABC's standards of blatant support for the government. Another state-controlled organization, South African Airways, continued playing the song on its in-flight music channel, and independent radio stations ignored the ban.

On a more serious level, the anti-South African campaign on the streets of Washington could not continue for long without being reflected at congressional level where demands grew for the withdrawal of the $3 billion directly invested in South Africa by American companies. With a quarter of the congressional committees chaired by blacks, the South African question soon found itself near the top of the political agenda. Suddenly it was not just another foreign policy issue. South Africa's race policies had become a key ingredient of American domestic politics. It was not going to rise and fall like Nicaragua or Middle East terrorism. No matter that most Americans were grossly ill-informed about South Africa, or that many of them (blacks included) had little interest in events there. It was nevertheless the kind of issue which, cleverly exploited, could separate the good guys from the bad guys, and which could tap American emotions over their own experience in dispensing political freedoms to the blacks. The issue looked similar to the civil rights struggle of the black American. Few people stopped to ask whether white Americans, if they had been a minority like the whites of South Africa, would have handed power over to the blacks. No, the issue seemed clear-cut: white oppressors against freedom-seeking blacks. Around that all sections of the Democratic Party could unite. Indeed it soon became apparent that any contender for the presidency in 1988 would do well to use South Africa as a vote-catching issue in his or her election platform.

Certainly Edward Kennedy did. He identified what was clearly a rising issue and leaped onto it with the instinctive political skill his family is famous for. Although Kennedy at that stage had not declared himself a candidate for 1988 the possibility was open for his running for the White House. Consequently, South Africa was an issue to latch onto, easily comprehensible, and neatly encapsulated within the nightly television news programmes. Kennedy's trip to South Africa in January 1985 was, therefore, aimed at giving him television exposure as champion of South Africa's blacks. The Kennedy advance men, who arrived in Johannesburg a few days before the senator, denied vehemently that Kennedy was undertaking the trip as part of a 1988 election bid. 'Anyone who believes that presidential elections in America are decided over issues like South

Africa betrays limited understanding of American politics', they said. And, of course, they were right. The flaw in their argument was that the American presidential elections are decided less by individual political issues than by the candidates' appeal on television. Kennedy, looking at a possible run at the White House in 1988, wanted to get on record his association with the black cause in South Africa with film of Kennedy among smiling blacks grateful for his support. As things turned out, South Africans (black and white) quickly spotted what many of them thought was a phoney. What started out as a slick political operation ended in disaster.

The public relations débâcle at the airport was followed by another setback for the image-building aspect of the tour, when South African officials outmanœuvred Kennedy's aides who were trying to keep the news cameras away from their chief's meeting with Pik Botha. Kennedy had to see Botha to avoid charges that he was not prepared to listen to the government's view but the last thing he wanted was to be photographed shaking hands with a representative of the very régime which America's anti-apartheid movement was depicting as evil incarnate. The aides wanted to keep the media back but Botha's officials contrived to admit them as the two politicians emerged from their meeting, much to Kennedy's evident displeasure.

The senator did not take kindly either to the introduction afforded him by the US ambassador to South Africa, Herman Nickel, at the start of a lunchtime meeting with businessmen. Courteously but firmly, Nickel warned Kennedy about the dangers of launching into an anti-South African campaign:

> I remember only too vividly a dark period in our not-too-distant past when anyone who did not conform with a particular brand of anti-communism ran the risk of being labelled – and libelled – as being 'soft on communism'. We do not need a repeat of this sordid chapter with respect to our policy towards South Africa. The real issue is not who is 'soft on racism' but how the United States can best use its influence to advance the delicately interdependent process of peaceful change in South Africa itself and peaceful change in relations between South Africa and her neighbours.

Nickel issued a further warning to the effect that 'the success of our policies is not measured in decibels'. Stung by Nickel's introduction, which essentially represented Reagan's views on dealing with South

Africa, Kennedy got up and said: 'I would like to thank Ambassador Nickel for his opening remarks . . . I think.'

Later in the trip the senator had to force his way through a demonstration by black protestors blocking the entrance to a trade union office which Kennedy was scheduled to visit. They belonged to AZAPO, whose commitment to a class struggle in South Africa meant that they viewed Kennedy as just another American capitalist who saw the struggle for political rights in South Africa in the same terms as the civil rights movement in his own country, an analysis which they entirely rejected.

As the visit wore on one sensed that the South African government only had to sit back and enjoy the spectacle of Kennedy putting his foot in it. The senator tried to recover some ground at the Onver-wacht resettlement camp in the Orange Free State, a site to which blacks who have been forcibly removed from their homes are relocated. The area is a fairly squalid place and Kennedy clearly saw it as an opportunity for some political mileage. The unfortunate official who was there to brief him on why so many people were living in such dreadful conditions had had little experience of being thrust before the world's television cameras, let alone being confronted by a professional politician like Kennedy. He was torn to shreds by the senator in front of the cameras in a totally ruthless piece of theatre staged solely for the purpose of the American TV networks. The conditions at Onverwacht spoke for themselves; Kennedy's savaging of the official was not necessary and did not contribute to an understanding of the situation there. In Durban Kennedy managed to insult Chief Buthelezi. In Cape Town Kennedy quoted from the Bible to a largely coloured audience, many of whose members were probably Muslim. The Kennedy party then went on to the Namibian capital of Windhoek where, after just three hours in the city, Kennedy was pronouncing on what was required to bring the territory to independence. Back in Johannesburg, Kennedy's final rally at Regina Mundi church in Soweto had to be cancelled as his security men considered it unsafe for him to attend because of hundreds of AZAPO demonstrators in the audience.

The visit achieved something unique in South African political life. It placed the leftist AZAPO movement on the same side as the government mouthpiece, the South African Broadcasting Corporation, both accusing Kennedy of opportunism. In the population at large, black and white, there was a feeling that Kennedy, given his previous history, was in no position to lecture others on how they should conduct their affairs. As the *Financial Mail* put it in its front-page headline: 'He's teaching us morals?' The media hype which surrounded the trip was epitomized in a cartoon in the liberal *Rand Daily Mail* which depicted Kennedy, his arms raised aloft and wearing a 'Ted 1988' badge, declaring to his audience: 'I am pleased with this opportunity that the people have of meeting me' – except that the people surrounding him were all members of the news media.

Kennedy returned from his South African trip a confused man. He was less certain that South Africa was a political runner. It bore a tangled message, one which would perplex the American people. There were grey areas, and American politics does not feed easily on issues which are not simply perceived. Kennedy realized that the potential for ending up with egg on one's face was strong. He saw too that the Democratic party, if it was going to stand a chance of winning in 1988, needed to become more centrist. Jesse Jackson's idea of a 'rainbow coalition' representing all minority groups was fine rhetoric but did not win elections. An issue like South Africa, which appealed to the blacks and the left, was not going to appeal to the centre ground of American politics where elections are won. Therefore Kennedy wanted to back away from the South African issue. But as the weeks went by and the actions of the Pretoria government continued to attract international hostility, it was obvious that the South African issue was still providing considerable political mileage. In addition Kennedy was already locked into the campaign in support of a Senate bill calling for economic sanctions.

Fearing that they were being outflanked by the Democrats on the South African issue, sections of the Republican Party moved quickly to join the moral crusade against apartheid. Thirty-five right-wing Republican congressmen sent an open letter to the South African ambassador to the US warning that they would seek to change American policy towards Pretoria unless the situation in his country improved. But the right wing was split. The leader of the fundamentalist Moral Majority movement, the Reverend Jerry Falwell, returned from a South African visit urging American support for Botha's reform programme and describing Bishop Tutu as a 'phoney', a remark he later qualified. The split among Republicans ensured that they would be unable to halt Democratic moves towards passing sanctions legislation. On 1 August, against the familiar nightly background of television news coverage showing turmoil in the townships, the House of Representatives passed a sanctions bill by 380 votes to 48. Six weeks later the Senate was on the point of passing the bill also, thereby challenging the president to invoke a veto in order to protect his policy of 'constructive engagement'.

Sensing a damaging political defeat, Reagan pre-empted the Senate vote by introducing his own sanctions package in the shape of an executive order. Reagan had had to reverse his opposition to sanctions in deference to congressional pressure even though his measures were hardly punitive. The president announced a ban on all computer exports to South African government agencies enforcing apartheid; restrictions on exports of nuclear goods or technology to Pretoria; and a ban on all new loans to the South African government except those related to social and educational projects open to all races. He also directed the Secretary of State to consult with America's allies on banning imports of the South African gold coin, the Krugerrand. In addition Reagan urged US companies doing business in South Africa to conform to the so-called Sullivan principles.

Established in 1977 by the Reverend Leon Sullivan, a black preacher and a director of General Motors, the Sullivan Code of Employment Practices is aimed at removing apartheid from the workplace of American companies operating in South Africa. The code embraces the principles of shop-floor desegregation: equal pay for blacks and whites doing comparable work; improvements in black training programmes and promotion; and spending on better community services for the blacks. By March 1985, 128 out of 350 American corporations in South Africa had become signatories and had voluntarily agreed to report on their employment practices to a US monitoring agency. The code is officially endorsed by the US State Department and the member countries of the European Economic Community operate a similar code affecting European-based companies in South Africa.

The South African debate in the House and the Senate has been accompanied by similar moves at state and city level. 'Disinvestment' (i.e. the withdrawal by foreign companies of their South African investments) got off the ground in the early 1980s. Before that the anti-apartheid campaigners had had little success in mobilizing shareholders against business dealings with South Africa. So the approach changed. The targets became the black mayors in the cities, also the state legislatures where blacks and other minorities are represented. On the university campuses there was a rush to get rid of South African-related shares. But the major universities remained sceptical, referring the question of selling off shares to committees of advisers. Columbia University in New York, despite student sit-ins, voted to disinvest only from companies which were not Sullivan signatories. Michigan State University resisted disinvestment calls, as did the University of California which has one-third of its investment in South African-related stocks. Harvard and Yale held firm also. In June 1985 the principals of leading American universities met in New York and rejected pressure for the total disinvestment of stocks which their universities held in American companies which did business in South Africa. 'We have an honest and strongly-held position that the corporate presence in South Africa is one of the positive forces for change', said Dr David McLaughlin, president of Dartmouth College. As for the state legislatures, the reaction to the campaign was mixed. Some states voted to sell all shares in US companies dealing in South Africa; others decided to sell shares in non-Sullivan companies. The constitutional entitlement of states and cities to lay down rules governing companies' foreign operations is also being tested in the courts, the question being: 'Can these bodies hijack foreign policy?'

But it was not the disinvestment of shares which worried companies so much as the threat to their procuring future contracts. During 1984 IBM, the American computer firm, were told that they would not obtain another contract in New York City if they carried on trading with South Africa. IBM feared that because its business in South Africa was minimal compared to that in New York, South Africa would have to be sacrificed. Companies like IBM have therefore mounted a strong campaign against anti-South African measures, so that the threat to their South African interests has, as of now, receded for the time being.

But given that their trade with South Africa is so small, why do these companies bother to fight? Why do US firms not just pull out and be rid of all the complications? To begin with, they believe they are doing a good job in South Africa, bringing prosperity to the black community and providing jobs for blacks. They know, too, that once they move out of the country it will be difficult to get back in. Also, for many of them, there is a matter of principle at stake. Withdrawing from South Africa would, as they see it, set a dangerous precedent, i.e. South Africa today, Chile or wherever tomorrow. Any interest group with a cause to peddle would start lobbying for disinvestment in companies doing business with any country which happened to be the current bête noire of the political activists. So, for both altruistic and hard-nosed business reasons, American companies are 'hanging in there' with determination.

Any debate about taking punitive measures against Pretoria must of course take place against the background of South Africa's strategic importance to the non-communist world, both in terms of its economic wealth and its geopolitical position as the guardian of the Cape sea routes.

South Africa says it is the western world's leading supplier of gold, vermiculite, manganese ore, ferromanganese and diamonds. It is the second-ranking supplier of platinum group metals, fluorspar, zirconium minerals and lead. South Africa is third in the world league table in supplies of antimony trioxide, titanium minerals, antimony concentrates, coal and asbestos, and fourth in supplies of silver. In addition, South Africa possesses 93 per cent of the manganese reserves in the West and 80 per cent of total world reserves. Manganese is mostly used in the production of iron and steel. As for platinum group metals, South Africa is the repository of 83 per cent of the world's reserves. As a precious metal, platinum is purchased both for jewellery and as an investment. The metal is also essential in oil refining, the purification of vehicle exhaust gases, and is used widely in the glass, ceramic, chemical and electro-chemical industries. Of the world's chrome reserves, 58 per cent is in South Africa, as well as 61 per cent of vanadium reserves. Clearly the West is not anxious for South Africa to slip into chaos and anarchy or to fall prey to the Soviet Union.

The country's position at the southern tip of Africa is also of importance, though to a lesser extent than its mineral wealth. The Cape sea route is one of the world's busiest sea lanes. The South African navy calculated that during 1980 6,450 ships passed the Cape of which 6,300 were western. Of these 3,700 were westward-bound, meaning that ten fully-laden vessels passed the Cape every day and sailed into the Atlantic. The fierce westerly winds and turbulent seas of the Roaring Forties between South Africa and Antarctica necessitate vessels hugging the South African coastline. The Cape sea lanes are also the main access route to the West for the oil tankers coming from the Gulf although following the 1975 reopening of the Suez Canal, closed because of Arab-Israeli conflicts, the amount of traffic taking the Mediterranean route has increased.

Some observers now say the importance of the Cape route is often overstated by South Africa and her friends. They see little sign of the 'total onslaught' upon South Africa by the Soviet Union that the Pretoria government has so often postulated as the looming danger threatening its position as the West's guardian in the region. The Soviets may be supporting some of the liberation movements and may be supplying several black states with weapons, goes the argument, but there is little sign of them developing the kind of infrastructure which would be required for a takeover bid in South Africa, for example sophisticated harbour facilities somewhere in southern Africa for the Soviet fleet, an absolute minimum for any such encroachment. But the strategic planners in Washington and in other western capitals are not planning for today's state of affairs, they are looking at tomorrow's possibilities and how all options can be covered. Another Middle East war could render the Cape route of vital importance once again; an Iranian victory in the Gulf War with Iraq could mean a stranglehold on the West's major oil routes; a sudden heightening of tension in Europe for whatever reason could spill over into other areas of the world where the superpowers are outfacing each other. The need for the West to have a south Atlantic staging post was highlighted by Britain's experiences in the 1982 Falklands War against Argentina. With only Ascension Island as a half-way house, Britain faced formidable hurdles in resupplying its naval task force and the islands, once recaptured. The Simonstown naval dockyard at Cape Town which was once used by Britain could again have a crucial role in any outbreak of hostilities, although its facilities might by now be somewhat antiquated. Strategists also take into account the electronic monitoring station at Silvermine near Cape Town which observes every aerial and sea movement in the south Atlantic and Indian Oceans although, again, its value is limited given today's satellite observance. These are the kind of considerations that western governments have to bear in mind when they contemplate taking measures against South Africa, measures which could, in some people's view, weaken the country and expose it to greater internal and external threats.

But the economic and strategic determinants are balanced by the desire in the United States to bring about meaningful change inside South Africa, to see the granting of full freedoms for all the population, regardless of race. The aim is no different to that of President Reagan's predecessor, Jimmy Carter, but the policy differs in emphasis. The Carter approach appeared to some to be based on the assumption that the United States occupied the moral high ground in its dealings with South Africa, a position which was guaranteed to antagonize Pretoria. The Carter administration was also seen as being too pro-black Africa to be able to influence South Africa effectively. A different line of attack was formulated in several articles shortly before the 1980 presidential election by Dr Chester Crocker, who was then director of African Studies at the Center for Strategic and International Studies at Georgetown University. The policy of 'constructive engagement' which eventually emerged was based on the Crocker premise that the United States' room for leverage in southern Africa was limited, but that the area was of importance to United States' interests. If peace and economic development could be brought to the region, went the theory, this would benefit not only the countries of southern Africa but also western economic and strategic interests vis-à-vis the Soviet Union. A second leg of the policy was to recognize South Africa's legitimate interests and to try to steer the country towards domestic reform, a crucial factor in achieving regional stability. Crocker spotted a move towards liberalizing apartheid by the Pretoria government and considered the most fruitful American policy would be to build upon this. 'Constructive engagement' was based on the precept that American interests lay in a strong South Africa (i.e. its economic wealth and position as an anti-communist bulwark should not be jeopardized), but a South Africa where American concepts of justice and political freedom applied. This aspect of the policy was encapsulated by Crocker's State Department deputy, Frank Wisner, in an address to the Hans Seidel Foundation in Munich on 3 November 1983. He stated:

> . . . we believe that apartheid is morally wrong. We believe that apartheid represents an approach to government fatally flawed in its premise: that people are not equal in the access they should have to deciding their system of government. As a multi-racial society we cannot concur in any system which arbitrarily classifies people according to race rather than allowing people to be self-classified on the basis of talent, merit and freedom of action. That said, we believe it is preferable to treat South

Africa's dilemma as a political problem involving participation rather than a moral issue involving inequity. In my experience 'moral problems' are often intractable. Moralistic interpretations of political conflicts lead to all-or-nothing confrontations.

The policy amounted to an unwritten agreement with Pretoria under which the United States would back away from anti-South African measures and rhetoric in return for which Pretoria would demonstrate genuine moves towards 'evolutionary' change and would co-operate in bringing Namibia to independence. Essentially, the policy amounted to giving Pretoria the benefit of the doubt. But, to be successful, the policy needed results and in the eyes of the opponents of 'constructive engagement' in America these have been singularly patchy. Critics would agree that reforms have been initiated, but then they would point to setbacks like the occasion when the South African police went out and shot dead twenty blacks in Uitenhage. On Namibia, Crocker's progress, as the critics see it, has been painfully slow. South Africa's commando raid into Cabinda would also suggest to them that Pretoria has little interest in real peace and is quite prepared to undermine American mediation efforts. As the internal violence in South Africa and the deadlock over Namibia continued the policy of 'constructive engagement' increasingly came under attack. Events within South Africa occasionally appeared to wrong-foot the administration. Following the Uitenhage police shootings Crocker stated that 'the use of force as the first recourse in that kind of situation is unacceptable'. Secretary of State George Schultz described the shootings as a 'deplorable tactic' which 'he was not prepared to defend', while Reagan said he 'deplored apartheid' but added that 'there is an element in South Africa that doesn't want a peaceful settlement . . . who want violence in the streets.' This may be the case, although given that an official inquiry had barely begun, Reagan's statement appeared to his opponents to be jumping the gun and suggested to them that under 'constructive engagement' South Africa could do pretty much as it chose without fear of an American response. This impression gained ground following South Africa's raid in Gaborone. At a subsequent news conference in Washington President Reagan suggested that Pretoria was having the same kind of problems with the ANC as his administration was experiencing with Shi'ite militiamen in Lebanon, who at that time were holding hostage in Beirut over thirty passengers and crew seized during the highjack of a TWA airliner.

The administration's reply to such criticism was to raise two crucial issues concerning the United States' approach towards South Africa and specifically the question of whether economic sanctions should be invoked. The first of these was whether sanctions would actually work and have their desired effect of forcing Pretoria to change its ways, and second, whether the blacks of South Africa would themselves welcome punitive anti-South African measures given that they could well be the first to suffer from them.

On the question of their effectiveness, the opponents of sanctions asked whether the best way of removing apartheid was to remove capitalism. For the critics it had too strong an echo of the kind of approach which had left post-colonial black Africa in chaos. The slogan of Kwame Nkrumah of Ghana, 'Seek ye first the political kingdom and all else will follow', sounded fine in 1949 if you were the aspiring leader of a soon-to-be-independent black African state fighting to establish a political base and for whom economic and other matters could be put onto the back burner. But the slogan would not produce wages to support families and the sad history of twenty-five years since decolonization has demonstrated not just the emptiness of the slogan but also its devastating destructiveness. The anti-sanctions lobby also cast doubt upon the idea of American companies pulling out of South Africa until apartheid disappears and then reappearing in some kind of black Utopia. 'Things don't happen like that', they say.

As to whether anti-South African measures would compel Pretoria to change its policy, past evidence is confusing. Without question the sports boycott has had far-reaching effects in the country, to such an extent that many sports are now multi-racial. Defenders of South Africa argue that as and when these sports become desegregated they should be readmitted into the Olympic and other international sports movements. But opponents, those who adhere to the 'no normal sport in an abnormal society' school of thought, hold that South Africa should not be allowed to compete internationally until the political system is reformed. White (and some black) South Africans are under no illusion that a return to international sport will happen before the country has a black president. Nevertheless if the desired intention of the sports boycott was to effect change it has certainly worked. The cancellation of the 1985 New Zealand All-Blacks' rugby tour, for example, was a crippling blow.

The effect of the cultural boycott has, however, been less certain. Indeed it could be argued that it is counterproductive. By depriving white South Africans of sustained exposure to western ideas and thinking, they are being encouraged, possibly, to remain within their laager mentality. It might perhaps be helpful if they were made more aware that the world is not a perfect place, and that the neatly-ordered society is rarely, if ever, achieved by any country, no matter how stable it is or however long its history of parliamentary democracy. Television viewers in South Africa are fed a diet of American TV serials in which whites and blacks in the US are seen mingling naturally. But the quality programmes produced by the British Broadcasting Corporation and Britain's independent television stations are rarely shown, mainly because of the ban imposed by the British actors' union Equity.

More pertinent to the argument of sanctions is an examination of how South Africa has withstood the oil and arms boycotts. Rich in nearly all vital commodities except oil, South Africa depends on 'liquid gold' for roughly a quarter of its energy requirements, though this figure should gradually diminish now that the country has its first nuclear power plant at Koeberg, north of Cape Town, which came on stream in March 1984. The fall of the Shah of Iran in February 1979, from whom South Africa was obtaining 90 per cent of its oil, together with the 1979 OPEC embargo on oil deliveries to South Africa, raised the prospect of the country having its oil supplies cut off. But Pretoria has succeeded in circumventing the ban both by obtaining supplies secretly and by developing its own oil resources.

The publication of detailed information about where South Africa obtains its oil is banned in the country itself under a number of security laws. But most observers agree that it is purchased on the spot or non-contracts market in Rotterdam, or through undercover deals involving shady middle-men. Independent analysts believe that Brunei and the Gulf states supply most of South Africa's oil. An insight into South Africa's secret oil dealings came in January 1980 when the supertanker *Salem* was scuttled off the coast of Senegal in west Africa having secretly offloaded its oil, which was destined for Italy, in Durban. The vessel was sunk in the hope of claiming the insurance on the vessel and on the shipment of oil, which would have been a double killing as the South Africans had already paid for the clandestine delivery.

While taking steps to ensure its oil imports, South Africa has also moved to develop its own oil resources, through an oil-from-coal enterprise at Sasolburg in the Orange Free State and at Secunda in the eastern Transvaal. Another plant is in the pipeline, the aim being to secure over half the country's fuel requirements from local resources by the turn of the century. The country is also poised to produce offshore natural gas from a field established off the Cape coast. For the foreseeable future, however, it seeems likely that South Africa will remain dependent on imported oil.

More effective has been the embargo on the sales of arms to South Africa which was introduced by the UN Security Council on 4 November 1977. The result of it has been that South Africa has developed its own arms manufacturing industry called ARMSCOR (Armaments Development and Production Corporation) which has made South Africa virtually self-sufficient in armour and artillery. Its G6 field gun is considered to be one of the most advanced weapons of its kind in the world. In early 1985 it was reported that 100 of the G5 155mm howitzers were sold to Iraq in a deal worth R1 billion, with payment likely to be made partly in crude oil. There have been reports that a number of black African states, including Somalia, are also importing South African weapons, which would be a significant move. Pretoria is desperate to get a foothold in the horn of Africa to obtain landing rights for South African Airways, thereby reducing by several hours its flights to European capitals which at present have to go around the bulge of Africa as SAA is denied overflying rights by most African states.

As an ultimate defence, South Africa's development of the nuclear bomb is strongly suspected in many quarters. The suspicion dates back to 22 September 1979 when an American satellite detected a mystery explosion somewhere over the south Atlantic. The Carter White House attributed the 'sighting' to the satellite being struck by a meteor, although the CIA reported to the National Security Council that the explosion was probably caused by a two- to three-kiloton bomb. In April 1985 the respected American columnist Jack Anderson reported that US intelligence, after a tip-off from Moscow, had established that as long ago as 1966 South Africa had been co-operating with Israel on a nuclear device and that since then American agents had kept track of a steady stream of visits to South Africa by Israeli technicians, nuclear scientists and defence experts. Co-operation between the two 'pariah states' in other areas of armaments development is well-documented. Co-operation on a weapon which either state might deploy in the event of a last-ditch stand would not be surprising.

The arms embargo has, though, left South Africa with a serious gap in some areas of its armed forces which ARMSCOR cannot fill. A new generation of fighter aircraft is urgently required. Attempts to replace the fleet of Shackleton coastal reconnaissance aircraft which were retired in November 1984 have also been unsuccessful, another sign perhaps that the West has scaled down the importance of the Cape sea route.

So the lesson to be learned from previous boycotts is that South Africa can get by, but with some gaping holes and at a cost. ARMSCOR is the main example of the self-sufficiency industries which have sprung up in the face of international boycotts. But such projects inevitably tie up investment in capital-intensive projects instead of channelling it into job-creating sectors. But, despite the economic strains which would be involved, South Africa would probably survive wide-ranging US sanctions. American interests in South Africa would quickly be bought up by Japanese, West German and other international firms. South Africans would take over the rest and continue to operate them, albeit on a smaller scale. However, there would be more concern if American car-manufacturing firms and all international computer companies pulled out. These South Africa would not be able to replace immediately. The degree to which the black workers would be affected is hard to quantify but there is general agreement that they would be the first to suffer. So how do the blacks feel about the prospects of the United States and others turning their backs on South Africa?

A wide-ranging survey on black worker attitudes financed by the US State Department was undertaken by Professor Lawrence Schlemmer of the University of Natal and the findings published in September 1984. On the key issue of whether black workers support disinvestment and sanctions as opposed to the policy of 'constructive engagement', Schlemmer found that 25 per cent were in favour of the former and 75 per cent the latter. The report suggested a black workforce which was angry and frustrated but which was neverthe-less cautious about committing itself to revolutionary violence or militant political action. A similar stance was taken by Zulu leader Mangosuthu Buthelezi, who campaigned hard against sanctions in the US. Schlemmer's findings were attacked in a critique by two other University of Natal academics, Dr Michael Sutcliffe and Dr Paul Wellings, who argued in a report prepared for the UDF that the disinvestment issue was extremely complicated and that Schlemmer's views on black workers' attitudes were based on a misrepresentation of the facts. A survey carried out among blacks living in urban areas by the Institute for Black Research (published in the *Sunday Times* of London in September 1985) found that more than 70 per cent of those questioned favoured the imposition of sanctions by the outside world although only a quarter of them wanted foreign companies to withdraw completely.

In the end it comes down to two irreconcilable viewpoints, neither of which can claim to be the correct one because neither has been put to the test. The advocates of 'constructive engagement' believe that American-led sanctions against South Africa could damage the country in such a way that it would be the blacks who would be most seriously affected. American companies are a force for reform in South Africa, they believe. They can knock heads in government and lobby in favour of further reform at a greater pace. Threats and boycotts would simply force P.W. Botha back into the laager and give the right wing a drum to bang.

The boycott supporters believe that nothing is to be lost by applying the pressure. It is the only effective way of forcing Pretoria to change course, they declare. If it means that the blacks will be hurt it is unfortunate but necessary, goes the thinking of the boycott supporters. Bishop Tutu has stated that it is perhaps time for the blacks to suffer for a generation, to make a sacrifice to win their political rights. The bishop is not convinced that the blacks would be the ones to suffer in the event of sanctions. As he once put it: 'When the ladder is falling over, surely it's those at the top who will get hurt most, not those at the bottom?'

CHAPTER 14

The South African Time-Bomb
Peaceful change or violent revolution?

South Africa is on the brink of an explosion. It is going to happen some time during the next quarter of a century and it is going to change the face of the country. That it will occur is as certain as night follows day. But it will not necessarily be the explosion that many people outside South Africa expect. A political revolution in the country may or may not happen – only a fool would predict. But the revolution which *will* take place concerns the number of people who will be living in the country come the twenty-first century: more specifically, the number who will have to be fed and the resources and economic and social planning which will be required to meet such an immense population explosion. It is this, rather than any imminent political upheaval, which is likely to influence the future of South Africa and determine how its political and economic life develops.

In the week that South Africa and Mozambique signed the Nkomati peace accord, a report circulated in the government which was to have far-reaching implications. Because of the Nkomati signing the report was overshadowed and its significance did not become apparent until later. When P. W. Botha read it he was stunned and ordered each member of his cabinet to study it. The report, compiled by the Department of Health and Welfare, was entitled 'Community development as a component of the population development programme' and within its pages was painted nothing less than a South African doomsday scenario.

The report said that the average population growth of South

Africa in 1982 was 2.3 per cent a year (whites 1.55 per cent, coloureds 1.8 per cent, Indians 1.76 per cent and blacks 2.8 per cent). The report warned: 'If this growth were to continue it would disturb the balance between population and natural resources in South Africa and could have far-reaching social and economic effects on South Africa and southern Africa, seriously jeopardizing stability and progress.' The scale of the problem was dramatically illustrated in the following table:

Projections for SA population if present population growth continues (in millions).

	Present growth per year (%)	1980	2000	2020	2040
Whites	1.55	4.40	5.81	6.64	7.03
Coloureds	1.80	2.53	3.79	5.40	7.57
Indians	1.76	0.81	1.16	1.55	1.99
Blacks	2.80	20.70	36.40	65.60	121.19
		28.44	47.16	79.19	137.78

Two conclusions stand out from the above table. First, that the South African population is going to multiply almost five times over the next six decades. Second, that whereas the whites are at present outnumbered almost 5–1 by the blacks, by the year 2040 this ratio will have risen to around 17–1.

The report stated bluntly that natural resources in South Africa are limited; for example, the country has sufficient underground and surface water for not more than 80 million people, and to sustain that number water would have to be imported. The report was of the opinion that: 'It is of fundamental importance that the population of South Africa, at the end of the following century, should have ceased growing and be 80 million.' This would necessitate an average number of 2.1 children per woman for all race groups before the year 2020. To reach that target the following objectives would have to be met:

	Present no. of children per woman	Target rate	Year in which target must be reached
Whites	2.08	2.1	1984
Coloureds	3.40	2.1	2000
Indians	2.70	2.1	1992
Blacks	5.20	2.1	2010

Clearly it is black population growth which is critical and the report admitted the chances of the blacks reaching their target birth rate by 2010 were slim. A more likely date was 2080–5.

The report sketched out the details of a vast population development programme aimed at curbing the birth rate and providing acceptable standards of living for a rapidly-growing population, a programme encompassing health, education, economic programmes, housing projects, urbanization and rural development. The report did not go into the political implications of such a project. Clearly, though, such an enterprise could not be achieved while apartheid continued to stifle economic development. There seems little doubt that if South Africa is to be able to continue to provide the quality of life which it boasts for all its people then several apartheid pillars will have to go.

How, for example, can effective birth-control systems be introduced when ill-educated, illiterate blacks continue to be dumped into the black homelands where no infrastructure exists to develop their communities? Studies have shown that high fertility, far from being the preserve of the more affluent classes, is most prevalent amongst the poverty-stricken. Such people need to be brought into the big cities, not kept away, so that they can be educated in birth-control and family care and have an opportunity of improving their financial and educational position. Urbanization, rather than ruralization, of the blacks is what is required. Consequently, laws on influx control and other restrictions on the movements and residence rights of blacks will have to go. The whites say they don't want Johannesburg or Cape Town to become like Cairo or Lagos with festering slums to which millions flock in search of work only to find there is no employment for them. The result can be a life of crime and squalor. It is a fair point. There are many countries in Africa whose cities are bulging because the land has been allowed to go to ruin. But compared to these countries South Africa, despite its recession, is a relatively rich land. If the country is able to create wealth and can put into action a programme of urbanization balanced by rural development, it should be possible to improve the standard of living of the black masses while steering the country away from the anarchy which will ensue if millions of blacks are left impoverished, feeling that the first-world opportunities which South Africa can offer are becoming fewer and that the country, or parts of it, is slipping into third-world chaos. But it is a big 'if'.

The world focuses on unrest in South Africa's black townships but this may prove minimal compared to what could happen in the homelands and rural areas if the time-bomb of economic deprivation and population explosion is not defused. A report published in 1985 by the Human Sciences Research Council forecast that under conditions of low economic growth anything between 3.3 and 9.7 million people (mostly black) will be unemployed by the year 2000. Regardless of any protest movements, guerrilla campaigns or international pressure, the greatest force for change in South Africa in the years to come may well prove to be the fundamental requirement of sustaining growth to meet the demands and aspirations of the rising black population. P.W. Botha knows it. His government knows it. Their confidence that peaceful change can be brought about in their country is based on the assumption that these demands and aspirations can be satisfied, that the blacks will continue to better themselves, that they will see an improvement in their housing and their general standard of living and that this will encourage them to opt for stability instead of revolution. In the end economic deprivation rather than the denial of political rights may turn out to be the more fertile breeding ground of upheaval.

Over the past two years or so the whites have had a foretaste of how black anger can explode when those demands are not met. Sharpeville, Uitenhage and Crossroads have all unnerved the whites in a way that has perhaps not been seen before. Flaring up in various parts of the country as a reaction to local grievances, the violence has become endemic. In some areas the police obviously could not handle the situation, and whites have grown accustomed to seeing troops on the streets. The deployment of the army was a reminder from the government of the formidable forces at its disposal should the internal unrest appear to be getting out of control. But the nightly television news pictures (although censored), of soldiers patrolling black townships have a double-edged effect. The whites are left feeling confident that the government is combating the situation, but it leaves them uneasy. It all looks rather like Israeli soldiers on the West Bank or the Syrians in Lebanon, except that their army is not holding down an occupied territory but is being deployed to suppress civil disturbances within South Africa itself. 'What is happening that requires such a show of strength?', ask some people.

The feeling of uncertainty is possibly greater than at the time of either Sharpeville 1960 or Soweto 1976. During those earlier periods of unrest the whites could at least fall back on an authoritarian government which was prepared to invoke sweeping and harsh security laws to defend the system. The whites knew where they stood. The policy of hard-line apartheid was a point of reference from which they could take their political bearings in turbulent seas. This time, though, the whites are not entirely sure what is going on: coloureds and Indians in parliament, a proposed new deal for blacks, Nelson Mandela to be reckoned with again, and all this at the same time that the black townships have been in flames. What is happening? Where is P.W. Botha leading them? Is reform paving the way towards peaceful change or opening the floodgates to black revolutionary violence? One columnist described P.W. Botha's reform plans as 'not so much a step in the right direction, rather a step into the unknown'. Many whites would agree. All that is certain is the knowledge among whites that they are being called upon to hand over some of the absolutist power they have enjoyed to date, but they are not clear what they are getting in return.

But just how far are the whites, or more particularly the political leaders of the whites, prepared to move in surrendering their power? This is, after all, what South Africa is all about, the key question which, at the end of the day, is the only one which counts. Changes of attitudes and policies there have certainly been. Five years ago, the government was still pledged to the policy of sending the individual race groups their separate ways. Now it's all about bringing everybody back together again. The homelands are no longer sacrosanct; the ideology of total separation is crumbling. Take these comments by the Minister of Co-operation and Development, Dr Gerrit Viljoen, in an interview with the magazine *Leadership* in early 1985. Asked whether apartheid was breaking down he replied:

In the sense of an absolute ideology, namely that everything can
be solved by complete separation of the people (though this was a
concept propounded by a very few), yes. If there is a breakdown
of anything, it is a breakdown of absolute, unqualified
ideological commitment to separation as the total solution to the
problem.

I think what we have come to realize is that while separation or
differentiation still has an important part to play, is an important
component of the solution, there are many areas in which
togetherness and sharing of opportunities and power play an
important part. And this, of course, is at complete variance with
the original and the ideological concept of apartheid.

In other words anything is negotiable, provided certain degrees of
separateness are retained, an approach which is enshrined in the
concept of 'group rights' for each ethnic section of the population. In
a pamphlet which caused something of a stir in National Party circles
during the early part of 1985, Dr Stoffel van der Merwe MP (one of
the enlightened Nationalist politicians) admitted that parts of old-
style apartheid did not meet the nation's requirements. On the other
hand the 'winner-takes-all' style of Westminster politics was not the
answer either. 'What was required', he wrote 'in multi-national
societies was an arrangement by which the minority would receive a
guarantee that it would not be disadvantaged, suppressed or destroyed by the majority.' Such a system would therefore have to be
based upon the principle of each population group retaining control
over its own affairs. The problem is, of course, that because the
whites have such an influential voice in most organs of state and in
most sections of the country's economic life, having control over
white affairs effectively means having control over the country as a
whole.

Could there be a solution under which whites would cede the right
to have the ultimate say over their own affairs? There has been
considerable discussion in South Africa about some kind of federal
option: a political structure which could well result in a black head of
government but with the whites, through some kind of weighted
representative system, retaining a stronger influence over decisions
than their numbers would merit. During 1985 government ministers, interestingly, began blowing the dust off a report which had
been allowed to lie on the shelves for some years because the

government objected to its findings. The report presented the conclusions of a commission chaired by Chief Mangosuthu Buthelezi on the future administration of the province of Natal and the black homeland of KwaZulu which, because of their proximity to each other, appeared to many that they should be joined together instead of separated into two distinct units as apartheid requires. The Buthelezi Commission brought together some of the finest minds in the country, including leading academics and politicians (but not Nationalists), and their conclusion was that Natal was an economic unit which should not be fragmented. It proposed a single government for the region as a whole based on a proportional representation system. The fact that the government is now taking another look at the Buthelezi report, having originally dismissed it, is a hopeful sign, in the view of many, that in the not-too-distant future, Natal and KwaZulu will be granted their own government and that this may be viewed as a 'dry run' for a wider federal system throughout South Africa. Addressing a provincial congress of the ruling National Party on 30 September 1985 P.W. Botha hinted at an eventual federal or confederal solution to the country's political problems.

A contribution to the federal/confederal debate had already come in June 1985 when South Africa's Associated Chambers of Commerce (ASSOCOM) expressed the view that the country's route back to international legitimacy lay in the eradication of racial laws through evolutionary change, coupled with devolved government which would accommodate the aspirations of the blacks. There would also have to be a system of checks and balances to ensure that one particular group did not seize power and then proceed to act against the interests of other groups, said ASSOCOM. Also several entrenched clauses would have to be included, relating to human rights, personal freedom and the rule of law.

The attraction of some kind of federal option is that it would in effect fudge the racial issue, thereby avoiding the 'all-or-nothing' settlement which the whites fear.

But would the blacks accept anything less than one man, one vote in a unitary state? Some of them would. Buthelezi, for example, would under certain conditions agree to dilute the principle in return for an ending of apartheid. And the ANC also? Probably not. The demand for majoritarian democracy on the basis of universal suffrage in a unitary state is fundamental to the ANC's struggle. But they would possibly be prepared to compromise; a transitional period with some reserved white seats in parliament might, at the end of the day, be a bargaining offer the ANC would be prepared to throw in. But 'entrenched clauses', Zimbabwe-style, is not what the whites of South Africa have in mind. Their faith in such guarantees, never very strong, was finally destroyed after Prime Minister Mugabe's 1985 election victory in Zimbabwe after which he threatened to hound those whites who had voted for Ian Smith and also sacked the white Minister of Agriculture Denis Norman who until then had run one of the most successful agriculture ministries in Africa. So clearly the gap between South Africa's whites and the black nationalists remains wide. But these are early days. The courtship between the government and the ANC, which began publicly with talk of Mandela's release, has barely started.

If in the future there is to be an accommodation between them, there will clearly have to be give and take on both sides. At the end of the day the most crucial factor for the whites may prove to be not so much the political guarantees they would require, but rather assurances about the nature of the economic system which would apply under a black-led government. Marxist socialism would have to be ruled out, though a mixed-market economy with some state intervention (similar to what South Africa has at present) might be acceptable. Sweeping nationalization would not be tolerated by whites and they would want guarantees about maintaining standards of education and a commitment to a strong defence force with white officers still occupying senior positions. The ASSOCOM submission stressed that the maintenance of 'economic freedom and the private enterprise ethic' would be important in any final constitutional plan for South Africa. The association also stated that there would have to be basic rules about the standard value of the national currency and the principles of taxation.

The economic shape of a future black-led South Africa was the subject of an intriguing meeting which took place at a remote lodge in Zambia between a group of prominent businessmen from Johannesburg, led by the head of Anglo American Gavin Relly, and an ANC delegation. The businessmen could justifiably claim that they had been in the forefront of the calls for change in their country and that it was only natural for them to meet leaders of the black organization which is generally regarded as representing most politically-conscious blacks. But the visit also revealed a distinct nervousness on their part, a perceptible shifting of bets. Whereas before, the Botha government had appeared to be the horse to back, by mid-1985 there was less certainty. Big business was taking steps to ensure that if the whole apartheid structure was about to disintegrate in a heap of chaos it would not go down with it.

Prior to the meeting the ANC leader Oliver Tambo had been to the United States and had been impressed with the arguments advanced by American business leaders who said that South Africa's future prosperity would depend on more, not less, capitalism. The South African team returned from the Lusaka meeting saying there had been what they called a refreshing lack of Marxist-Leninist rhetoric at the talks. The two sides expressed the hope they would meet again. Once news of the talks leaked out Botha expressed his strong opposition to the business leaders' meeting the ANC, though whether he was quite so vehemently hostile when the talks were still secret is uncertain.

And then the inevitable question: 'Will peaceful change or a revolutionary bloodbath confront South Africa in the years to come?' History, of course, is on the side of the latter. Proponents of this school of thought would hold that the tide of black nationalism which has swept Africa since the early 1960s, often removing by violence whatever obstacles stood in its path, will not leave South Africa – the last bastion of white rule – untouched. But South Africa is different in many respects to those other countries. It has a white race which has nowhere else to go, a strategic importance which the West will not easily let slip into Marxist hands and a defence force (possibly supported by a last-ditch nuclear bomb capability) which can withstand any offensive threat which, under present political circumstances, might arise. So one has to look for more hopeful signs and here, as the author Alan Paton has put it, it is necessary to be optimistic because to be pessimistic about South Africa does not bear thinking about. Is there cause for optimism?

Few ruling parties in the world have admitted so directly or implicitly that the policies which they have enforced over the years have been so misguided, have caused so much hardship to people and were so desperately in need of revision. South Africa's National Party under its leader P.W. Botha has changed direction in a way which could not have been foreseen a few years ago. In Afrikaner terms the changes have been remarkable and could herald further significant reforms in the future.

The government is also beginning to learn the lesson that solutions

prescribed in advance by the whites will stand little chance of
drawing the blacks to the negotiating table. The feature of Mr
Botha's new forum on constitutional change affecting the blacks is
that nothing is on the table at the outset, although as is evident his
main problem is how to find authentic black leaders who will trust
him sufficiently to sit down and thrash out a future for the country.

As for the black nationalists, it is perhaps remarkable that despite
four decades of being subjected to apartheid they have not launched
a guerrilla war equivalent to that mounted by the Palestine Liberation Organization against Israel. The evidence of modern international terrorism is that even the most sophisticated defence umbrella
is not invulnerable to the fanatical martyr. This may change of
course. A bomb at Amanzimtoti near Durban in December 1985,
which killed five whites, suggested some militants are prepared to
strike at softer civilian targets.

But while the revolution may not be imminent there is little doubt
that the past two years have seen the introduction into the politicized
townships of revolutionary elements determined to overthrow the
system by violence if necessary. The country seems destined to
witness further unrest, therefore, which will be matched by repressive action by a government seeking to introduce reform at its own
pace and within the boundaries which it decides upon. Even if the
unrest tails off the gaps between periods of violence are likely to
become shorter.

What is reassuring about South Africa though is that people on
both sides of the argument are applying their minds to a possible
solution. Violence certainly occurs, committed by both sides, but it is
rarely the mindless, fanatical kind of violence that one sees in the
Middle East, for example. There is a high level of political debate
about how these different peoples who somehow find themselves
thrown together at the foot of Africa should resolve their differences.
In that sense, one has cause for hope. And those who wish the best for
South Africa would probably share the views of the former Anglo-
American chief Harry Oppenheimer who told the American Foreign
Policy Association in New York on 11 October 1984:

> South Africans, even white South Africans, are not really worse
> than other people, they are just ordinary men and women who
> find themselves face to face with problems which require quite
> exceptional qualities of courage, magnanimity and faith for the
> solution. The hour may be late, but the way of peaceful change
> still deserves a chance.

Select Bibliography

Anderson E.W. and Blake G.H., 'The Republic of South Africa as a supplier of strategic minerals', Johannesburg, Occasional Paper published by the South African Institute of International Affairs, 1984.

De Klerk W.A., *The Puritans in Africa – A Story of Afrikanerdom*, London, Rex Collins, 1975.

Geldenhuys D., *The Diplomacy of Isolation – South African Foreign Policy Making*, Johannesburg, Macmillan South Africa, 1984.

Giliomee H. and Schlemmer L., *Up Against the Fences – Poverty, Passes and Privilege in South Africa*, Claremont, South Africa, David Philip, 1985.

Hachten W.A. and Gifford C.A., *Total Onslaught*, Johannesburg, Macmillan South Africa, 1984.

Harrison D., *The White Tribe of Africa*, London, British Broadcasting Corporation, 1981.

Human Sciences Research Council, *The South African Society: Realities and Future Prospects*, Pretoria, HSRC, 1985.

Labour Monitoring Group, 'Report: The November Stay-Away' published by the *South African Labour Bulletin*, Johannesburg, May 1985.

Lamb D., *The Africans*, New York, Random House, 1983.

Lodge T., *Black Politics in South Africa since 1945*, Johannesburg, Ravan Press, 1983.

Longford E., *Jameson's Raid*, Johannesburg, Jonathan Ball, 1982.

Mandy N., *A City Divided – Johannesburg and Soweto*, Johannesburg, Macmillan South Africa 1984

Morris Donald R., *The Washing of the Spears*, London, Jonathan Cape, 1965.

Pakenham T., *The Boer War*, London, Weidenfeld & Nicolson, 1982.

Platzsky L. and Walker C. for the Surplus People Project, *The Surplus People – Forced Removals in South Africa*, Johannesburg, Ravan Press, 1985.

Reader's Digest, *Illustrated Guide to Southern Africa* (2nd edn) Cape Town, The Reader's Digest Association South Africa, 1980.

Reitz D., *Commando – A Boer Journal of the Boer War*, London, Faber & Faber, 1929.

Ritter E.A., *Shaka Zulu*, St Albans, Panther, 1958.

Schlemmer L., 'Black Worker Attitudes – Political Options, Capitalism and Investment in South Africa', Durban, Centre for Applied Social Sciences, University of Natal, Durban, 1984.

Selby J., *A Short History of South Africa*, London, George Allen & Unwin, 1973.

South African Department of Foreign Affairs and Information, *South Africa, 1984 – Official Yearbook of the Republic of South Africa*, Johannesburg, Chris van Rensburg Publications, 1984.

South African Institute of Race Relations, *Survey of Race Relations in South Africa 1976*, Johannesburg, 1977.

South African Institute of Race Relations, *Survey of Race Relations in South Africa 1982*, Johannesburg, 1983.

South African Institute of Race Relations, *Survey of Race Relations in South Africa 1983*, Johannesburg, 1984.

South African Institute of Race Relations, *Race Relations Survey 1984*, Johannesburg, 1985.

South African Research Service, 'South African Review 11', Johannesburg, Ravan Press, 1984.

Southern African Catholic Bishops' Conference, 'Report on Police Conduct during Township Protests August-November 1984'.

Surplus People Project, Western Cape, 'Khayelitsha – new home, old story,' Cape Town Surplus People Project.

Thompson L. and Prior A., *South African Politics*, Cape Town, David Philip, 1982.

Van Der Merwe, Professor R., 'The Eastern Cape – Problem Child or Pacesetter?', Port Elizabeth, Paper to University of South Africa Seminar, 1983.

West M. and Morris J., *Abantu*, Cape Town, C. Struik, 1976.

Wilkins I. and Strydom H., *The Super-Afrikaners*, Johannesburg, Jonathan Ball, 1978.

Wilson M. and Thompson L. (eds), *The Oxford History of South Africa* volumes 1 and 2, Oxford, Oxford University Press, 1975.

Wisner F., 'Southern Africa: An American Perspective Today', published by the South Africa Foundation in *South Africa International*, Johannesburg, January 1984.

Index